D1242058

TEXAS ARCHEOLOGY

R. KING HARRIS

TEXAS ARCHEOLOGY

Essays Honoring
R. King Harris

Edited by KURT D. HOUSE

INSTITUTE FOR THE STUDY OF EARTH AND MAN

Reports of Investigations: 3

Claude C. Albritton, General Editor

SMU PRESS · DALLAS

© 1978 • INSTITUTE FOR THE STUDY OF EARTH AND MAN
SOUTHERN METHODIST UNIVERSITY • DALLAS

Incorporated on May 11, 1966, the INSTITUTE FOR THE STUDY OF EARTH AND MAN is a graduate research center for the departments of Anthropology, Geological Sciences, and Statistics. The Institute was founded by William B. Heroy, its purposes being, as stated in the Bylaws, ". . . to encourage, foster, promote, and advance research and development and education in the fields of the Anthropological and Geological Sciences and other related fields of scholarship within Southern Methodist University."

Communications should be addressed to:

The Institute for the Study of Earth and Man
111 N. L. Heroy Science Hall
Southern Methodist University
Dallas, Texas 75275

Library of Congress Cataloging in Publication Data
Main entry under title:

Texas archeology.

(Reports of investigations—Institute for the Study of Earth and Man; 3)
   Bibliography: p.
   CONTENTS: Krieger, A. Introduction—Wendorf, F. The changing roles of amateurs and professionals in Texas archeology.—Wetherington, R. Anthropological perspectives in Texas archeology. [etc.]
   1. Texas—Antiquities—Addresses, essays, lectures. 2. Archaeology—Methodology—Addresses, essays, lectures. 3. Harris, R. King—Addresses, essays, lectures. I. Harris, R. King. II. House, Kurt, 1947-   III. Series: Dallas. Southern Methodist University. Institute for the Study of Earth and Man. Reports of investigations—Institute for the Study of Earth and man ; 3.
F388.T387   976.4   78-10491
ISBN 0-87074-170-5

Contents

Preface

AMATEURS AND PROFESSIONALS alike practice the science of anthropology today, and it is with the past and future relationships of these individuals that this volume is concerned. While some wish to draw rigid dividing lines between these types, the honoree of this volume is an example of how unwise and for the most part useless it is to be concerned with such categories. There is one title, however, which both of these types may deserve, one which ignores the false boundary between amateur and professional: both may be *scientists*, honestly employing the scientific method and processes. Neither has sole claim to this approach, and therefore neither has sole claim to the title *scientist*, which is so often misconstrued as meaning "professional." Amateurs and professionals alike can earn the title *scientist*, and it belongs as much to the businessman who spends his coveted spare time sorting and cataloging artifacts and writing reports after the thrill of digging is over as to the academic professional who practices rigorous scientific methodology while recruiting newcomers to the field. A proper scientist humbly respects the knowledge he acquires, whether he is a young professional learning from a grizzled amateur, or whether the exchange of knowledge is in the opposite direction. The ideal situation, of course, is where exchanges occur in both directions in the unified archeological effort.

The adherence to a single rule binds the young professional and the experienced amateur together and separates them clearly from the nonscientific pot hunter or professional artifact salesman whose shallow interest is in the artifacts alone. The scientific practitioner, be he amateur or professional, wants more than anything to derive a maximum amount of information from the site excavation because he realizes that excavation is destruction of a part of human history. This sobering realization carries with it the responsibility to gain all the information the site will yield. Among the rewards for these efforts is our learning a deep respect for the Indian maiden who created the pot we study and try but fail to duplicate, for the ancient flintknapper of the parallel-flaked projectile point we contemplate, and for the history of human groups who gathered around campfires long since extinguished, but to whom we are nevertheless related.

In the development of archeology its practitioners have shown an increased interest in botanical, zoological, ecological, geological, and behavioral data. Even as professional archeologists met with experts in these fields to affirm the importance of these new kinds of data (Taylor, 1957), some farsighted amateurs were already in the field collecting exactly these data. But were the standards of those regarded as amateurs as scientific as the standards of professionals? Krieger (1957, p. 231) said of two of these amateurs: "Although the discoverers are amateur archeologists, they have been conducting field work on a professional level in this area for many years." One of the men referred to by Krieger was Wilson Crook, Jr., who has contributed a paper to this volume honoring the second individual of whom Krieger wrote. This second individual is R. King Harris, and it is to this man and his extraordinary contributions to Texas archeology that this *Festschrift* is dedicated.

The primary purpose of this volume is to honor King Harris, and at times when other goals and standards conflicted with this purpose, they were silently and quickly sacrificed in order to accomplish this single goal efficiently.

But our idea of quickly producing a volume worthy of the man stretched into three years, countless letters, and publication delays, all surrounded by an aura of secrecy that became increasingly difficult to guard. Not until a week ago, as I write this, was the secret inadvertently lost, and I am sorry that we were not all there to share in what was described as the "wonderment, amazement, and absolute disbelief" of King Harris that a volume honoring him was in progress. The papers contained in this *Festschrift* are as diverse as the interests of King Harris, but they are united in the belief that good archeology can be practiced by qualified persons regardless of amateur or professional status in the field.

In the archeological milieu there is no better place to be than in Texas, with its large area, diverse habitat zones, and healthy academic institutions which remain viable for the purpose of training and helping us to understand our past. It is appropriate, too, that the volume originated and was produced in King's home area of Texas, and was published under the sponsorship of the Institute for the Study of Earth and Man, where he worked for six years and where he is still a consultant.

R. King Harris was born November 5, 1912, in Dallas, Texas, the eldest of the three sons of Samuel Wylie Harris and Henrietta Benjamin King. While in elementary school he became a Boy Scout and it was here, through the influence of his troop leader, Fred Kenamacher, that Indian artifacts sparked what was to become a lifelong interest in anthropology. In 1931, after completion of high school, he enrolled in Southern Methodist University, but his father's illness, the need to support his family, and the Depression necessitated his withdrawal after a year and a half. The stories of his subsequent founding of the Dallas Archeological Society and founding influence on and membership in the Texas Archeological Society and other organizations are aptly described in the papers by Krieger and Crook, his fellow researchers, and by Wendorf, one of his early students.

How the goals, approaches, and theory have changed in the dynamic field of anthropology since those formative days of Texas archeology is discussed in the papers by Wetherington, Webb, and House. The contributions of remarkably broad scope by Story, Humphreys and Singleton, and Gilmore, together with the specialized paper by Gregory, cover some of the main areas of interest of the honoree and illustrate his varying approaches to problems of different magnitudes. The last paper by Crook deserves a special category; in it almost all of the former topics are combined in a delightful, readable, and firsthand account of King's archeological adventures, together with his first formally published bibliography. The papers have a remarkable cohesiveness, illustrating King's specific interest areas, and the topics were chosen for this reason. Most of the papers were written in 1975, and several of the authors expressed concern when in 1977 their papers were still unpublished. Delays of several types prevented the early publication I had envisioned, but I do not believe this kept us from accomplishing our goal.

I wish to thank most of all the unselfish contributors to this volume, who are some of King's closest friends and without whose support and suggestions this volume could not have been produced. I am grateful also for the editorial assistance of Drs. E. Mott Davis and Edward I. Fry. Special thanks go to Claude Albritton and William Heroy, Jr., members of the Executive Committee of the Institute for the Study of Earth and Man, sponsor of the volume, and to the Lee F. Clayton Memorial Fund for a grant to help support its publication. In addition, I appreciate the long-suffering patience and guiding expertise of Margaret L. Hartley, Charlotte T. Whaley, and the rest of the personnel at the SMU Press. It is hoped that this effort by a few of his friends has finally acknowledged to all of his friends the debt owed to R. K. Harris by all of those who engage in Texas archeology. These friends, many of whom we hope are pleased readers, may find this a more satisfactory tribute than the inadequate credit so often encountered in the literature: Harris, R. K. 19___: personal communication.

KURT D. HOUSE

Southern Methodist University
Dallas, Texas
September, 1978

BIBLIOGRAPHY

Krieger, A. D. 1957. "Notes and News—Early Man." *American Antiquity*, 22 (3): 321-23.

Taylor, W. W., ed. 1957. *The Identification of Non-artifactual Archeological Materials*. National Academy of Science, National Research Council, Washington, D.C.

TEXAS ARCHEOLOGY

Introduction

ALEX KRIEGER

THIS INTRODUCTION is not concerned with the articles in this volume, which I am sure have been well chosen by the editor, Kurt House. Rather, it concerns the man to whom it is dedicated, R. King Harris, his wife, Inus, and the other remarkable members of the Dallas Archeological Society.

The Harris family cannot, in fact, be separated from the Society, for they have been its driving force and inspiration for more than thirty-five years. (And, for all I know, considering King's great size, he might have given his fellow members a beating now and then to make them work harder!)

Over the years the Dallas group, though numerically small, has undertaken scores of site surveys, surface collections, and controlled excavations, always at great personal sacrifice. They cannot fairly be called "weekend archeologists," for their weekday nights, weekends, holidays, and vacation times alike were filled with the chores of writing up notes, cataloging, drawing ground plans, sketching and photographing artifacts and burial contents, typing, and getting out the *Record*, their small but valuable publication. As far as I know, none of them had any money to spare; their drive and enthusiasm came from the heart, and from the sure knowledge that they were doing something valuable with their time. (I wouldn't say spare time either, in their case, for I doubt that they ever had any.)

I should like to offer definitions of the amateur and the professional archeologist. The first step is to exclude from either category the looters. These people are of no help to science; in fact, they are usually just the opposite: a nuisance, if not worse. There are tens of thousands of outright looters scattered over the land, in this country and abroad. They tear from the ground whatever they can, totally unconcerned with the destruction of information that might be of scientific value. They keep or sell or trade their loot. We would have to include here those who carry on the idiotic search for "Spanish gold" all over the southwestern United States, ripping into caves, mounds, ruins, and whatnot in their frantic search for treasure that the looter *knows* is hidden somewhere. In southwestern Texas we once ran across one of these obsessed idiots who said he had "dug up" some two or three hundred caves and felt he was getting closer to the one that had the gold!

Possibly even more numerous than the looters are the hobbyists. They at least have some appreciation of the artifacts they find, and they can be taught to keep records, such as notes on site locations and catalogs of their findings. Most of them keep what they find, readily answer questions as best they can, and allow professionals to study and photograph the collections. While at the University of Texas (there was only one campus then, in Austin), I made at least a hundred trips to work over these collections and extract whatever information I could. I was invited to eat with the family, sometimes to stay overnight, and so on. These intelligent hobbyists were more than willing to form local archeological societies in many parts of the state, and I spent a great deal of time during those seventeen years helping them to organize, catalog, write notes, and read up on comparable material from other parts of Texas and from surrounding states. From about 1940 to 1956 the membership of the Texas Archeological and Paleontological Society (the name was shortened to Texas Archeological Society during that period) rose from about fifty to five hundred, with numerous local chapters. The increase was, I am sure, largely due to increased enthusiasm over what these good people were doing to expand archeological knowledge in Texas and adjoining states. The local societies actually "policed" themselves, casting out those who were essentially looters or who were just uncooperative and would not learn.

It is important to note, too, that during the middle 1950s, when the first antiquity laws were being created, many of these local archeological societies were of great value in reporting the presence of looters who were destroying sites in areas ranging from one to five or six counties. Thus the looting could at least be reported to state and federal authorities; and it could be discouraged by putting pressure on the looters themselves and/or those who owned the land on which the sites were located.

Professional archeologists comprise a third group. In the 1940s and 1950s, as is true even today, some of us amused ourselves by trying to define a "pro." I can recall some emphatic statements to the effect that "a professional archeologist is one who is paid for it." Such statements came from people in other states, but the definitions were just as applicable in Texas. As a matter of fact, however, I was the only person in the entire state of Texas who was paid full time as a research scientist/archeologist. There were four or five others in the state whose careers were in archeology, but they had to be teachers first and then somehow had to find "extra" time to do field work. Grants for such work could not be obtained from the universities then. (At the University of Texas the whole annual departmental budget for travel and miscellaneous expenses during those years was $400, and my share was a maximum of $150 per year.) One had to go through a long and laborious routine to get a little money from some federal agency, and a fifty-fifty average of success was considered excellent. A large, fat grant of over $10,000 for a single excavation at a promising site was thought of as "out of this world." Almost all of these grants were for archeological and historical sites that were to be destroyed by dam construction and the resulting reservoir flooding. Grants for archeological investigation at sites for highway construction, urban expansion, state and federal parks, etc., were still in the future.

Given such state and/or federal funds, the professionals enjoy conditions for salvaging archeological and historical material on a scale they had never dreamed of before. Today's younger generation cannot be expected to know what conditions we were up against then. Grants of a hundred thousand dollars are now common; a sum of three hundred thousand dollars for a two-year project surprises no one these days.

There is another category, one that is extremely important and that should be recognized wherever it exists in our country. It is in this category that King Harris and the Dallas Archeological Society belong. The Dallas group were neither hobbyists nor professional archeologists who were "paid for it." They were what is called an "amateur" group, which may be defined as a group of people who are not on a university campus and are not paid for their work, as over against professional archeologists who *are* on university campuses and are paid faculty salaries. Often I have wondered how much difference there is between them. I have known professionals who have their Ph.D.'s and all that, and yet are fools when it comes to thinking out archeological problems. Conversely, I have known amateurs who are extremely intelligent, completely dedicated, do not count the hours they spend, and are of incalculable value to archeology if only the professionals will recognize them and work with them. A definition? I don't really have one as yet for this unique group, except such phrases as "professional amateur" or "unpaid professional." Neither of these seems quite right, and I guess it does not matter too much at the moment. What does matter is that these intelligent people are of as much value to the advancement of knowledge as the professionals (paid), and they should be recognized.

King, I salute you as close friend and valued colleague!

The Changing Roles of Amateurs and Professionals in Texas Archeology

FRED WENDORF

INTRODUCTION

TEXAS ARCHEOLOGY is now rapidly changing as a direct result of recent legislation, both federal and state. This legislation reflects an increasing public awareness of the significance and value of our archeological and historical heritage; it includes the Texas Antiquities Act, passed in 1969; the federal National Environmental Protection Act, also passed in 1969; and the Archeological and Historic Conservation Act of 1974 (known as the Moss-Bennett bill). These three most important legislative actions reinforce a public policy to protect our heritage from needless destruction, and, for the first time, provide truly effective means for its preservation. By recognizing the value of our archeological and historical heritage, however, the legislation also has circumscribed significantly the freedom which archeologists, both amateurs and professionals, have traditionally enjoyed in the study and use of this heritage. The protection of our resources, which was sought by so many of us for so many years, has been obtained, but at a price—a price which we can accept, but which must be recognized.

One important result of the new legislation will be a significant change in the roles played by amateurs and professional archeologists in Texas. In discussing these changes it may be useful to consider the roles which each has played in the development of archeology in this state.

7

HISTORICAL BACKGROUND

The debt which archeology owes to amateur enthusiasts for its origin and early development has often been noted (see Oakley, 1964; Willey and Sabloff, 1974). Important contributions by these early amateurs occurred during the first half of the last century, when their discoveries and forceful arguments caused the scientific world to reexamine the basic premises concerning the antiquity of man and thus irrevocably changed our whole world view and our understanding of man's place in nature. These amateurs were sometimes trained in such professions as medicine, law, or theology, but many others had little formal training of any kind and held semiskilled or unskilled positions. All of them, however, shared a keen intellectual curiosity, the ability to observe, and the openness to interpret what they saw without depending on those preconceived notions which so often blinded the more formally trained to the significance of the phenomena which they recorded. It seems likely that these early pioneer archeologists were able to make their important contributions primarily because they lacked the rigidity which often accompanies formalized training. These amateurs simply trusted their own senses implicitly and refused to accept the prevailing view that the artifacts and the fossils that they found could not be real. It is significant that these early "amateurs" not only found the data, but interpreted them, and made the data and their interpretations available to the broader community through lectures and publications.

DEVELOPMENT OF TEXAS ARCHEOLOGY

The beginning phase of archeology in Texas, however, cannot be traced to this early "period of discovery." There is very little surviving evidence of interest in Texas archeology during the nineteenth century, although there must have been numerous amateurs who collected artifacts, and some of them, perhaps, conducted excavations. The first archeological reports dealing with Texas, however, are by individuals who would probably be classified as professionals, regardless of their academic training (Bandelier, 1892; Mallery, 1886, 1888-89; Fewkes, 1902). Most Texas amateurs at this early stage seem to have been collectors, and their service to the development of archeology was primarily in locating sites for the professionals. If they conducted their own investigations, the results have not survived in published form (see bibliography in Campbell, 1952, 1958).

In reality, there was very little interest in Texas archeology during this period. On the national scene, the public's imagination, and much of the professional's interest, was focused on the question of the mound builders and the spectacular mounds to be found in the Mississippi Valley and elsewhere in the eastern United States, or on the large pueblo ruins and the painted pottery found in the American Southwest. Even slightly later, during the first twenty-five years of this century, most of the occasional publications on Texas archeology were concerned with either the mounds in the eastern part of the state or the pueblos and caves in the western sections (Hill, 1906; Moore, 1912; Pearce, 1919).

In 1926, however, with the discovery of the Terminal Pleistocene bison kill site at Folsom, New Mexico, and the slightly earlier find of similar age near Colorado City, Texas (Cook, 1927), widespread interest was suddenly generated in Texas archeology, much of it initially focused on the problem of Early Man in the area. It was this interest which led to the 1928 founding of the Texas Archeological and Paleontological Society by a group of amateur enthusiasts under the leadership of Dr. Cyrus N. Ray, a chiropractor, at Abilene, Texas. It may not be entirely accurate to say that archeology in Texas began with the organization of the Texas Society in 1928, but it is clear that the real stimulus of interest in the prehistory of Texas can be traced to this group.

The Texas Society provides an excellent illustration of the role played by amateurs in the development of archeology throughout the United States during the first half of this century. It is the amateurs who have been responsible, through their efforts in developing and supporting regional societies, for the initiation of the publication outlets where archeological data are now recorded and preserved. Almost all of the numerous regional and national journals dealing with archeology in the United States had their inception either totally through amateur sponsorship or with strong participation by nonprofessionals. Thus, one of the important contributions of amateur archeologists has been in facilitating communication.

Since its inception, the Texas Society has provided the organizational structure around which most of those interested in Texas archeology, both amateur and professional, have functioned. The first *Bulletin* of the society was published in 1929, and volume 45 of the series was issued in 1974. The *Bulletin*, traditionally, has provided an outlet for both amateurs and professionals, although in recent years the contributions by professionals have become more frequent, reflecting the dramatic increase in the number of professional archeologists working in Texas from the late 1950s onward. In the first five volumes, the ratio of amateur to professional authors was approximately 3:1; in the most recent volumes, however, the ratio was reversed to 2:3 in favor of professional authors.

Professional archeology, which is here defined as the employment of an individual to do archeology, began in Texas just after World War I with the work by J. E. Pearce at the University of Texas. Most of the work done by Pearce was in the burnt rock mounds of Central Texas, with some testing in the mounds of East Texas. It is significant that archeology was viewed as a routine academic program and was supported by the university administration as legitimate faculty research.

In the 1930s, with the WPA and similar public works programs, professional archeology had its first major boost in Texas. Extensive excavations, funded with federal money, were conducted by the University of Texas under the general supervision of Pearce. Several archeologists were employed to supervise these excavations, and others were brought in by the university to teach. The Department of Anthropology in Austin grew rapidly during this period.

It was during the thirties that other Texas institutions also began professional archeology, some of it financed by federal funds. Significantly, all of these programs were under the leadership of individuals who, while lacking formal training in archeology, had a long interest in the subject as amateurs. Many had played important roles in the organization of the Texas Archeological and Paleontological Society. Thus, Floyd Studder in the museum at West Texas State University, W. C. Holden at Texas Tech University, Victor J. Smith at Sul Ross State Teachers College, and R. K. Harris at the Hall of State Museum in Dallas all moved from amateur status into the ranks of the professional archeologists during this period of accelerated development. The number of archeologists active in Texas and the pace of archeological research in the area reached the point where a Council of Texas Archeologists was organized in Alpine at the November, 1939, meeting of the Texas Archeological and Paleontological Society. The officers of the council included J. G. McAllister (president), A. T. Jackson (vice president), and T. N. Campbell (secretary), all of the University of Texas. Three newsletters were issued, but the council had a short life and did not survive the decline in Texas archeology which occurred with the onset of World War II. It was, nevertheless, one of the most important periods in Texas archeology, for both the chronological and cultural frameworks

within which the interpretation of Texas archeology still functions were
established during this period.

While professional archeology in Texas virtually ceased during
World War II, the close of hostilities found a significant increase underway with the onset of the River Basin Archeological Salvage Program
(Krieger and Hughes, 1950; Wheat, 1953), again federally funded and
initially centered at the University of Texas. In the 1950s, however,
other institutions also added archeologists to their staffs, particularly at
Texas Tech University, West Texas State University, and the University
of Texas at El Paso. Another important development was the creation
of the Office of State Archeologist in 1959. A state-related archeological
salvage program was begun in that office almost immediately thereafter,
often with funds provided by other state agencies. In the 1960s archeological programs were also initiated at Southern Methodist University,
Texas A&M University, and East Texas State University. More recently
archeological programs have begun at the University of Texas at San
Antonio and North Texas State University, and archeologists have joined
the faculties at several junior colleges. Statewide, more than fifty individuals are now employed as archeologists on a full-time basis, and
more than twice that many advanced graduate student archeologists have
part-time and full-time employment in the field. The total of public
funds available for archeological research in the state now exceeds
$500,000 a year and shows every sign of continued increase. Archeology
has become an important scientific and cultural activity.

THE PRESENT SCENE

Much of this recent growth for archeology can also be largely attributed to efforts initiated by the amateur to broaden public support for
archeology. This public support is the third and most recent major area
(after the acquisition of data and the encouragement of communications)
where amateurs have contributed to the development of Texas archeology. The awakening of public awareness to the social and cultural
values possessed by our archeological heritage, and the creation of public
policy to protect these resources, is a most significant new development
in American and Texas archeology; amateurs have been an effective lobby
for new antiquities legislation, both state and national, generated to
support this policy.

In Texas the first successful activity of this type led to the initial
establishment of the Office of State Archeologist in 1959, but it required

the persistent efforts by members of the society over several legislative sessions before favorable results emerged. The enactment of the Texas Antiquities Code in 1969, on the other hand, was not the result of specific efforts by the amateur community. Rather, it came from widespread public anxiety over the looting and destruction of an extremely valuable treasure-laden shipwreck off the Texas coast. That this looting was done by a group from outside the state served further to enhance public outrage. Protective attitudes are quickly aroused when outsiders try to take something of value from us, even though up to that point we had failed to appreciate its value and had done little to protect it.

The new federal legislation, particularly the Moss-Bennett bill, was strongly supported by the entire archeological community, and amateur support was crucial for the final outcome. Amateurs were able to convey the breadth of public concern and generate a broad base of congressional support which underlay the passage of that legislation. Many Texas amateur archeologists participated in this successful effort.

During this period of increased political activism by archeologists, a gradual change in the attitude of amateurs toward the data of archeology has become apparent. The same arguments which persuaded the general public of the value of our archeological heritage—as a unique and nonrenewable resource—led to an increased appreciation of the uniqueness of the archeological record, and this in turn has led to interest by amateurs in training in the techniques of archeology in order that their investigations may result in the maximum recovery of data and the minimum loss of resources. This was the major impetus behind the formal field schools which the society has offered in recent years for its members, and their value is attested by the several hundred individuals who attended these schools, some of them more than once.

The Changing Roles

The new antiquities legislative acts, both federal and state, are designed to prevent the needless destruction of our archeological and historical resources. Among other things, these laws provide that archeological sites on public lands, or those on projects which involve public funding, can be investigated only by qualified archeologists. But who is a qualified archeologist? For the first time we are faced with the problem of determining not only who is qualified as an archeologist, but also what kinds of training and experience are necessary to achieve this position. Although these questions mostly concern those employed as archeologists, they necessarily affect all those engaged in archeological research, regardless of their professional status.

Largely because of this new legislation, the Society for American Archeology has taken initial steps toward the certification of archeologists, and both the National Park Service at the federal level and the Texas Antiquities Committee for the state have begun the process of defining educational and experience qualifications for an archeologist. It is significant that all of these efforts, thus far, have recognized the several routes whereby an archeologist can achieve competence. The simplest to identify, possibly the easiest to achieve, and probably the most frequent route to be used will be through traditional formal training and advanced degree programs available at many universities. It is also evident that many of the most skilled archeologists today, as in the past, lack formal training or degrees in archeology. Thus, a mechanism whereby these most valuable participants in our community will be included has been built into the certification procedures. Certification through this route will not be easy and will require demonstrated competence fully equivalent to that expected of academically trained applicants, but the door should always be open to dedicated and competent amateurs to achieve certification and to assure that the King Harrises of the future will not be excluded.

One effect of this certification process and the formal inclusion within the group of Certified Archeologists of the highly qualified amateur archeologists will be an erosion of the dichotomy between professional and amateur archeologists which has gradually emerged with the increased professionalism of archeology in recent years. The important distinction will not be the source of employment, but rather the competence and skills of the individual, and those amateurs who make significant contributions to archeology will receive the formal recognition and status they so richly deserve.

BIBLIOGRAPHY

BANDELIER, A. F. 1892. *Final Report of Investigation among the Indians of the Southwestern United States Carried on Mainly in the Years from 1880 to 1885.* Papers of the Archaeological Institute of America. American Series. Boston.

CAMPBELL, T. N. 1952. *A Bibliographic Guide to the Archaeology of Texas.* Archaeological Series, 1. Dept. of Anthropology, University of Texas, Austin.

————. 1958. "Texas Archaeology: A Guide to the Literature." *Bulletin of the Texas Archeological Society* 29:177-254.

COOK, H. J. 1927. "New Geological and Paleontological Evidence Bearing on the Antiquity of Mankind in America." *Natural History* 27:240-47.

FEWKES, J. W. 1902. "Pueblo Settlements near El Paso, Texas." *American Anthropologist* 4:57-75.

HILL, R. T. 1906. "On the Origin of the Small Mounds of the Lower Mississippi Valley and Texas." *Science* 23(592): 704-6.

KRIEGER, A. D. 1946. *Culture Complexes and Chronology in Northern Texas.* University of Texas Publication no. 4640.

————, and HUGHES, J. T. 1950. "Archaeological Salvage in the Falcon Reservoir Area: Progress Report No. 1." Mimeographed. Austin.

MALLERY, G. 1886. "Pictographs of the North American Indians: A Preliminary Paper." *Annual Report of the Bureau of American Ethnology* 4:3-256.

————. 1888-89. "Picture-Writing of the American Indians." *Annual Report of the Bureau of American Ethnology* 10:3-807.

MOORE, C. B. 1912. "Some Aboriginal Sites on Red River." *Journal of the Academy of Natural Sciences of Philadelphia* 14:1-163.

NEWELL, H. P., and KRIEGER, A. D. 1949. *The George C. Davis Site, Cherokee County, Texas.* Memoirs of the Society for American Archaeology, no. 5.

OAKLEY, K. P. 1964. "The Problems of Man's Antiquity." *Bulletin of the British Museum of Natural History*, vol. 9, no. 5, London.

PEARCE, J. E. 1919. "Indian Mounds and Other Relics of Indian Life in Texas." *American Anthropologist* 21:223-34.

SAYLES, E. B. 1935. *An Archaeological Survey of Texas.* Medallion Papers, no. 17. Gila Pueblo: Globe.

SELLARDS, E. H. 1952. *Early Man in America.* Austin: University of Texas Press.

SUHM, D. A.; KRIEGER, A. D.; and JELKS, E. B. "An Introductory Handbook of Texas Archaeology." *Bulletin of the Texas Archeological Society*, vol. 25.

WHEAT, J. B. 1953. "An Archaeological Survey of the Addicks Dam Basin, Southeast Texas." Bureau of American Ethnology Bulletin no. 154, pp. 143-252.

WILLEY, G. R., and SABLOFF, J. R. 1974. *A History of American Archaeology.* San Francisco: W. H. Freeman Co.

Anthropological Perspectives
In Texas Archeology

RONALD WETHERINGTON

FOR THE MAJOR PART of their history, systematic archeological investigations in Texas have been dominated by a concern for cultural chronology and classification. The last ten years have witnessed a shift in concern toward cultural and ecological functions and processes, a concern which has achieved significance only in the last five or six years.

This brief sketch is an evaluation of the shift in emphasis, the reasons for it, and its importance for Texas archeology.

BACKGROUND

In its earlier development as well as in its current status Texas archeology has been affected by three factors, and each has played a unique part in influencing both the earlier and the more recent interests.

The first factor is the strong amateur interest and commitment which have always characterized archeology in Texas. Even before the organization of the Texas Archeological and Paleontological Society in 1928, amateur groups were active. Local archeological societies, such as those at El Paso (established in 1922), Dallas (1936), and Houston (1947), have long been initiators of archeological investigations in Texas. With increasing guidance by professionals, these local groups as well as the Texas Archeological Society itself have come to serve the profession with scientific skill and dedication. The first TAS-sponsored excavation, at the Gilbert Site in 1962, marks one of the important milestones in the

15

turn to professionalism among amateur groups. R. King Harris was assistant director of that project and has been instrumental in the encouragement of amateurs.

The second influential factor in the orientation and emphasis of archeology in the state is Texas' unique geographical character. Its range of arid to temperate climates, and woodland to parkland to plains environments, has always given it multidimensional cultural characteristics. This is as true in the industrial present, with our concern for water, fuel, and transportation resources, as it was in the prehistoric past. Moreover, Texas' special geographic position makes it a crossroads in cultural movement.

Several cultural provinces overlapped within the state during prehistoric times. In expressing his interest in standardizing terminology, Krieger (1945) emphasized the confluence of the southwestern, southeastern, plains, and several Mexican culture areas in the state. The same mélange characterized the early historic picture, when French and Spanish settlers carved the territory into new provinces. The diverse geographical characteristics of Texas have strongly influenced the kind of archeology which is done here and the kinds of problems that are posed by archeologists working here.

The third factor stems from the early need to manage water resources in Texas, resulting in the ongoing line of reservoirs along the major rivers and their tributaries. This development encouraged the survey and salvage operations which have dominated archeological discovery and interpretation in Texas. Salvage archeology has become an increasingly important enterprise and one which has grown in magnitude. Reconnaissance sponsored by the Bureau of American Ethnology and the River Basin Surveys in the late 1940s and into the fifties set the stage for larger scale and more numerous reservoir surveys during the sixties and early seventies. Professional groups under the auspices of the Texas Historical Survey Committee, the Texas Archeological Salvage Project, and more recently the Archeology Research Program at Southern Methodist University have drawn heavily on various local, state, and federal fund sources to conduct surveys, collections, and excavations before land development projects are underway. Most of these have been along river sites for proposed reservoirs, with the consequence that archeological resources and settlements along major drainage systems are becoming increasingly well known. The nature and tempo of this kind of investigation have influenced the kinds of questions asked of archeologists as well as the kinds of data sought through archeological research.

The change in orientation from typological-historical to cultural-ecological concerns has characterized American archeology in general during the past decade. This change, with its European and American components and its methodological and philosophical dimensions, has been well documented elsewhere (Binford, 1968; Longacre, 1970; Martin, 1971; Taylor, 1972) and needs no elaboration here. It is certainly true that the manifestations of this shift in archeological research in the Texas area are responses to a more nationwide trend. The professional training of many of the younger archeologists in Texas has emphasized the newer concepts and their methodologies. The local factors noted above, however, have also been influential, and these deserve elaboration, for they have contributed to the more traditional typological-historical approach.

THE TRADITIONAL CONCERN FOR CLASSIFICATION AND CHRONOLOGY

A look at site reports, conference statements, and most of the remaining literature over the past twenty to thirty years demonstrates that the goals of archeology in Texas have been essentially three: (1) to characterize the prehistoric and early historic cultures, principally in terms of describing their technological contents; (2) to define their geographic distributions and boundaries; and (3) to reconstruct their chronological sequences.

The means for achieving these goals were correspondingly descriptive and nomenclatural. Artifact types, particularly among arrowheads and pottery, achieved a growing importance as the key to understanding cultures and their relationships and differences (Suhm, Krieger, and Jelks, pt. 2, 1954; Suhm and Jelks, 1962). These in turn have led to extensive diagnostic trait lists, inventories of artifacts defining the spatial and temporal distributions of particular "cultures." The resultant compendia of stages, phases, aspects, and foci (Suhm, Krieger, and Jelks, 1954; Jelks, Davis, and Sturgis, 1958) have dominated cultural classification in Texas archeology. The factors previously discussed have influenced this approach. Archeology in Texas received from amateur groups not only its impetus but also its direction and sustaining productivity.

The first stage in the development of a science and the first step in scientific analysis is classification. This is not just a logical prerequisite to understanding phenomena; it is also a relatively straightforward, empirical procedure, and it characterized the earlier amateur efforts. The growth of amateur archeology in Texas has reflected the desire to describe cultural manifestations in terms of their artifact types and to define their spatial and temporal limits in terms of culture areas and cultural periods. As amateur work became more professionally oriented with the aid of trained archeologists, research strategy did not change from a descriptive culture-history culture-area focus. Rather, existing methodologies became more refined. The development of a research philosophy oriented to explanation rather than description and to functional interpretation rather than classification, which characterizes the latter stages of a science's maturation, has come only recently. Again, while this can be partially explained by the general trend in archeology, the more specific factors noted above have played a part.

The geographic factor is identified synchronically in the regional differences in archeological manifestations: the elaborate Caddoan complex in the eastern part of the state; the occasional sedentary, pueblo-influenced groups in the panhandle and Trans-Pecos; the Plains-related expressions to the north; the southern hunting-collecting pattern reminiscent of the so-called "Desert Culture" adaptations.

No unified interpretive strategy was easily identified in the presence of this diversity. A description of the differences, based on comparative type- and trait-lists, provided essentially a ready-made, self-generating uniformity and a common method of descriptive analysis.

The intraregional differences, moreover, were revealed chronologically and historically. Early records provided an excellent basis for an ethnohistorical approach to prehistory (Newcomb, 1958) and its resulting historical methodology. To this end, likewise, exhaustive trait lists and artifact typologies were appropriate means.

Finally, the fact that most archeological data have come from or are limited to surveys has played well to the philosophy that if we can classify and date the vast quantity of surveyed sites, we can understand the cultures represented, in both their historical development and their intraregional and interregional relationships.

In summary, until recently Texas archeology has had limited objectives restricted largely to time- and space-related problems of description/classification. This is not because the data have not been available for more functional cultural-ecological analyses (although frequently the appropriate data have not been collected), but rather because the contexts in which data recovery has occurred have not encouraged alternative objectives.

The Cultural-Ecological Approach

Beginning in the late 1960s a shift in orientation began to take place in Texas archeology. The interest in what artifacts, middens, and their distributions could reveal about the site itself and the culture of its occupants came to replace the concern for how these data fit into existing artifact, cultural, and chronological classes. Self-defined cultural patterns began to replace normatively defined cultural categories as objectives of analysis.

Archeologists came to realize that where such traditional classifications stop, an analysis of cultural pattern and social process begins (Campbell, 1972); that, moreover, the developing of traditional classifications frequently builds typological, spatial, and temporal fences around the data, preventing fuller analysis. This shift in orientation becomes clear, for example, to one who examines the contents of the *Bulletin of the Texas Archeological Society* since about 1968. As previously noted, this shift is partly a result of major changes in American archeology.

To appreciate the genuine contributions of the shift one must look behind the new, frequently ponderous, and occasionally obfuscating terminology of the "new archeology": the change may be characterized as a rather fundamental revision of (1) what archeology is or should be, and (2) what archeologists do or can do with their resources.

The first dimension of this new perspective is the assertion that archeology is not simply culture history, a systematic chronicle of past events, but is more appropriately the anthropological study of past societies. This formal assertion helped to legitimize efforts to reconstruct more of the cultural system than its technology and more of human behavior than subsistence and ceremony. The further legitimization of these efforts must lie in their successful application.

The second dimension of this new perspective is the assertion that archeological data are the sufficient resources required for valid reconstruction and interpretation. Such interpretation is not, therefore, limited by the availability of comparative data or the adequacy of ethnohistorical records for analogy. With appropriate models of the past, hypotheses regarding social organization or adaptive processes can be rigorously drawn which are testable by the archeological data alone. This assertion brought to archeology a more mature, more comprehensive scientific methodology.

These two dimensions of the change, the first reflecting a basic philosophy, the second a new methodology, opened new vistas for research and provided new objectives to supplement, and in some cases substitute for, the traditional objectives. Archeology has become, to those espousing the new claims, a more holistic behavioral science. Its aims are to reconstruct and interpret the social (familial, economic, political, religious, etc.) institutions of past human groups and their cultural (technological, behavioral, conceptual) mechanisms of integration and adaptation.

In order to identify and describe these groups, institutions, and mechanisms one must first employ typological and chronological procedures, but these become handmaidens rather than goals, and in the process are themselves changed.

The influence of this shift in perspective and philosophy on Texas archeology came from professional archeologists working in the area and from their students. The strong base of amateur groups in the state felt this influence through personal contact, conferences, local meetings, field work, and formal field schools. Professionals such as Joel Shiner, Frank Hole, and James Sciscenti played important roles in stimulating this shift in emphasis (see Shiner, 1971). Excavations at Kerrville under the direction of Alan Skinner, then a student, were among the first to employ a research design based on preexcavation hypotheses (see Skinner, 1974).

Other factors, however, were also instrumental in the change. One of these was the new ecological focus given survey and salvage archeology by increased public concern for preserving and protecting the environment. This concern was reflected in the National Environmental Policy Act of 1969, the Texas Antiquities Act of 1969, and more recently by the Archeological and Historic Conservation Act (the Moss-Bennett Bill) of 1974. The first of these in particular has encouraged an ecological perspective in archeology, as it requires assessment of the impact of proposed alterations on the physical, biological, and cultural resources of an area. Filing the required environmental impact statement necessitates a multidisciplinary evaluation and encourages an interdisciplinary synthesis. While such a synthesis has not yet reached its potential in print, the change in perspective toward a culture-process and cultural-adaptation theme has been significant (see Sciscenti, 1972).

Even a straightforward inventory of the diverse environmental and cultural factors which describe human ecological processes is important in this light. It makes clear the recognition that such interaction in the preindustrial past was not only highly influential but frequently intense. It strongly suggests the possibility that the interregional and intraregional variations in culture, from major settlement types to minor stylistic patterns, may be more responses to this interaction than reflections of historical tradition. Finally, it engenders the idea that cultures did not survive, adapt, and interact in terms of artifact types and cultural foci; these are merely labels which, if misapplied and overemphasized, obscure attempts to understand and explain the entities they define.

There were numerous other factors which influenced the change of the late sixties, among them the growing professionalism of amateurs, the training of amateurs in the more comprehensive aspects of archeological research, and the introduction and expanded use of statistics and computers.

THE SIGNIFICANCE OF THE CHANGE

The results of the newer philosophy and its approaches are evident in numerous articles, monographs, and theses. Most striking, perhaps, are the differences seen in the kinds of questions asked, for these elicit new methodologies. A representative contrast may be seen in work on the Caddoan area of northeastern Texas and adjacent areas of Louisiana, Arkansas, and Oklahoma.

The formalization of the Caddoan Conference, beginning with its second gathering in 1950 and continuing irregularly since then, was to share and exchange information and discuss major problems of Caddoan archeology. Most of the meetings have been concerned with refining taxonomy, accuracy of trait lists, origins and internal development of Caddoan culture, and external relationships and influences (Davis, 1959). In a review of the area, Webb (1958, pp. 53-55) listed a number of suggestions for future research, almost all of which were concerned with verifying trait lists and searching for Caddoan origins and external influences. At that time the understanding of what constituted and characterized early culture in the Caddoan area was essentially limited to the trait lists of artifacts and architecture categorized by Krieger's modified McKern System of cultural classification. Excavations and analyses were largely restricted to filling in the gaps of chronology and geography. Distributional patterns within a site were of interest mainly to insure recovery of all diagnostic material, rather than to identify functional complexes. Webb (1958, p. 57) stated: "Since many sites in this area cover more than one culture period . . . a careful check should be made of the kinds of artifacts, evidences of middens, house patterns, etc., in various parts of the site."

A little over a decade later the Caddoan area was being approached from a different viewpoint by several workers. Survey, excavation, and analysis were being conducted within theoretical frameworks designed to test models of social structure and interaction. One paper approached the problem of explaining the shift from concentrated, nuclear settlements of the Gibson Aspect to the smaller, dispersed settlements of the Fulton Aspect. Anderson (1972) wrote: "The aim of this (methodological) procedure is to excavate sites not just because few sites of a particular period have been dug, and it is intuitively felt that more are necessary, but because excavation will provide understanding of cultural adaptation, adjustment, and development." Another paper (Woodall, 1972) approached the problem of defining tribal boundaries among the Caddo of Fulton Aspect as one means of interpreting social complexity and intergroup activity.

This is not to say that the new approaches have exclusively addressed new problems. The more traditional problems of geographic distribution of a culture, its relationship to others, and its ethnohistoric connections remain important. There is, however, a difference in approaching them. Typology and chronology are not goals, but tools to help achieve goals. Discovery of the antecedents of historic tribes is no longer restricted to identifying linear traces back through time by virtue of trait continuity and geographic proximity. More than this, early historic documents together with archeological data can provide models of social size, distribution, complexity, and interaction which can allow the prediction of what might characterize earlier manifestations and where they might be. Such approaches have already proven successful (Gilmore, 1968).

The insistence that typology is a tool to aid interpretation (Shiner and Shiner, 1968) has encouraged the collection and analysis of all artifacts and deemphasized concentration on the most "visible" or well-known "types." The results have increased our understanding at many levels, from the technology of stone-tool manufacture (Sollberger, 1968), to identification of functional components within a site (Shiner, 1969), to the more ambitious attempts to analyze and interpret a site comprehensively in terms of its technology (Blaine et al., 1968).

Advantages and Liabilities of the New Perspective

The newer philosophy which underpins archeological research in Texas, the goals of interpretation and explanation which that philosophy has established, and the methodologies and techniques by which the goals are approached all augur well for the future. Equally auspicious are the great wealth of archeological resources in the state, the growth of professionalism in amateur groups, and the increasing availability of public and private funds for the conduct of research. Aside from the value of specific returns from the new orientation, there are at least four general advantages which accrue, even to the more traditionally oriented archeologists.

First is the emphasis on greater scientific precision in all aspects of archeological research: more precise control of provenience information, better field sampling procedures, more detailed attention to the attributes used in taxonomy, and more explicit awareness of the line between description and explanation.

Second is the increased use of multidisciplinary expertise, from the individual consultant to the large-scale survey. The knowledge that archeological data contain more locked-in potential than previously realized encourages wider-ranging contacts and participants, and all of the disciplines profit. The final step in this process is interdisciplinary synthesis, a synergistic enterprise which is certainly realized in Texas archeology.

Third is the search for more data-testable problems through the use of explanatory models. Building such models involves the kind of inductive-hypothetical thought that stimulates specific problem-oriented research. It likewise allows one to specify the kinds of empirical data which will test the validity of the model. Consequently, this new perspective on scientific procedure sensitizes one to both the explanatory power of empirical data and the reciprocal relationship of "fact" and "theory."

Fourth is the identification of archeological problems as cultural problems, the archeologist as ethnographer. The ultimate goals are cultural, not typological. Recovered technology (artifacts, architecture) reflects, at least potentially, the whole of the cultural pattern. This view, briefly mentioned previously, expands the frontiers of scientific explanation for which description is only a first step.

The assessment of the prospective value of a new perspective or a new methodology in science ought to be tempered with at least a pinch of parsimony, particularly when its virtues come to be extolled by a cult of followers, which has happened with the "new archeology." There are two very real dangers in the new perspective, noted by others in other contexts, which could threaten its virtues.

There is first the danger of dogmatism: the fallacious claim that everything not "new" is "old" and therefore obsolete—worse, unscientific. A colleague has even asserted that anything published before the sixties is largely useless! Pouring out the baby with the bath is a syndrome typical of scientific watersheds. It has occurred several times in the history of the physical and biological sciences.

It is dangerous for obvious reasons: in confusing means and ends, data and methodology, it seeks to nullify everything prior to it. But data analyzed by an inaccurate methodology or invalidly interpreted are not themselves rendered inaccurate or invalid. While refining methodologies should replace less appropriate ones, the objectives of the latter are not necessarily inappropriate for the science.

While the goals of intragroup interaction or cultural-ecological explanation are laudable, these goals must not sweep away those of culture history, cultural origins, or even attempts to reveal migration and diffusion. Different goals are appropriate, obviously, to different circumstances. The critical key is not what goals are set, but how validly they are approached.

A second danger is the fallacy of scientism: the "feeling" (since it is usually not articulated) that the more "scientific" the approach to a problem, the more likely its solution. The notion that *the* scientific approach to a problem is the deductive approach is an example. (In fact, deduction is itself not truly scientific at all.) Scientism takes many forms and, like the fallacy of dogmatism, also has a tendency to recur through history. It was a major characteristic of nineteenth-century positivism.

In one expression it confuses methodology and technique, the latter replacing the former. An example would be to analyze a data set by complex statistical technique without an appropriate methodology which establishes the prior assumptions and predictive hypotheses. In another expression it views quantitative analysis as the necessary and sufficient condition for the conduct of science. Variables not subject to quantification are judged irrelevant.

The danger here is also obvious. The value of statistical tests is conditional and derivative. Failure to appreciate this contributes to the myth of the machine. The advent of "statistical thinking" by itself is no less pernicious than the traditional "typological thinking" it replaces. Cumulative graphs are inherently no better and no worse than the standard trait lists. If archeology refuses to deal with imponderables, ignores data which cannot easily be quantified, it cannot truly come to terms with the culture it pursues.

Both of these dangers must be avoided. The newer perspectives and methodologies must take care not to promise more than can be delivered, nor to deliver less than they should.

There is good reason to believe that the next decade will witness both a refinement and a maturation of these newer approaches in Texas archeology, that the innovations will be more than just semantic and the techniques more than just novelties, that we will gain much in our understanding of the interaction of early cultures with their environments, and that in the process the more traditional problems of developmental sequences and spatial distributions will be clarified.

BIBLIOGRAPHY

ANDERSON, K. M. 1972. "Prehistoric Settlement of the Upper Neches River." *Bulletin of the Texas Archeological Society* 43:121-98.

BINFORD, L. R. 1968. "Archeological Perspectives." In *New Perspectives in Archeology*, ed. S. R. and L. R. Binford, pp. 5-32. Chicago: Aldine.

BLAINE, J. C.; HARRIS, R. K.; CROOK, W. W.; and SHINER, J. 1968. "The Acton Site. Hood County, Texas." *Bulletin of the Texas Archeological Society* 39:45-94.

CAMPBELL, T. N. 1972. "Systematized Ethnohistory and Prehistoric Culture Sequences of Texas." *Bulletin of the Texas Archeological Society* 43: 1-12.

DAVIS, E. M., ed. 1959. "Proceedings of the Fourth Conference on Caddoan Archeology." *Bulletin of the Texas Archeological Society* 30:1-34.

GILMORE, K. 1968. "The San Xavier Missions: A Study in Historical Site Identification." Master's thesis, Southern Methodist University.

JELKS, E. B.; DAVIS, E. M.; and STURGIS, H. B. 1958. "A Review of Texas Archeology," pt. 1. *Bulletin of the Texas Archeological Society* 29.

KRIEGER, A. 1945. "Some Suggestions on Archeological Terms." *Bulletin of the Texas Archeological Society* 16:41-51.

LONGACRE, W. A. 1970. *Archeology as Anthropology: A Case Study*. Anthropological Papers of the University of Arizona, no. 17. Tucson: University of Arizona Press.

MARTIN, P. S. 1971. "The Revolution in Archeology." *American Antiquity* 36:1-8.

NEWCOMB, W. W. 1958. "Indian Tribes of Texas." *Bulletin of the Texas Archeological Society* 29:1-34.

SCISCENTI, J., ed. 1972. *Environmental and Cultural Resources within the*

Trinity River Basin. Institute for the Study of Earth and Man, Southern Methodist University.

SHINER, J. 1969. "Component Analysis for Archaic Sites." *Bulletin of the Texas Archeological Society* 40:215-30.

——, ed. 1971. "The Amateur Archeological Field School." *The Record* 27:3, Dallas Archeological Society.

SHINER, M., and SHINER, J. 1968. "Suggestions to Authors." *Bulletin of the Texas Archeological Society* 39:163-66.

SKINNER, A. S. 1974. "Prehistoric Settlement of a 'Natural Area.'" Ph.D. dissertation, Southern Methodist University.

SOLLBERGER, J. B. 1968. "A Partial Report on Research Work Concerning Lithic Typology and Technology." *Bulletin of the Texas Archeological Society* 39:95-110.

SUHM, D. A.; KRIEGER, A.; and JELKS, E. B. 1954. "An Introductory Handbook of Texas Archeology." *Bulletin of the Texas Archeological Society* 25.

——, and JELKS, E. B. 1962. *Handbook of Texas Archeology: Type Descriptions.* Austin: Texas Archeological Society and Texas Memorial Museum.

TAYLOR, W. 1972. "Old Wine and New Skins: A Contemporary Parable." In *Contemporary Archaelogy,* ed. Mark P. Leone, pp. 28-33. Carbondale: Southern Illinois University Press.

WEBB, C. H. 1958. "A Review of Northeast Texas Archeology." *Bulletin of the Texas Archeological Society* 29:35-62.

WOODALL, J. N. 1972. "Prehistoric Social Boundaries: An Archeological Model and Test." *Bulletin of the Texas Archeological Society* 43:101-20.

Changing Archeological Methods and Theory In the Transmississippi South

CLARENCE WEBB

EXCITING CHANGES have taken place in archeological method and theory over the forty years that King Harris and I have been engaged in the discipline. For most of that time we have been primarily concerned with archeological studies in Texas, Louisiana, Oklahoma, and Arkansas, the states that share the diagonal axis of the Red River. Much of this territory is incorporated in the Caddoan area and much of it is in the Trans-Mississippi South, a biogeographical construct introduced by Frank Schambach (1970) at the Thirteenth Caddo Conference held at the Balcones Research Center in 1971. The Trans-Mississippi South incorporates as a natural area the oak-hickory southeastern Woodland environment that occurs west of the lower Mississippi Valley, interposed between the valley and the plains; it largely coincides with the four-state Caddoan archeological area, with some extension beyond its usual boundaries. Most of the interests that King Harris and I have shared are encompassed within the two constructs—archeological and physiographic— but to some extent our studies have ranged from the low plains to the Mississippi.

Forty years ago nearly all who engaged in archeology in this area were amateurs—untaught, self-taught, or with rudiments of the craft taught by individuals who had academic connections in other, sometimes related, fields. Professors J. E. Pearce and W. C. Holden in Texas, Fred Kniffen in Louisiana, S. C. Dellinger in Arkansas, J. Willis Stovall in

Oklahoma, Major Webb in Kentucky, Wrench in Missouri, and Jones in Alabama, had their training in such fields as history, geography, zoology, or sciences other than archeology. Nevertheless, they did some creditable archeological work, established museums, laid the groundwork for departments of anthropology in their institutions, and fostered the early careers of professionals such as Tom Campbell, Robert Bell, Bob McGimsey, Bill Haag, Tom Lewis, David DeJarnette, and Jim Ford. Credit should also go to some of the pioneers who were active in local archeological societies, the Houston society and several others, and contributed to such publications as Frank Watts's *Central Texas Archaeologist* of the 1930s and the *Dallas Record*, which Robert Hatzenbuehler and King Harris took turns editing in the 1940s.

The Texas Archeological and Paleontological Society was the pioneer of the statewide organization, and its bulletin has the longest record of continuous publication in the field. The society was established before 1930 under the leadership of Cyrus N. Ray, the crusty but indomitable spirit of Abilene, and it continued under his presidency, with the bulletin under his editorship, for nearly two decades. In 1940 W. C. Holden became editor, and he has had a number of distinguished successors. In 1953 the Texas Archeological and Paleontological Society became the Texas Archeological Society.

The original name was an indication that paleontology was an important part of the society's early interests, as was geology. The society's activities centered in the plains of western Texas and the panhandle. Early man and the extinct animals that he hunted were focal. E. H. Sellards, Glen Evans, Grayson Meade, Ray, and Holden were frequent contributors to programs and publications. Ray attracted well-known students of early man, geology, and the Southwest, encouraging them to visit the area, do field work, and participate in programs of the society. The programs were sometimes more noted for heat than for light, but times were never dull. Involved were people like Warren Moorehead, Ernest A. Hooten, J. Alden Mason, Frank Bryan, Harold Gladwin, M. R. Harrington, E. S. Renaud, Ales Hrdlicka, W. C. McKern, A. E. Jenks, and Lloyd A. Wilford, the latter two (Jenks and Wilford, 1938) concerned with the Sauk Valley skeleton research. One of James B. Griffin's early pottery descriptions, that of sherds from the Abilene area (1935), was published in the *Bulletin*. (He has recently said, "I knew very little about it at the time and even less now.") This paper included a description and chemical analysis by Frederick Matson, of the University of

Michigan, of a white aplastic temper that Matson showed to be calcium phosphate, presuming it to be derived from limestone beds or fossil bone. Later, Alex Krieger and I showed a microscopic study that this temper of Leon Plain pottery in central Texas and of ceramics in East Texas and northwestern Louisiana is crushed bone.

The methodology of the early excavations and studies in central and western Texas related largely to the geological and extinct animal associations, and to the morphology of the projectile points. The absence of relatively exact time markers and, sometimes, the vagaries of excavation led to heated discussions.

In the mid-1940s, during a trip to the Texas Panhandle, Krieger, my son, and I participated briefly with Glen Evans in an excavation of the Plainview bison kill (Sellards et al., 1947). We were taken by Floyd Studer and Judge Pipkin to visit the Alibates quarries and the Antelope Creek ruins, where I observed for the first time the curious West Texas custom of the individuals' leasing of archeological search rights on entire ranches—and the avid defending of them.

During the mid-1930s a minimal amount of work occurred in East Texas, southern Arkansas, and northwestern Louisiana. A. T. Jackson was excavating burial sites and houses in East Texas and securing collections for the Austin Museum, including pottery and pipes and ornaments, about which he wrote descriptive articles in the *Bulletin of the Texas Archeological and Paleontological Society* (Jackson, 1933, 1934, 1935). The archeology of Titus County was reported by Goldschmidt (1935), following a summer's work by a field party from the University of Texas. He first presented evidence of cultural stratigraphy in the Caddoan area of East Texas, began the identification of Titus Focus, and discounted the prior opinion by Jackson that cultural subareas in East Texas corresponded to the four major river systems. Dickinson (1936), Lemley (1936), and Lemley and Dickinson (1937) published reports of the Crenshaw site in southwestern Arkansas and of studies along Bayou Macon in the southeastern part of that state. In 1936 King Harris was on the program of the Texas society at its Abilene meeting, with a description of sites on the upper Trinity River. This was my first meeting, and, I believe, my first acquaintance with King.

Elsewhere, many of the excavations and explorations were specimen-related, made on behalf of museums or by nonprofessionals for private collections. Dellinger was exploring the Ozark bluff shelters of northern Arkansas. Numerous local or regional collectors were actively digging into graves and collecting, buying, or manufacturing artifacts up and down the Mississippi Valley (an activity that is still going on); museum people had to develop some expertise in detecting fraudulent objects. The Great Depression stimulated the hunting and selling of pottery; Mississippi pots from the St. Francis, wagonloads of pottery from the Carden Bottoms on the Arkansas River, and many thousands of artifacts from Poverty Point site found their way into museums and private collections throughout the nation. Toward the latter part of this period the great "mining" rape of Craig Mound at Spiro took place. Museum directors as well as amateurs and admitted artifact dealers were contaminated by the loot, but—to their credit—some hardy individuals and tough societies resisted the temptation to exploit the sites and opposed the looting process. For example, Henry Hamilton (1952) and Harry Trowbridge (1938) traced many of the Spiro objects and recorded them for archeology.

With the Depression came Works Progress Administration (WPA) archeology and the first large influx of professionally trained archeologists into the area. The first relief labor program was at the Marksville site in Louisiana, under Frank M. Setzler and James A. Ford; but the real prototype was the Tennessee Valley Authority (TVA) series of explorations and excavations in the Norris, Wheeler, and Pickwick Basins, between 1934 and 1939. This was organized and directed by Major William S. Webb. For the first time huge crews exposed entire villages and completely excavated mounds or immense shell middens. To the credit of Major Webb, within eight years of the program's inception there resulted three massive reports (W. S. Webb, 1938, 1939; W. S. Webb and DeJarnette, 1942), completely illustrated, with special sections on physical anthropology and osteology by Funkhouser, Newman, and Snow; ceramics by Griffin and Haag; tree-ring dating by Florence Hawley; molluscs by J. P. E. Morrison; geology by Walter Jones; and ethnographic and comparative artifact studies and conclusions by Webb or DeJarnette.

In the Trans-Mississippi South the WPA methods and results were more variable and less spectacular. The economic need for the use of manpower sorely tried the newly found expertise of professional archeologists in managing budgets, in transporting and supervising raw crews numbering from dozens to hundreds, in doing a massive volume of archeological work, and in handling specimens that numbered into the multiplied thousands. There is little wonder that scant attention was paid to processual debris and debitage, small floral and faunal remains, and other minutiae. There were floods of specimens and skeletal material, stacks of excavation reports, maps, and logs, and masses of photographs and drawings. Storage facilities were packed, analyses lagged far behind, and final publications were scarce or late—some are still waiting in the wings or are stored in attics.

Out of this exasperating welter of sweat and worry, however, some outstanding beginnings of analysis and synthesis did result. Kniffen brought Ford to Louisiana State University and with his help imported, for the WPA program, trained individuals who were destined to become well known in their own right. Included in the group were Gordon Willey, John Cotter, George Quimby, R. S. (Stu) Neitzel, Arden King, Edwin Doran, and Carlisle Smith. Ford (1936) had used an unwieldy system of pottery sherd classification in his analysis of collections from Louisiana and Mississippi, and had employed it in establishing the sequence of Marksville, Coles Creek, Deasonville, Tunica, Caddo, and Natchez ceramic complexes. Out of his and Willey's dissatisfaction with the system and their experiences in the Southwest, they worked out the binomial system of pottery nomenclature with Griffin in the 1937 Conference on Pottery Classification for the Southeastern United States. Ford and Willey (1941) used this system in the Louisiana WPA projects between 1938 and 1941. It was adopted by the nascent Southeastern Archeological Conference (Haag, 1939), later used by Caldwell and Waring in Georgia, and eventually became standard throughout the eastern United States.

I had been encouraged by Griffin and Ford to develop pottery types in northwestern Louisiana. I used the binomial system (i.e., "Belcher Engraved") in a report of pottery types from the Belcher Mound, published in the *Bulletin of the Texas Archeological and Paleontological Society* (C. H. Webb and Dodd, 1941)—the first use of this system for Caddoan ceramics in the bulletin. Later I assisted Krieger in extending the binomial or trinomial (i.e., "Holly Fine Engraved") system throughout the Caddoan area.

Ford and his coworkers in central Louisiana, and Phillips, Ford, and Griffin (1951) in the Lower Mississippi Valley Survey used the techniques of meticulous stratigraphic study, vertical as well as horizontal distribution of artifacts, resolution of artificial and natural levels, histograms and overlays in presentation of data, pottery sherd seriation (previously used, but reintroduced by Ford), and correlation of cultural occupations with Fisk's monumental river geology reports to establish the prehistoric sequences of the lower valley. The Poverty Point-Tchefuncte-Marksville-Troyville-Coles Creek-Plaquemine-Natchez or the alternate Poverty Point-Tchula-Marksville-Baytown-Coles Creek Early and Late Mississippian sequences served as fulcrums around which other cultural complexes of the eastern United States have been oriented or with which they have been compared.

In Oklahoma, excavations were conducted at the Spiro group and other prehistoric Caddoan sites, also in pre-Caddoan Archaic and early ceramic sites in the Arkansas River valley and eastern Oklahoma (Orr, 1952; Bell and Baerreis, 1951). Hopewell related materials were reported and the Fourche Maline complex of Late Archaic and Early Woodland sites was outlined. By long-range comparisons, Fourche Maline was assumed to cover a Poverty Point-Tchefuncte-Marksville time span. Among the workers in Oklahoma were Forrest Clements, Kenneth Orr, David Baerreis, Lynn Howard, Rodney Cobb, and Phil Newkumet.

Concurrent with the Oklahoma archeological activities during the late 1930s were the WPA excavations in East Texas which included the George C. Davis site near Nacogdoches and the Hatchel Mound near Texarkana. McAllister was department chairman at the University of Texas, T. N. Campbell was department archeologist, and Perry Newell was field archeologist for the Davis excavations between 1939 and 1942. Krieger came to the university as research associate in 1941, completed the Davis publication (Newell and Krieger, 1949) after Newell's death, established artifact types that later appeared in the Texas handbook, and developed cultural entities and chronologies for Texas and the Caddoan area. J. Charles Kelley, Campbell, and Donald J. Lehmer were working in southwestern and central Texas.

Between 1935 and 1942 Monroe Dodd, Jr. and I made surface collections in northwestern Louisiana, excavated a small cemetery at Smithport Landing (C. H. Webb, 1963) which demonstrated early Caddoan nonceremonial burial and village wares, salvaged two large burial pits at the Gahagan site (C. H. Webb and Dodd, 1939), and were excavating the Belcher Mound (C. H. Webb, 1959) as another salvage program. I exchanged visits with Ford and Willey, then with Newell and Krieger. At Ford's recommendation we excavated the Belcher Mound by the peeling technique, rather than the then popular "cake-slicing" technique, completely exposing the occupations and house floors one at a time. I believe that this was the first Caddoan mound to be so excavated.

The concept of interrelationships over the four-state area was beginning to ferment. Eventually, in January, 1942, Krieger and Newell from Texas, Baerreis and Cobb from Oklahoma, and Beecher and I from Louisiana spent a weekend together at my home studying archeological data. We confirmed or established ceramic types, compared materials from the several states, and laid the groundwork for areal cooperation that culminated, in 1946 and after World War II, in the First Caddo Conference (symposium) at the University of Oklahoma (Krieger, 1947).

This initial conference, under the cochairmanship of Alex Krieger and Kenneth Orr, set several patterns that were followed at Caddo conferences for many years: (1) no written papers; (2) round table discussions with one or more leaders for each chosen topic; (3) full audience participation; (4) representation from each of the states and from outside of the area; and (5) a minimum of formality. The expressed purposes of the meetings were to assemble data relative to the definition of cultural units, to seek agreement on these identities and their relationships, to integrate them with those found in surrounding areas, to discuss the broader implications of these correlations in terms of the Southwest, Mississippian, the Southeast, the Plains, and Mexico, and to try to define the major unsolved problems in the area.

An attendance of forty-one persons at the first conference included representatives from the four states. Those from outside of the area were: Chapman, the Hamiltons, and Wrench from Missouri; Spaulding and Trowbridge from Kansas; Deuel, MacNeish, and McGregor from Illinois; Neumann from Indiana; Griffin from Michigan; Dr. and Mrs. Mera from New Mexico; and Armillas, Du Solier, and Noguera from Mexico. King Harris and I participated, and we have attended most, if not all, of the subsequent Caddo conferences, which in 1978 totaled twenty-one. Griffin continued to attend frequently, and often he, Krieger, and Ford led spirited discussions of cultural and temporal relationships between Caddoan, Mississippian, and Lower Valley manifestations. As they came to the area or developed within it, others took over frequently as discussion leaders: Robert Bell, Hester and Mott Davis, C. R. McGimsey, Don Wyckoff, Michael Hoffman, Dee Ann (Suhm) Story, Hiram Gregory, James Brown, Frank Schambach, Harry Shafer, Terry Pruitt, Ned Woodall, and Martha Rolingson.

The Caddo conferences and other meetings in the area after the mid-1940s often reflected archeological trends that were occurring throughout the eastern United States. There was, of course, the desire to use artifacts and excavation findings for the reconstruction of culture history, replacing the collection of artifacts for esoteric pleasure. Then a lot of new ground was broken in artifact typology, in the attempt to advance from cumbersome individual artifact description to the establishment of *types* (comparable to the *species* concept in botany and zoology) as more effective tools. With the introduction of the binomial or trinomial system in nomenclature, much additional study entered into questions of how attributes should be quantified in the formulation of types. Arguments were, and still are, rife over subjective versus mathematical formulations, the latter concept emphasized by Spaulding (1953) and reinforced by the advent of computer technology. In artifact classification there are those who lump types and those who prefer to split types in finer detail; there are arguments over relative values of attributes. Some people, such as Ford, Willey, and I working in Louisiana; Krieger, Suhm, and Jelks in their papers in the Texas handbook; and Bell and Perino in their studies in the Oklahoma projectile point handbooks, prefer to establish types as simple and sharp tools. Others, including Phillips, Williams, Brain, Halley, and Belmont in working with the Harvard University surveys in the Yazoo and Tenas Basins; Duffield, Johnson, and McClurkan in dealing with East Texas lithics; and Schambach in studying Arkansas ceramics, have preferred the type-variety concept, with further study of modes, in their attempts to clarify changes in time and relationships in space. Still other serious students have questioned artifact formulation by named types and varieties lest this method might interfere with the recognition of individual and local technologies.

Similarly, there have been varying ideas of the ways in which artifact types and other cultural traits should be manipulated or combined in the demonstration and comparison of prehistoric culture units. The Texas and Caddoan taxonomists initially adopted the McKern Midwestern system of site (component)-focus-aspect-phase-pattern (the latter two seldom used). Progressively, however, they modified the original purity by adding, overtly or covertly, temporal and historic connotations. Students in the Lower Mississippi Valley and eastward have modified the McKern system to use the site (component)-phase-period formulation of cultures and chronologies, sometimes expressing their restiveness by substituting terms like *stages* or *characterizations*. The words *period* and *complex* have meant different things to different people.

On a larger scale, discussions of trends, broad sweeps of cultural transmission, and even grandiose generalizations have been essayed or proposed. The WPA era resulted first in the establishment of local and regional chronologies; then came an outstanding series of syntheses and interpretations. Griffin, Ford, Willey, Phillips, William H. Sears, Joseph R. Caldwell, Jesse D. Jennings, and Alex Krieger were prominent in these endeavors. The outstanding volume of a quarter-century ago was *Archaeology of Eastern United States*, edited by Griffin (1952) and dedicated to Fay-Cooper Cole. Others have followed, including the Rice Institute symposium, which resulted in the publication of *Prehistoric Man in the New World*, edited by Jennings and Norbeck (1964). Ford (1952) published the results of one of the early attempts at widespread comparisons and demonstrations of culture movements—from Florida to the Caddoan area—in his "Measurements of Prehistoric Design Developments in the Southeastern States." Krieger's (1946) "Culture Complexes and Chronology in Northern Texas, with Extension of Puebloan Datings to the Mississippi Valley," and Bell's study of Caddoan extensions into the plains are other examples.

Many debates have centered around the concepts of independent invention versus culture diffusion, or of man-the-innovator versus man-the-culture-bearer. The latter was one of the favorite arguments between Jim Ford and me, with Ford expounding on Leslie White's culture diffusion theory and with me holding for my concept of individualistic and humanistic action.

King Harris and I contributed to the knowledge of the Caddo-European contact period along Red River. His studies were of sites like Roseborough Lake, Womack, and Kaufman (Harris, 1953, 1967; Harris and Harris, 1967; Harris et al., 1965; Skinner et al., 1969) in the northeastern corner of Texas, south of Red River and above the Fulton Bend. Although the materials he worked with included both native and trade objects, perhaps King's finest contribution was an exhaustive compilation of trade bead types and datings. My work was in the Natchitoches area, with reports of late Caddoan pottery types, presumably from the Natchitoches tribe, and trade materials (C. H. Webb, 1945). Later reports from the Colfax Ferry site concerned a 1790-1805 occupation by Pascagoula-Biloxi groups. Hiram Gregory

(Gregory and Webb, 1965) joined me in describing trade bead types from the Natchitoches vicinity and subsequently wrote his doctoral dissertation (1973) at Southern Methodist University on the Spanish post at Los Adaes, with a careful study of European beads, ceramics, and other trade or native objects found in his exploration at the site.

At the other end of the time spectrum, Harris and I were involved in studies of early man in the Trans-Mississippi South. Wilson W. Crook, Jr. and Harris (1952, 1954) described two sequent Archaic cultures near Dallas. Then they discovered and reported the Lewisville site (Crook and Harris, 1957, 1958), with radiocarbon dating of charcoal from a hearth reported to be older than 38,000 B.C. The date and site have elicited much discussion and some controversy, especially since a Clovis point was found in Hearth 1. In recent years there has been less reluctance to accept a date this early for man in the Americas, as radiocarbon datings much earlier than the accepted range for Clovis have been reported from other sites, including recent datings of approximately 16,000 years ago from rock shelters in Pennsylvania and Tennessee.

King and I shared an interest in San Patrice culture. I had initially described San Patrice points and Albany type sidescrapers from northwestern Louisiana in the *Bulletin of the Texas Archeological and Paleontological Society* (Webb, 1946). Lathel Duffield's published findings (1963) at the multicomponent Wolfshead site in East Texas indicated San Patrice antedated Archaic horizons. He also gave some evidence of the associated tool types and delineated three varieties of San Patrice type. More recently (Webb, Shiner, and Roberts, 1971) we reported isolated San Patrice components, stratigraphically below Archaic materials, at the John Pearce site near Shreveport. Here the San Patrice varieties *Hope* and *St. Johns* were associated with side-notched Keithville points, Albany sidescrapers, and a complete assemblage of microlithic tools made from flakes and blades. King Harris found a San Patrice point in the Wood Pit site at a level deeper than material from which a radiocarbon date of approximately 4000 B.C. was secured (personal communication). Gagliano and Gregory (1965) and C. H. Webb (1948) had previously demonstrated the presence of a wide variety of Paleo-Indian point types in Lousiana, including Clovis, Folsom, Angostura, Scottsbluff, Plainview, Meserve, Dalton, San Patrice, and Pelican types.

The third field in which King Harris and I have collaborated concerns the Poverty Point culture. Although this culture is primarily centered in the Lower Mississippi Valley and adjoining portions of the Gulf Coast, it reached the Ouachita River to the west and influenced late Archaic cultures across southwestern Arkansas to the Red River. Following brief reports (Webb, 1944, 1948) that I made in *American Antiquity*, and later the Jaketown report of Ford, Phillips, and Haag (1955) and the Ford and Webb (1956) publication by the American Museum of Natural History, many of us have joined in pursuing this intriguing culture. The work of the Lower Mississippi Valley Survey has continued under the sponsorship of Peabody Museum, Harvard University, with Phillips's (1970) monumental Lower Yazoo Basin report. Other aspects of Poverty Point have been investigated by Stephen Williams and Jeffrey Brain. Before his untimely death, Ford (1966) published a stimulating article outlining the Formative Period in the southeastern United States, and then later a widely acclaimed book (Ford, 1969) which compared Poverty Point, Adena-Hopewell, Olmec, and Chavin cultures of the American Formative during the millennium before the time of Christ.

Poverty Point has now (C. H. Webb, 1977) been documented as a widespread culture of the American Formative, involving five river systems and more than 125 documented sites, with its cultural climax and politico-religious center at the index site.

Many other people have contributed to studies of Poverty Point: in Louisiana, Sherwood Gagliano, Jon. L. Gibson, William Haag, Hiram Gregory, Donald G. Hunter, William G. Neitzel, Robert Neuman, William Baker, Carl Alexander, Richard Shenkel, Carl Kuttruff, and many other members of the Louisiana Archaeological Society; in Arkansas, Frank Schambach, Cynthia Weber, Martha Rolingson, Dan Morse, Harvey McGehee, and others of the Arkansas Archaeological Society; in Mississippi, John Connaway, Sam McGahey, Richard Marshall, L. B. Jones, Thomas H. Koehler, and dozens of members of the Mississippi Archaeological Association in the Yazoo Basin and on the Gulf Coast. Beyond these states, our study of the cultural influence and trade connections has involved professional and nonprofessional students in Missouri, Tennessee, Florida, and most of the southeastern tier of states. The Poverty Point collections of King Harris and several of his Dallas friends were among the eighteen collections Ford and I classified and tabulated during the 1960s. Additionally, King (personal communications) found earth ovens and a bead-maker's kit at the site which were important additions to the technology; he also reported on jasper bead-making in Walker County, Alabama (Harris, 1950).

In the most recent epoch in the archeology of the Trans-Mississippi South there is involvement in archeological surveys and feasibility studies in conjunction with river basin, dam site, highway, and other kinds of public—or private—earth-altering operations. Contract archeology is an outstanding example of applied science. It has the advantages of governmental funding of research and publication, and the affording of employment to many graduate students and full-time archeologists. It demonstrates to the government and to the public the important role of archeology in developing and preserving the national and state heritage in history and prehistory. But it has the disadvantages of confining efforts largely to limited studies and restricted excavations at the expense of problem-oriented research, and it can condition departments, universities, and legislatures to depend on federal financing, with the attendant possibilities of restrictive or unimaginative directives or the withdrawal of support.

The establishment of a state archeologist's office in each of the states and the development of active state archeological societies have been important advances. With the latter have come society-sponsored field schools and supervised excavations. Also, in Arkansas there are training programs for amateurs which offer certification of training accomplishments and qualification for certain degrees of independent responsibilities. This program is being watched with interest by other state societies. C. R. McGimsey and Hester Davis came to Arkansas in connection with river basin salvage and were appointed to university positions. They worked with an active state archeological society to develop a favorable atmosphere in the state legislature. This has resulted in funding to support a statewide network of regional survey offices and anthropological staffing of the state universities.

Don G. Wyckoff has been most prominently associated with the Oklahoma River Basin Survey Project and the Oklahoma Research Institute for more than a dozen years. He and his associates have produced an outstanding series of survey reports. In East Texas, Robert Stephenson, Edward Jelks, Lathel Duffield, E. Mott Davis, Curtis Tunnell, and others have been connected with river basin surveys. Departments of Anthropology at the University of Texas at Austin, Southern Methodist University, Texas A&M University, and Stephen F. Austin University have been active in East Texas studies.

The burgeoning expansion of archeological programs during the last two decades has been paralleled, nationally and regionally, by a spirit of introspection and inquiry into motives, methodology, and mission. The social anthropologist, elevated to an atmosphere of social awareness and surrounded by an aura of rightness (if not righteousness), looks down at the dirt archeologist and demands to know how immediate and relevant his work is. The archeologist, possibly feeling guilty because he enjoys his work and forgetting that the pursuit of knowledge does not have to be immediately relevant in order to be useful, responds by trying to orient his science toward individual people rather than toward cultural-historical situations. Let us hope that the injection of sociology into archeology will have happier results than those achieved by sociologists in government, education, welfare, and the judicial-correctional systems.

The theoreticians are looking for a new paradigm. Readers of archeological literature have become accustomed to this word, which the dictionary translates as "show side by side," as a pattern or an example; but in reference to anthropology or archeology Leone (1972) expands the term to mean "a theory or set of propositions assumed or known to govern the operation of an isolated body of phenomena." A paradigm is a set of laws to some, a guiding and shining light to others. One might also get acquainted with words like strategy (as "excavation strategy"), models, systems analysis, cultural dynamics, interaction spheres, ecotones, manufacturing trajectory, exchange hypothesis, functionalism, and pragmatism—they are all present in archeological literature today.

What is the "new archeology"? For a reasonably balanced presentation of the subject, I recommend *Contemporary Archaeology: A Guide to Theory and Contributions*, a compilation of thirty-three essays, edited by Leone (1972). A more in-depth study is *New Perspectives in Archeology* by Binford and Binford (1968). There is also other good work by Flannery, Service, Sahlins, Deetz, Levi-Strauss, and—nearer to dirt archeology—Struever. These seem to typify the modern schools that challenge Leslie White, Kroeber, and Taylor, just as these latter challenged, but never supplanted, the original American anthropological theoretician Franz Boas. From our area and especially with regard to research design in contract archeology there are the studies of Raab and Klinger (1977) or Schiffer and House (1975).

There is dissatisfaction with the results of former periods of archeology, which have been described by Willey (1968) as speculative (up to the mid-nineteenth century), descriptive (to the early twentieth century), descriptive-historic (to 1950) and comparative-historic (since 1950). Willey and Phillips (1958) said "the ultimate aim of archaeology is science but at the present stage the practice has more of the character of history."

The present desire, as I fathom it, is to replace the study of culture history with the study of culture process, thence to deduce or formulate the laws and dicta of culture change and the dynamics of cultural transformation, which will then be made available (confidently) as guidelines for society. To be relevant, it is said, the reconstruction of the prehistoric past must be applied to man's future.

Specifically, Binford and Binford (1968) states that processual archeology is the deductive generation of multiple hypotheses from general anthropological theory that are then tested by sophisticated quantitative methods. This is the hypothetico-deductive approach; with it, to quote Leon (1972), "People are now said to be doing science as opposed to writing history, deducing as opposed to inducing, testing hypotheses (models) as opposed to speculating, and so on down the whole litany of procedural requirements for being legitimate as opposed to tainted." The present view seems to be that the new archeology can handle a new range of problems, like social organization, ecological relationships, demographic and paleonutritional assays, and the relationships of material culture to technology and economics. These are laudable aims to which all archeologists should address themselves as the opportunities are presented, but the attempt to force them in the face of inadequate evidence can produce ludicrous results. It remains to be seen how much better the results of the new school are than those of the old (anything before 1960); so far, I have seen more words than results.

An unfortunate aspect of the new dogma is the conviction—sometimes implied, too often expressed—that traditional archeology was erroneous or futile, that only the new approach is scientific, that no excavation is worthwhile unless it is problem-oriented, that scientific results can be secured in the excavation of a site only if the work is done according to modern sampling theory, that deduction is scientific and induction is not (even though the terms are often confused), and that anyone who practices anything other than the new archeology is, ergo, doing "bad" archeology. After fifty years in one science and forty in another, with some experience in research in each and with much contact with excellent scientists in both, I must observe: (1) no individual or school of thought has a corner on the market for earnestness or intellect; (2) most scientists worth their salt use both deduction and induction; (3) much of scientific progress is about 80 percent dogged perseverance and 20 percent sound methodology, intuition, and luck (witness for perseverence Ehrlich's 605 chemical compounds before he found the 606th that was the "magic bullet," and for a combination of luck and brilliance the almost accidental discovery of penicillin by Fleming); (4) there are many paths to science and most breakthroughs represent the apex of a large pyramid of antecedent studies and clarifications; and (5) unfortunately, most scientists who seek to elevate their own stature by attacking or deriding their contemporaries are suffering feelings of insecurity or inferiority.

History may be no more futile than process. Moreover, anyone reporting on human behavior would do well to remember the newspaper reporter's dictum, "who, what, where, when, why—and how." And, if history *can* be separated from process and human behavior, I happen to prefer history. King Harris and I feel we have paid our debt to society by service rendered in our other professions; archeology is to us a pure intellectual joy, and no polemics can succeed in making us feel guilty.

There is no question that many methods are now available, often from other sciences, to assist and excite the archeologist. Radiocarbon dating has stabilized chronology, and other isotopes are reaching into the distant past. In our area Du Bois is doing outstanding work with archeomagnetic studies at Oklahoma, and Bell, at the same institution, is measuring hydration of obsidian from El Inga. Cynthia Weber arranged for thermoluminescence studies of Poverty Point baked clay objects by Aitken and Huxtable at Oxford, England. Palynology, flotation techniques, paleonutritional techniques, tree-ring dating in this area, specialized studies of flint knapping, the application of computer techniques, and many other advances offer avenues of approach for the future. This is a time for experience-sharing and cooperative working in an exciting science, not for procedural bickering and theoretical snobbishness.

BIBLIOGRAPHY

BELL, R. E., and BAERREIS, D. A. 1951. "A survey of Oklahoma Archaeology." *Bulletin of the Texas Archeological and Paleontological Society* 22:7-100.

BINFORD, S. R., and BINFORD, L. R., eds. 1968. *New Perspectives in Archeology.* Chicago: Aldine Publishing Co.

CAMPBELL, T. N. 1959. "A List of Radiocarbon Dates from Archaeological

Sites in Texas." *Bulletin of the Texas Archeological Society* 30:311-20.
CROOK, W. W., JR., and HARRIS, R. K. 1952. "Trinity Aspect of the Archaic Horizon: The Carrollton and Elam Foci." *Bulletin of the Texas Archeological and Paleontological Society* 23:7-38.
_____. 1954. "Traits of the Trinity Aspect Archaic: Carrollton and Elam Foci." *The Record* 12 (1):2-16.
_____. 1957. "Hearths and Artifacts of Early Man near Lewisville, Texas, and Associated Faunal Material." *Bulletin of the Texas Archeological and Paleontological Society* 28:7-97.
_____. 1958. "A Pleistocene Campsite near Lewisville, Texas." *American Antiquity* 23:233-46.
DICKINSON, S. D. 1936. "Ceramic Relationship of the Pre-Caddo Pottery from the Crenshaw Site." *Bulletin of the Texas Archeological and Paleontological Society* 8:56-70.
DUFFIELD, L. 1963. "The Wolfshead Site: An Archaic-Neo-American Site in San Augustine County, Texas." *Bulletin of the Texas Archeological Society* 34.
FORD, J. A. 1936. *Analysis of Indian Village Site Collections from Louisiana and Mississippi*. Department of Conservation, Louisiana Geological Survey, Anthropological Study no. 2.
_____. 1952. *Measurement of Some Prehistoric Design Developments in the Southeastern States*. Anthropological Papers of the American Museum of Natural History, vol. 44, no. 3.
_____. 1966. "Early Formative Cultures in Georgia and Florida." *American Antiquity* 31(6):781-99.
_____. 1969. *A Comparison of Formative Cultures in the Americas*. Smithsonian Contributions to Anthropology, vol. 11. Washington, D.C.: Smithsonian Institution Press.
_____; PHILLIPS, P.; and HAAG, W. G. 1955. *The Jaketown Site in West-Central Mississippi*. Anthropological Papers of the American Museum of Natural History, vol. 45, no. 1.
_____, and WEBB, C. H. 1956. *Poverty Point: A Late Archaic Site in Louisiana*. Anthropological Papers of the American Museum of Natural History, vol. 46, no. 1.
_____, and WILLEY, G. B. 1941. "An Interpretation of the Prehistory of the Eastern United States." *American Anthropologist* 43(3):325-63.
GAGLIANO, S. M., and GREGORY, H. F. 1965. "A Preliminary Survey of Paleo-Indian Points from Louisiana." Louisiana Studies, vol. 4, no. 1. Louisiana Studies Institute, Northwestern State University.
GOLDSCHMIDT, W. R. 1935. "A Report on the Archaeology of Titus County." *Bulletin of the Texas Archeological and Paleontological Society* 7:89-99.
GREGORY, H. F. 1973. "Eighteenth Century Caddoan Archeology: A Study

in Models and Interpretation." Ph.D. dissertation, Southern Methodist University.

————, and WEBB, C. H. 1965. "European Trade Beads from Six Sites in Natchitoches Parish, Louisiana." *Florida Anthropologist* 18 (3), pt. 2, pp. 15-44.

GRIFFIN, J. B. 1935. "Report on Pottery Sherds from near Abilene, Texas." *Bulletin of the Texas Archeological and Paleontological Society* 7:57-69.

————, ed. 1952. *Archeology of Eastern United States.* Chicago: University of Chicago Press.

HAAG, W. G. 1939. "Description of Pottery Types." *Newsletter of the Southeastern Archaeological Conference* 1(1-6).

HAMILTON, H. W. 1952. "The Spiro Mound." *Missouri Archaeologist,* vol. 14.

HARRIS, R. K. 1950. "Preliminary Report on Site 3 Walker County, Alabama." *The Record,* vol. 9, no. 2 (November-December 1950).

————. 1953. "The Sam Kaufman Site, Red River County, Texas." *Bulletin of the Texas Archeological Society* 24:43-68.

————. 1967. "Reconnaissance of Archaeological Sites in Fannin, Lamar and Red River Counties, Texas." In *The Archaeological, Historical and Natural Resources of the Red River Basin,* edited by Hester Davis. University of Arkansas Museum.

————, and HARRIS, I. M. 1967. "Trade Beads, Projectile Points and Knives." In *A Pilot Study of Wichita Indian Archeology and Ethnohistory,* edited by E. B. Jelks, pp. 129-63. Report to The National Science Foundation, grant 964.

————; HARRIS, I. M.; BLAINE, J. C.; and BLAINE, J. L. 1965. "A Preliminary Archaeological and Documentary Study of the Womack Site, Red River County, Texas." *Bulletin of the Texas Archeological Society* 36:287-363.

JACKSON, A. T. 1933. "Some Pipes of East Texas." *Bulletin of the Texas Archeological and Paleontological Society* 5:69-86.

————. 1934. "Types of East Texas Pottery." *Bulletin of the Texas Archeological and Paleontological Society* 6:38-57.

————. 1935. "Ornaments of East Texas Indians." *Bulletin of the Texas Archeological and Paleontological Society* 7:11-28.

JENKS, A. E., and WILFORD, L. A. 1938. "The Sauk Valley Skeleton." *Bulletin of the Texas Archeological and Paleontological Society* 10:136-68.

JENNINGS, J. D., and NORBECK, E., eds. 1964. *Prehistoric Man in the New World.* Published for Rice University by University of Chicago Press.

KRIEGER, A. D. 1946. *Culture Complexes and Chronology in Northern Texas, with Extension of Puebloan Datings to the Mississippi Valley.* University of Texas Publication no. 4640.

_____. 1947. "The First Conference on the Caddoan Archaeological Area."
    American Antiquity 12(3):198-207.

LEMLEY, H. J. 1936. "Discoveries Indicating a Pre-Caddo Culture on Red
    River in Arkansas." *Bulletin of the Texas Archeological and Paleonto-
    logical Society* 8:25-55.

_____, and DICKINSON, S. D. 1937. "Archaeological Investigations on
    Bayou Macon in Arkansas." *Bulletin of the Texas Archeological and
    Paleontological Society* 9:11-47.

LEONE, M., ed. 1972. *Contemporary Archaeology: A Guide to Theory and
    Contributions.* Carbondale: Southern Illinois University Press.

NEWELL, H. P., and KRIEGER, A. D. 1949. *The George C. Davis Site, Chero-
    kee County, Texas.* Memoirs of the Society for American Archaeology,
    no. 5.

ORR, K. G. 1952. "Survey of Caddoan Area Archaeology." In *Archeology of
    Eastern United States*, edited by James B. Griffin. Chicago: University
    of Chicago Press.

PHILLIPS, P. 1970. *Archaeological Survey in the Loyer Yazoo Basin, Missis-
    sippi, 1949-1955.* Papers of the Peabody Museum of Archaeology and
    Ethnology, Harvard University, vol. 60.

_____; FORD, J. A.; and GRIFFIN, J. B. 1951. *Archaeological Survey in
    the Lower Mississippi Valley, 1940-1947.* Papers of the Peabody Muse-
    um of Archaeology and Ethnology, Harvard University, vol. 25.

RAAB, L. M., and KLINGER, T. C. 1977. "A Critical Appraisal of 'Signifi-
    cance' in Contract Archaeology." *American Antiquity* 42(4):629-34.

SCHAMBACH, F. 1970. "Pre-Caddoan Cultures in the Trans-Mississippi South:
    A Beginning Sequence." Ph.D. dissertation, Harvard University.

SCHIFFER, M. B., and HOUSE, J. H. 1975. *The Cache River Archaeological
    Project: An Experiment in Contract Archaeology.* Arkansas Archeo-
    logical Survey, Publications in Archeology, Research Series, no. 8.

SELLARDS, E. H.; EVANS, G. L.; MEADE, G. E.; and KRIEGER, A. D. 1947.
    "Fossil Bison and Associated Artifacts from Plainview, Texas." *Bulletin
    of the Geological Society of America* 58:927-54.

SKINNER, S. A.; HARRIS, R. K.; and ANDERSON, K. M., eds. 1969. *Archae-
    ological Investigations at the Sam Kaufman Site, Red River County,
    Texas.* Southern Methodist University Contributions in Anthropology,
    no. 5.

SPAULDING, A. C. 1953. "Statistical Techniques for the Discovery of Artifact
    Types." *American Antiquity* 18:305-13, 391-93.

TROWBRIDGE, H. M. 1938. "Analysis of Spiro Mound Textiles." *American
    Antiquity* 4(1):51-53.

WEBB, C. H. 1944. "Stone Vessels from a Northeast Louisiana Site." *Amer-
    ican Antiquity* 9(4):386-94.

————. 1945. "A Second Historic Caddo Site at Natchitoches, Louisiana." *Bulletin of the Texas Archeological and Paleontological Society* 16:52-83.

————. 1946. "Two Unusual Types of Chipped Stone Artifacts from Northwestern Louisiana." *Bulletin of the Texas Archeological and Paleontological Society* 17:9-17.

————. 1948. "Evidences of Prepottery Cultures in Louisiana." *American Antiquity* 13(3):227-32.

————. 1956. "The Role of the Nonprofessional in the Local Society." *American Antiquity* 23(2), pt. 1, pp. 170-72.

————. 1959. "The Belcher Mound: A Stratified Caddoan Site in Caddo Parish, Louisiana." *Memoirs of the Society for American Archaeology*, no. 16.

————. 1963. "The Smithport Landing Site: An Alto Focus Component in De Soto Parish, Louisiana." *Bulletin of the Texas Archeological Society* 31:143-87.

————. 1974. "Can the Professional and the Amateur Archaeologist Co-operate?" *Louisiana Archaeology* 1:1-7.

————. 1977. *The Poverty Point Culture.* Geoscience and Man, School of Geoscience, Louisiana State University, vol. 17.

————, and DODD, M., JR. 1939. "Further Excavation of the Gahagan Mound: Connections with a Florida Culture." *Bulletin of the Texas Archeological and Paleontological Society* 11:29-126.

————. 1941. "Pottery Types from the Belcher Mound Site." *Bulletin of the Texas Archeological Society* 13:88-116.

————; SHINER, J. L.; and ROBERTS, E. W. 1971. "The John Pearce Site (16CD56): A San Patrice Site in Caddo Parish, Louisiana." *Bulletin of the Texas Archeological Society* 42:1-49.

WEBB, W. S. 1938. *An Archaeological Survey of the Norris Basin in Eastern Tennessee.* Bureau of American Ethnology Bulletin no. 118.

————. 1939. *An Archeological Survey of Wheeler Basin on the Tennessee River in Northern Alabama.* Bureau of American Ethnology Bulletin no. 122.

————, and DEJARNETTE, D. L. 1942. *An Archaeological Survey of Pickwick Basin in the Adjacent Portions of the States of Alabama, Mississippi and Tennessee.* Bureau of American Ethnology Bulletin no. 129.

WILLEY, G. R. 1968. "One Hundred Years of American Archaeology." In *One Hundred Years of Anthropology*, edited by John O. Brew. Cambridge: Harvard University Press.

————, and PHILLIPS, P. 1958. *Method and Theory in American Archaeology.* Chicago: University of Chicago Press.

Some Comments on Anthropological Studies Concerning the Caddo

DEE ANN STORY

BECAUSE MUCH OF MY INTEREST in the Caddo has been generated by
R. K. Harris, it is in appreciation of his generous sharing of ideas and
information that I have written this essay on the subject.

It is widely agreed (Fletcher, 1959a, p. 179; 1959b, p. 638; Powell,
1966, pp. 88, 134; Swanton, 1942, pp. 5-6) that the word *Caddo* is
derived from a native term for *chief*, either directly from *kä-ede* or as
an abbreviated form of *kä-dohädä'cho* (real chiefs). Since the French
customarily shortened tribal names by using only the first syllable of
the proper term, it is most probable that *Caddo* stems from their usage
(Mildred Wede, letter dated Feb. 3, 1975).

Unfortunately, there is no similarly simple anthropological explanation of the term. *Caddo* and *Caddoan* have come to have linguistic,
ethnographic, archeological, and even geographical connotations. They
have served to designate (1) a linguistic family, (2) a subdivision of
related dialects within the family, (3) a collective term for perhaps as
many as twenty-five tribes or bands, (4) a possible confederacy on the
Red River, (5) a tribe or band within that possible confederacy, (6) certain prehistoric and historic archeological manifestations, and (7) the
geographic region containing these archeological remains. A paper which
could untangle and disassociate even some of the usages is obviously desirable, though probably at least several decades too late. As an alternative, this brief essay attempts to place anthropological concern with the

46

Caddo into a broad perspective and to evaluate critically the current status of research on the Caddo. Throughout, the focus is on *Caddo* and *Caddoan* as they have been applied to historic Indian groups and archeological remains in Northeast Texas, Northwest Louisiana, Southwest Arkansas, and Southeast Oklahoma.

LINGUISTIC STUDIES

It was through linguistics that *Caddo* initially assumed a broad and significant anthropological meaning. Taylor (1963a, 1963b) and Chafe (1973) provide excellent discussions of *Caddo* as a linguistic construct.

Although a Caddo (Hasinai) word list was apparently collected as early as 1687 by Henri Joutel, it was not until Americans gathered data in the early 1800s that a systematic analysis could begin (Taylor, 1963a, p. 51). The first important classification of American Indian languages did not appear until 1936, when Albert Gallatin published *A Synopsis of Indian Tribes within the United States East of the Rocky Mountains, and in British and Russian Possessions in North America* (Powell, 1966, pp. 88-99; Taylor, 1963a, p. 51). This remarkable work identified twenty-eight linguistic groups and laid the foundation for the many classifications which followed. Adaize, Caddo, and Pawnee were included in the Gallatin scheme as separate languages. By the 1850s the relatedness of Pawnee and Caddo began to be perceived, usually by reference to the "great Pawnee" or "Pani" family. The affinity of the two languages is recognized by Powell's oft-cited 1891 classification, but under the rubric Caddoan rather than Pawnee. As Powell (1966, p. 135) explained:

> The Pawnee and Caddo, now known to be of the same linguistic family, were supposed by Gallatin and many later writers to be distinct, and accordingly both names appear in the Archaeologia Americana as family designations. Both names are unobjectionable, but as the term Caddo has priority by a few pages preference is given to it.

Powell lists the principal tribes comprising the Caddoan linguistic family as including Pawnee, Arikara, Wichita, Kichai, and Caddo.

Adai appears in both Gallatin and Powell as a distinct language, although Powell (1966, pp. 121-22) acknowledges that it could be affiliated with Caddoan. Since Adai is available only as an internally inconsistent list of about 250 words collected by Sibley in 1802 (Powell, 1966, p. 122), its classification remains an unsolved problem. Swanton (1942, p. 6) accepts it as Caddoan, while Lesser and Weltfish (1932, pp. 2, 14) are ambivalent. They conclude that it was probably a divergent dialect of Caddo. Linguistic placement of the Eyeish (or Hais), a group sometimes culturally identified as Caddo, is impossible. Sibley (1922, p. 12) indicated that he collected a vocabulary from an "Aiche" woman in exchange for a shawl. The list apparently has not survived and Eyeish has long been an extinct language.

In essence then, the definition of the Caddoan family has changed little since 1891. As presented by Lesser and Weltfish, (1932, p. 2) it includes:

I. Pawnee, Kitsai, Wichita
  A. Pawnee
    1. South Band or Pawnee proper
    2. Skiri
    3. Arikara
  B. Kitsai
  C. Wichita
    1. Wichita proper
    2. Tawakaru, Weku
II. Caddo
  A. Caddo proper
  B. Hainai
  C. Adai?

Lesser and Weltfish characterize the relationship between these languages as follows:

Pawnee, Wichita, and Kitsai are, in relations to each other, about equally divergent, save that Kitsai in phonetic structure and some forms is probably closer to Pawnee than Wichita is to Pawnee. All three, however, are mutually unintelligible. Caddo is the most divergent of the four languages.

The possibility that the Caddoan family of languages bears a remote generic relationship to other major linguistic groups, particularly to Iroquoian and Siouan, has been suggested from time to time for over a century (Chafe, 1973, pp. 1190, 1193). The most famous and controversial grouping was that proposed by Edward Sapir in 1929 (pp. 138-39). In this classification Sapir lumped the languages spoken by North American Indians into six great stocks or suprafamilies. Iroquoian and Caddoan were joined into one subgroup, which was classed with Siouan and a number of other languages into a stock called Hokan-Siouan. Documentation supporting a relationship between Caddoan and either Iroquoian or Siouan, however, was not published until 1973. In this year Chafe presented evidence of what were judged to be genetically derived similarities between these groups and suggested that the resulting stock be termed Macro-Siouan. Other more distant ties have been proposed, especially for Siouan (and by extension Caddoan); but, like Sapir's Hokan-Siouan stock, they are still highly speculative.

From this review it should be evident that classification problems— primarily the composition and internal relationships of the Caddoan family, and secondarily the broader and more ancient affiliations—have been the dominant concerns in Caddoan linguistics. There are, to be sure, some exceptions such as the kinship inferences drawn by Spier (1924), Troike's (1957) acculturation study, which relied heavily on linguistic data to document interaction between Tonkawa and Hasinai groups, Chafe's (1968) use of Caddoan examples in dealing with phonological theory, and the areal-typological approach of Sherzer (1973). It nonetheless remains true that linguistic attention to the Caddo, and to the Caddoan family of languages, has been on the whole quite meager. Sound descriptive data are still sorely lacking and detailed, anthropologically oriented linguistic research is necessarily severely hampered. Encouragement, however, is to be found in Chafe's observation that Caddo survives as a language and that among its speakers are "remnants of the earlier dialect differences . . . distributed among them in a manner that could repay further study." (1973, p. 1165).

Ethnographic Studies

By the early 1890s, when the Caddo were first visited by an anthropologist, James Mooney (1896, pp. 1092-1103; Swanton, 1942, p. 118), they had suffered greatly from more than two hundred years of Spanish, French, and Anglo-American pressure. Perhaps it is because they were so disturbed that the Caddo largely escaped the flurry of field work conducted among American Indians, particularly by Bureau of American Ethnology personnel and students of Franz Boas. The little field work that has been published (Mooney, 1896; Dorsey, 1905a, 1905b; Parsons, 1941; Swanton, 1931, 1942; Spier, 1924) is based generally on brief visits and few informants. It also has tended to be narrowly focused, emphasizing only certain aspects of cultural behavior, such as folk tales (Dorsey, 1905a) or participation in the Ghost Dance (Mooney, 1896). Sadly, there is no detailed well-balanced ethnology derived from intensive, firsthand observation and interview by a trained professional. Elsie

Clews Parsons's *Notes on the Caddo*, which is based mainly on data obtained in the 1920s from an informant then living in New York City, remains the most inclusive, up-to-date description of Caddo culture.

Fortunately, the documentary sources have not been equally neglected, and it is primarily from observations made from the late seventeenth through mid-nineteenth centuries that we know the various groups now commonly identified as Caddo. The two major monographs, John R. Swanton's *Source Material on the History and Ethnology of the Caddo Indians* (1942) and William J. Griffith's *The Hasinai Indians of East Texas as Seen by Europeans, 1687-1772* (1954), are ultimately derived from these documents. In addition, there are numerous historical studies (see, for example, bibliographies by Glover, 1935; Castañeda, 1936-58; Swanton, 1942; Griffith, 1954; Neuman and Simmons, 1969) which contain invaluable information. While the primary and secondary ethnohistoric accounts are far too voluminous and complex to be reviewed in this essay, a few general observations are offered.

Perhaps most importantly, the limitation of Caddo as an ethnohistoric construct should be stressed. Although this point was clearly made a decade ago by Williams (1964, p. 545), it merits reiteration. Caddo is a concept of convenience which for the period ca. A.D. 1690-1800 has come to include about twenty-three, or perhaps twenty-five, distinct bands or tribes. Ignoring the difficult problems of correlating names and locations given in the documents at different times and by different observers, these groups are most often identified (Swanton, 1942, pp. 7-14; Newcomb, 1961, pp. 200-202) as:

Near or above the Great Bend of the Red River:
    Kadohadacho   Upper Natchitoches
    Upper Nasoni   Nanatsoho

Near San Augustine, Texas:
    Eyeish

Between the Great Bend and Vicinity of Natchitoches:
    Yatasi
    Petit Caddo

Vicinity of Natchitoches, Louisiana:
    Lower Natchitoches
    Doustioni

Near Robeline, Louisiana:
Adai

Ouachita River, near Arkadelphia, Arkansas:
Cahinnio

Lower Ouachita River:
Ouachita

On the Upper Neches and Angelina Drainages (the so-called "Hasinai" or "Tejas" Indians):

Nabiti	Neche
Nadaco	Nacogdoche
Lower Nasoni	Nabedache
Hainai	Nacono
Nacao	Nechaui
Nacachau	

The justifications for lumping these groups together have never been discussed in detail but apparently include linguistic affinity, geographical distribution, native statements of relatedness, and historical events. That the groups were in fact very similar culturally and that most of them were organized in terms of confederacies (Bolton, 1908, p. 251; Swanton, 1942, p. 7) has not been challenged seriously enough. *Confederacy* is a term almost certainly inappropriate when applied to the groups in the Natchitoches area. In the case of others, particularly those in the Great Bend region of the Red River, confederacy may be appropriate, but it could be a late phenomenon, resulting from pressure by Europeans or Osages.

As a single sociopolitical entity, Caddo does not emerge until after the 1850s after there had been much displacement, reduction in numbers, and considerable amalgamation with other groups. It was in 1874, while on the reservation of the Wichita and Affiliated Tribes near Fort Cobb, Oklahoma, that the remnants of the various Caddo groups, along with the Delaware and probably other Indians, formally agreed to unite and be known thereafter as the Caddo Indians (Foreman, 1946, p. 284). The uncritical projection of this unity into the past is an obvious oversimplification, especially when we are generating hypotheses against which prehistoric archeological data are to be tested. Significant cultural variations in both time and space could well have existed among the various tribes, and observations made at a specific village at a specific time should not be taken to apply necessarily to all places and times. Given the time span involved, we should also be prepared for differences in acculturation stemming from variations in the European cultures and displaced Indians with whom the various Caddo groups were associated. Whenever possible, specific dates and names should be used rather than *Caddo* and generalized cultural descriptions.

In view of the desirability of particularizing our approach in terms of more functional social entities—Hainai, Kadohadacho, Village of El Loco, etc.—it is regrettable that the historic sources pertaining to specific tribes or settlements are not equally rich in ethnographic details. At a fairly early date some groups, such as the Cahinnio and Ouachita (Swanton, 1942; Williams, 1964, p. 546), disappear from the documents as distinct entities. Others, for example the Nechaui (Hatcher, 1927, p. 215; Bolton, 1908, p. 267), are known only as names and vague locations. By contrast, it is the Hasinai—the so-called principal tribes resident in the Upper Neches and Angelina drainages (Bolton, 1908, pp. 253-55)—that between ca. 1690 and 1840 experienced the most prolonged and intimate contact with Europeans, especially the Spanish and Anglo-Americans. The most in depth descriptions are for the Hasinai groups; but even these accounts are disturbingly few. Swanton makes this quite clear when he discusses the sources from which he compiled his monograph (1942, pp. 2-3):

> In the subjoined material there are but a few original notes, the greater part, as the title [of his monograph] implies, being a compilation from the productions of earlier writers, including mainly the letters and reports of the missionaries Francisco Casañas de Jesus Maria Francisco Hidalgo, Isidro de Espinosa, and José de Solís, the Historia and Memorias of Juan Agustín Morfi, and the relations of La Salle's companion, Henri Joutel.

We have come to depend very heavily upon Spanish sources, both as primary documents and, more often, as known through translations and historic interpretations. This situation introduces certain geographical and temporal limitations, as well as a Spanish (especially missionary) cultural screen through which the recorded native behavior has been filtered. One has to suspect that this reliance upon Spanish material reflects the outstanding archival research of such competent historians as Eugene Bolton (1908, 1912, 1914, 1915) and Carlos Castañeda (1936-1958), and that the French and Anglo-American accounts have not been as thoroughly combed for tidbits of ethnographically relevant information.

As with the language of the Caddo, much remains to be learned about their culture(s). The almost 1,800 persons now listed on the tribal roll (Marquis, 1974, p. 167) merit attention, not to seek survivals of the past but to understand the Caddo as a viable segment of contemporary society. Historically significant information can come only from the historic documents, and we must view the work of Swanton and Griffith as beginnings, not ends. New sources surely remain to be discovered and old ones, especially the primary accounts, need to be critically reexamined and more carefully utilized. The ethnohistoric research presently underway by Mildred Wedel, who is working with the badly neglected French sources, and by T. N. Campbell, who is combing materials pertaining to Texas Indians, is certain to provide new information and new perspectives.

PHYSICAL ANTHROPOLOGY STUDIES

Published information on the biology of Caddo populations has been derived primarily from analyses of skeletal remains from archeological sites. The concern with living groups has been quite limited and to my knowledge includes only Hrdlicka (1908), Dixon (1923), and Gray and Laughlin (1960). Hrdlicka reports on pathological and genetic anomalies observed by reservation personnel. The Caddo appear only in his table 9, in a listing (item 40) that uselessly includes them with nearby Oklahoma tribes: the Kiowa, Apache, Wichita, and Comanche. Dixon's treatment of the Caddo[1] in his book *The Racial History of Man* (1923, pp. 423, 426-29) is also cursory and is based mainly on unpublished metric data collected by Franz Boas for the Chicago World's Columbian Exposition of 1893. On the strength of head and nose form, Dixon classed the Caddo as basically a "Plains" type but, along with the Tonkawa, as displaying features which represented a survival of physical elements once dominant on the southern plains.

Using blood group gene frequencies, Gray and Laughlin almost forty years later reached essentially the same conclusion, with more specific and useful samples. This most recent study is the only one of the three to deal with the living Caddo in a fashion that today might

[1] The few crania also included by Dixon as Caddo (1923, p. 428) are based on observations published by Allen in 1896. In examining this reference I found that Allen identified the skulls in question as "Arickaree." The basis for this identification and exactly what Dixon meant by *Caddo* are not specified.

be called significant. It represents an interesting, though clearly problem-fraught, attempt to unravel the genetic affiliations of the Caddoan-speakers: the Pawnee, Wichita, and Caddo.

Whether studies are biological or cultural, however, it is almost certainly too late to extract much of the past from the living Caddo. Growth and nutrition research would seem to be far more promising and relevant both to the Caddo and to contemporary physical anthro-pology. As yet there is little indication that such studies are being con-ducted or even contemplated.

By contrast, the health status of prehistoric populations—insofar as it can be assessed from skeletal remains—has been a fairly consistent concern in the analysis and interpretation of materials from archeological sites. Particular attention has been given diseases affecting the mouth and teeth (Colquitt and Webb, 1940; Webb, 1944; Goldstein, 1948; Keith, 1973), with interesting inferences for modern dentistry being pointed out in one study (Colquitt and Webb, 1940, p. 2417). Observa-tions on other kinds of pathologies and on mortality rates typify most recent papers, at least when the skeletal collection is in fair condition. Good examples are to be found in Brues (1958, 1959), Butler (1969a), and Buikstra and Fowler (1975).

Detailed study of the crania is another well-established tradition in the analysis of Caddoan, and other, skeletal remains. It is especially evi-dent in the works of the earlier researchers, most notably Hrdlicka (1909, 1912, 1927, 1940) and to a lesser degree Goldstein (1941) and Stewart (1940). Determination of racial affinity was apparently one of the major objectives of the seemingly endless observations and measurements possible on well-preserved skulls. Evidence of cranial de-formation has also been consistently sought, as deformation has long been recognized as being frequent in collections from Caddoan sites. Usually it is only one of many observations made (e.g., Butler, 1969b); but one paper (Bennett, 1961) deals solely with cranial deformation among Caddo Indians, and two others (Neumann, 1941; Stewart, 1941) have utilized Caddoan materials in establishing types of deformation. Somewhat surprisingly, deformation has attracted little interest from a behavioral point of view. Bennett has attempted to define the practices which probably produced various types of modification to the skull and has briefly presented distributional data, concluding that deformation was a matter of individual choice. Gregory (1963) has published a brief note on skull deformity as a means of enhancing personal appearance.

No one appears to have tried to determine, however, whether or not cranial deformation co-varies with certain cultural traits. Is it, for example, closely associated with artifacts believed to signify special social position?

More commonly asked questions concern the affiliations of the skeletal remains found at archeological sites (e.g., Stewart, 1940; Brues, 1958). Neumann (1952, 1954), in the most encompassing classification of Amerindian material developed thus far, has defined eight varieties. Maples (1962) is apparently one of the few to compare Caddoan series with Neumann's types. Using skeletal remains from eight Caddoan sites in Texas (Sanders, Womack, Hunt, Farrar, Allen, Hatchel, Moore, and Mitchell), Maples noted, among other conclusions, (1962, pp. 25-26) a close morphological relationship with Neumann's Walcolid and Lenapid varieties. However, a more recent study (Long, 1966) has convincingly cast doubt on the validity of Neumann's varieties. It is thus unlikely that such affiliations are of any real significance. The typological approach to skeletal remains has simply never been very productive.

The problems confronting any sort of meaningful analysis of skeletal remains are manifold and difficult to surmount. Ideally, a study should be based on a population in a biological sense, and should examine this population in terms of the genetic and environmental factors that interact in complex ways to affect the phenotypic characteristics of its members. The most serious problems are (1) the extraction of a valid population sample from the archeological record, (2) the uncertainty surrounding the heritability of many skeletal attributes, (3) the physical limitations in the reaction of the skeleton to environmental conditions (especially disease, nutrition, and injury), and (4) the frequently poor preservation of bones in archeological sites. Some of these problems we must accept as inherent; others can at least in part be overcome, particularly if there is a closer interaction between the physical anthropologist and the archeologist. The objectives of an analysis must be more explicitly and more realistically related to both the nature of the sample and the levels of confidence possible.

The crucial definition of a breeding population must depend heavily upon a critical evaluation of the cultural evidence. On an archeological level this is most effectively conceived as a cultural problem rather than a biological problem. In the Caddoan area the recognition of the parameters of population is facilitated by (1) the widespread occurrence of cemeteries which may yield large samples from a definable spatial context, and (2) the common inclusion of offerings in graves which aid temporal and cultural alignments within and beyond one site. The tendency, however, to equate a cemetery sample with a population is not necessarily justified. It may result in an improbable biological assemblage of materials for study, or a disadvantageous reduction in sample size. In view of the need for statistically adequate samples, the possibility of ranging beyond one site should always be considered. Well-documented and well-curated skeleton collections are of key importance and should be receiving far more attention than they have received to date. Moreover, the scientific value of fragile skeletal remains could probably be enhanced by archeologists familiarizing themselves with up-to-date techniques of preservation, and by having a physical anthropologist visit the site to advise on collecting procedures and to make a preliminary *in situ* analysis.

Given reasonable preservation and sample size, we should expect a skeletal analysis at a minimum to yield demographic data, to draw inferences on health status, and to comment on the relative homogeneity or heterogeneity of the sample, as a whole and as sorted in sex categories. When these data are integrated with information on cultural behavior, such as mortuary practices, social organization, and subsistence patterns, they become highly useful. When they stay isolated in an appendix they are of little value to either physical anthropology or archeology.

ARCHEOLOGICAL STUDIES

Whether measured by the published literature or by the number of researchers currently active, it is evident that the dominant anthropological concern with the Caddo has been from the perspective of archeology. It is equally apparent that much of Caddoan archeology remains poorly explained. Well-sampled and well-reported sites are relatively few in number, and data lacking good contextual associations are major sources of information.

As an archeological term *Caddoan* has interrelated cultural and spatial dimensions. The Caddoan area centers geographically near the Great Bend of the Red River and encompasses much of the contiguous portions of Arkansas, Louisiana, Oklahoma, and Texas. It does not coincide with a commonly recognized natural region, nor does it lend itself to simple geographical reference.[2] It is an area delineated by the extent

---

[2] These circumstances have no doubt contributed to the occasional, confused usage of "Caddoan area" in distributional studies of non-Caddoan remains (e.g., Orr, 1952). A workable solution to this terminological problem was proposed by Frank Schambach

of certain archeological remains—in actual practice, primarily ceramics —which are presumed to represent the Kadohadacho, Hasinai, etc., and their prehistoric cultural ancestors. The defining ceramics are difficult to characterize in general but are more or less distinctive in specific temporal, spatial, and functional contexts—at the type level and at the attribute level.

Other archeological traits which have been listed as characteristically Caddoan (E. M. Davis, 1961, pp. 86-89; Hoffman, 1969, p. 43) include circular houses with temporary center posts, certain clay pipe forms, and shaftlike burial pits with elaborate offerings. These, however, are even less serviceable than pottery. They vary greatly by kind of settlement as well as by time and place of occurrence. Even more importantly, it is being increasingly recognized (e.g., Brown, 1975) that material traits alone contribute little to the understanding of social entities and relationships, political organizations, or economic adaptations.

The ways in which Caddoan archeological remains are characterized and explained are very much functions of the conceptualizations and methodologies in vogue at the time of study. There have been about seventy years of investigation, and Caddoan archeology, like Caddoan culture, has a history of development. Since reasonably inclusive and up-to-date summaries of this history are available (H. A. Davis, 1969; E. M. Davis, 1970; Neuman, 1970; Hoffman, 1970; Wyckoff, 1970), this review will briefly discuss what I see as three major phases in Caddoan research. These are presented in roughly historical sequences and are admittedly generalized characterizations based largely on published materials.

The first several decades of fieldwork in the Caddoan area focused on the recovery of specimens for display and for answering very broadly framed questions about lifeways of the past. It was a time of basic discovery, with the quantity and quality of artifacts found serving as the main measures of success of an excavation. The emphasis was on large sites and, even more particularly, on the cemeteries they contained. Contextural relations were often poorly recorded and nonartifactual debris (faunal remains, chipping debitage, and the like) were only incidentally collected, or completely ignored. This specimen-oriented approach domi-

---

at the 1971 Caddo Conference. In an as yet unpublished paper read at this conference, Schambach introduced Trans-Mississippi South as a natural area and defined the Caddoan area as a cultural province which occurs in portions of the Trans-Mississippi South. (See Webb, this volume.)

nated much of the institutionally supported fieldwork from the time of
C. B. Moore in the late 1900s to the close of the WPA at the outbreak
of World War II. It still continues today, mainly in the form of the
unwitting private collector.

In spite of the sampling biases and the often skimpy documentation,
the collections amassed during this early era of Caddoan archeology are
major resources for study. They are the contributions of many individuals,
only a few of whom can be singled out here. C. B. Moore and M. R.
Harrington certainly deserve mention as pioneer researchers. Moore is
especially remembered for his prompt and lavishly illustrated publications of 1908, 1909, and 1912. These reports attracted attention to a
region that had largely escaped serious notice, and they remain as the
sole or primary sources of published information on a number of important sites, including Gahagan, Haley, Friday, and Foster on the Red
River, and Glendora and Keno on the Ouachita River.

M. R. Harrington, commissioned in 1916-17 by the Heye Foundation
to continue Moore's work, was apparently the first in print (1920) to
associate archeological remains with a historic Caddo Indian group, the
"true Caddo" (Kadochacho), and to make interpretations by reference
to ethnohistoric accounts. Subsequent historic associations (Jackson,
1934; Walker, 1935; Dickinson, 1941; Webb, 1945; Harris, 1953)
seemed to cinch Harrington's pronouncement and, though periodically
criticized (Krieger, 1947; E. M. Davis, 1961) "Caddo" and "Caddoan"
have become deeply entrenched in the archeological literature.

The years following Harrington's work in southwestern Arkansas saw
a gradual increase in fieldwork, as well as a shift toward more locally
based excavations by both private individuals and institutionally affiliated
archeologists. The late 1930s were especially active times, with major
WPA excavations being conducted in eastern Oklahoma and northeastern
Texas. Public work projects in Louisiana and Arkansas, however, resulted
in few or no investigations at Caddoan sites. Rather, this task fell to
dedicated nonprofessionals such as Clarence H. Webb and Harry J.
Lemley.

By the outbreak of World War II and the termination of the WPA
program, cultural complexities in the Trans-Mississippi South and Caddoan archeology were becoming apparent. For example, pre-Caddoan
material had been identified in Arkansas (Dickinson, 1936; Dickinson
and Lemley, 1939); a Caddoan sequence was being developed in Louisiana (Webb and Dodd, 1941); comparative studies of materials from

Caddoan sites in Texas had been undertaken (e.g., Jackson, 1933, 1934, 1935, 1938); and Caddoan culture complexes were beginning to be defined in Oklahoma (Orr, 1941).

From the recognition that Caddoan archeology could not be explained as a single culture complex emerged a second major phase of research, one of systematic description and synthesis. This cultural-historical approach crystallized in the early 1940s and reached a peak in the summaries published in the 1950s (Bell and Baerreis, 1951; Orr, 1952; Suhm, Krieger, and Jelks, 1954). It had been stimulated by a new generation of highly trained archeologists who had begun their professional careers (many on WPA projects) and who were formulating new approaches to artifact typologies (e.g., Rouse, 1939) and to cultural taxonomies (e.g., McKern, 1939), as well as publishing broad chronologic schemes (e.g., Ford and Willey, 1941).

The way to systematic ordering of Caddoan archeology was led by one such archeologist from the University of California at Berkeley, Alex D. Krieger. Krieger came to Texas in the late 1930s as supervisor of the WPA Austin lab. In 1941 he began his comparative Caddoan studies, and by 1943, in a paper presented at the Third Round Table Conference in Mexico City (Krieger, 1944), was able to outline two major time periods, the Gibson (early) and Fulton (late) aspects, and twelve foci. The definition and chronologic placement of Caddoan complexes, particularly their alignment with the better established sequences in the Southwest, Lower Mississippi Valley, and Mesoamerican, became dominant themes in many of Krieger's subsequent publications. His broad command of New World prehistory and his ability to synthesize a wide variety of information are quite evident in his two major contributions to Caddoan archeology: *Cultural Complexes and Chronology in Northern Texas* (1946) and *The George C. Davis Site* (Newell and Krieger, 1949).

In Texas, Krieger provided a continuity with the WPA investigations. In Oklahoma, it was Kenneth G. Orr and David A. Baerreis. Orr is best known for his analysis of the Spiro Site (1946) and his summary article on Caddoan archeology (1952). Baerreis has also published on Caddoan materials in the Arkansas River drainage (1954, 1955, 1957). In 1951, he collaborated with Robert E. Bell to produce a good example of the syntheses of this period, "A Survey of Oklahoma Archeology."

While Oklahoma and Texas were centers of institutionally supported research during the 1940s and on into the early 1950s, significant con-

tributions were also being made by amateurs and by professionals working outside the Caddoan area. The latter include most notably James A.
Ford and James B. Griffin, both of whom injected an invaluable perspective (see especially Ford, 1951; Griffin, 1950, 1952, 1961). Particularly outstanding among the nonprofessionals active during this
period are C. H. Webb in Louisiana, R. K. Harris in Texas, and Dr. and
Mrs. T. L. Hodges in Arkansas.

By the late 1950s fieldwork in the Caddoan area was again on the
increase, largely as a result of renewed federal support of archeological
projects in Arkansas, Oklahoma, and Texas. What had begun in 1946
as modestly funded reservoir surveys, generally under the auspices of the
Smithsonian Institution (e.g., Bell, 1948; Stephenson, 1948), had by
1958 shifted to cooperative agreements between local institutions and
the National Parks Service, and to expanded survey and excavation programs. The opportunities to answer many unresolved questions of typology, taxonomy, and chronology seemed close at hand.

Gradually, however, it was becoming evident that not all of the
weaknesses were in the data. E. B. Jelks, for example, noted in his
analysis of Texarkana Reservoir excavations (1961, p. 74):

> Differences in quantitative representation of pottery types at Knight's
> Bluff, Sherwin, and the Hatchel Site (type site of the Texarkana Focus) em-
> phasize a general observation that a focus (as that classifactory unit has
> been applied in the Caddoan Area) is not necessarily a closely integrated
> complex of traits found with little or no variation from site to site.

The time-space constructs were not adequately expressing, much less
explaining, the observable variations between and within sites. From
dissatisfaction with the limited objectives of the taxonomic approach
arose new directions in American archeology. The most significant of
these crystallized in the early 1960s, mainly in the writings of Lewis L.
Binford (1962a, 1962b). Known variously as processual, scientific, and
new archeology, it basically takes the position that the residue of the
past can be comprehended only in the context of generalizing principles
of human behavior. The strategies of processual archeologists have been
classed (Flannery, 1973) as falling into two camps: one which seeks
covering laws of human behavior and tests them by statistical correlation, the other which seeks regularities of human behavior in the framework of systems theory.

The new archeology has had a profound impact on Caddoan research, even though there are still relatively few full-blown processual studies, such as James A. Brown's analysis of Spiro mortuary behavior (especially Brown, 1971, 1975) and segments of the Lake Palestine project (Gilmore, 1973; Anderson et al., 1974). This is most evident in the increased concern with nontemporal dimensions of artifacts (e.g., Woodall, 1969; Shafer, 1973), subsistence systems (e.g., Keller, 1974), intrasite variability (e.g., Story, 1972), settlement patterning (e.g., McCormick, 1973), and, in general, interpretations framed in behavioral terms. There is new optimism but there are also new and complex demands. Projects are certain to become more costly and time-consuming and to require specialized facilities and expertise that are presently difficult to obtain. Since the still *in situ* sample for study is daily being reduced, it is imperative we quickly and intelligently meet the new challenges of what we have come to call Caddoan archeology.

BIBLIOGRAPHY

ALLEN, H. 1896. "Crania from the Mounds of the St. Johns River, Florida: A Study Made in Connection with Crania from Other Parts of North America." *Journal of the Academy of Natural Sciences of Philadelphia* 10 (4): 367-448.

ANDERSON, K. M.; GILMORE, K.; McCORMICK, O. F. III; and MORENON, E. P. 1974. *Archaeological Investigations at Lake Palestine, Texas.* Southern Methodist University Contributions in Anthropology, no. 11.

BAERREIS, D. A. 1954. "The Huffaker Site, Delaware County, Oklahoma." *Bulletin of the Oklahoma Anthropological Society* 2:35-48.

————. 1955. "Further Material from the Huffaker Site, Delaware County, Oklahoma." *Bulletin of the Oklahoma Anthropological Society* 3:54-68.

————. 1957. "The Southern Cult and the Spiro Ceremonial Complex." *Bulletin of the Oklahoma Anthropological Society* 5:23-38.

BELL, R. E. 1948. "Recent Archeological Research in Oklahoma." *Bulletin of the Texas Archeological and Paleontological Society* 19:148-54.

————, and BAERREIS, D. A. 1951. "A Survey of Oklahoma Archaeology." *Bulletin of the Texas Archeological and Paleontological Society* 22:7-100.

BENNETT, K. A. 1961. "Artificial Cranial Deformation among the Caddo Indians." *Texas Journal of Science* 13 (4): 377-90.

BINFORD, L. R. 1962a. "Archaeology as Anthropology." *American Antiquity* 28 (2): 217-25.

————. 1962b. "Archaeological Systematics and the Study of Cultural Process." *American Antiquity* 31 (2): 203-10.

BOLTON, H. E. 1908. "The Native Tribes about the East Texas Missions."
Texas State Historical Association Quarterly 11 (4): 249-76.

―――――. 1912. "The Spanish Occupation of Texas, 1519-1690." *Southwestern Historical Quarterly* 16 (1): 1-26.

―――――, ed. 1914. *Athanase de Mézières and the Louisiana-Texas Frontier,
1768-1780.* 2 vols. Cleveland: Arthur H. Clark Co.

―――――. 1915. *Texas in the Middle Eighteenth Century.* Reprint. Austin:
University of Texas Press, 1970.

BROWN, J. A., 1971. "The Dimensions of Status in the Burials at Spiro."
In *Approaches to the Social Dimensions of Mortuary Practices,* ed. J. A.
Brown, pp. 92-112. Memoirs of the Society for American Archaeology,
no. 25.

―――――. 1975. "Spiro Art and Its Mortuary Context." Dumbarton Oaks Conference on Death and the Afterlife in Pre-Columbian America (Oct. 17,
1973), pp. 1-32.

BRUES, A. M. 1958. "Skeletal Material from the Horton Site." *Bulletin of the
Oklahoma Anthropological Society* 6:27-32.

―――――. 1959. "Skeletal Material from the Morris Site (CK-39)." *Bulletin
of the Oklahoma Anthropological Society* 7:63-70.

BUIKSTRA, J., and FOWLER, D. 1975. "An Osteological Study of the Human
Skeletal Material from the Bentsen-Clark Site." Appendix in *The Bentsen-Clark Site, Red River County, Texas: A Preliminary Report,* by L.
Banks and J. Winters. Texas Archeological Society, Special Publication
no. 2, pp. 79-97.

BUTLER, B. H. 1969a. Appendix I: "Analysis of the Human Skeletal Remains." In *Archaeological Investigations at the Sam Kaufman Site, Red
River County, Texas,* ed. S. A. Skinner, R. K. Harris, and K. M. Anderson. Southern Methodist University Contributions in Anthropology, no.
5, pp. 115-36.

―――――. 1969b. Appendix III: "The Skeletal Material from the Bison Site,
Area B." In *Archaeological Excavations in the Toledo Bend Reservoir,
1966,* by J. N. Woodall. Southern Methodist University Contributions
in Anthropology, no. 3, pp. 84-93.

CASTAÑEDA, C. E. 1936-1958. *Our Catholic Heritage in Texas, 1519-1936.*
7 vols. Austin: Van Boeckmann-Jones Co.

CHAFE, W. L. 1968. "The Order of Phonological Rules." *International Journal of American Linguistics* 34:115-46.

―――――. 1973. "Siouan, Iroquoian, and Caddoan." In *Current Trends in Linguistics,* ed. T. A. Sebeok. *Linguistics in North America* 10:1164-1209.
New York: Mouton.

COLQUITT, W. T., and WEBB, C. H. 1940. "Dental Diseases in an Aboriginal
Group." *Tri-State Medical Journal* 12 (4): 2414-17.

DAVIS, E. M. 1961. "Proceedings of the Fifth Conference on Caddoan Archeology." *Bulletin of the Texas Archeological Society* 30:77-143.

————. 1970. "Archeological and Historical Assessment of the Red River Basin in Texas." *Archeological and Historical Resources of the Red River Basin,* ed. H. A. Davis. Arkansas Archeological Survey, Publications on Archeology, Research Series, no. 1, pp. 25-65.

DAVIS, H. A. 1969. "A Brief History of Archeological Work in Arkansas up to 1967." *Bulletin of the Arkansas Archeological Society* 10 (1-3): 2-8.

DICKINSON, S. D. 1936. "Ceramic Relationships of the Pre-Caddo Pottery from the Crenshaw Site." *Bulletin of the Texas Archeological and Paleontological Society* 8:56-69.

————. 1941. "Certain Vessels from the Clements Place, an Historic Caddo Site." *Bulletin of the Texas Archeological and Paleontological Society* 13:117-32.

————, and LEMLEY, H. J. 1939. "Evidences of the Marksville and Coles Creek Complexes at the Kirkham Place, Clark County, Arkansas." *Bulletin of the Texas Archeological and Paleontological Society* 11:139-89.

DIXON, R. B. 1923. *The Racial History of Man.* New York: Charles Scribner's Sons.

DORSEY, G. A. 1905a. *Traditions of the Caddo.* Carnegie Institution of Washington, Publication no. 41.

————. 1905b. "Caddo Customs of Childhood." *Journal of the American Folk-Lore Society* 18:226-28.

FLANNERY, K. V. 1973. "Archeology with a Capital S." In *Research and Theory in Current Archeology,* ed. C. L. Redman, pp. 47-53. New York: John Wiley & Sons.

FLETCHER, A. C. 1959a. "Caddo." In *Handbook of American Indians North of Mexico,* ed. F. W. Hodges, pt. 1, pp. 179-83. American Bureau of Ethnology Bulletin no. 30 (1907). Reprint.

————. 1959b. "Kado Hadacho." In *Handbook of American Indians North of Mexico,* ed. F. W. Hodges, pt. 1, pp. 638-39. American Bureau of Ethnology Bulletin no. 30 (1907). Reprint.

FORD, J. A. 1951. *Greenhouse: A Troyville-Coles Creek Period Site in Avoyelles Parish, Louisiana.* Anthropological Papers of the American Museum of Natural History, vol. 44, pt. 1.

FORD, J. A., and WILLEY, G. R. 1941. "An Interpretation of the Prehistory of the Eastern United States." *American Anthropologist* 43 (3): 325-63.

FOREMAN, G. 1946. *The Last Trek of the Indians.* Chicago: University of Chicago Press.

GALLATIN, A. 1836. "A Synopsis of the Indian Tribes within the United States East of the Rocky Mountains, and in British and Russian Possessions in North America." In *Transactions and Collections of the American Antiquarian Society (Archeologia America)*, vol. 2.

GILMORE, K. K. 1973. "Caddoan Interaction in the Neches Valley, Texas." Ph.D. dissertation, Southern Methodist University.

GLOVER, W. B. 1935. "A History of the Caddo Indians." *Louisiana Historical Quarterly* 18 (4): 872-946.

GOLDSTEIN, M. S. 1941. "Crania from East Texas." *News Letter of the Southeastern Archaeological Conference* 2 (4): 5.

_____. 1948. "Dentition of Indian Crania from Texas." *American Journal of Physical Anthropology*, 6 (1): 63-84.

GRAY, P. M., and LAUGHLIN, W. S. 1960. "Blood Groups of Caddoan Indians of Oklahoma." *American Journal of Human Genetics* 12 (1): 86-94.

GREGORY, H. F. 1963. "Skull Deformation: An Indian Beauty Mark." *Louisiana Studies* 2 (3): 52-53.

GRIFFIN, J. B. 1950. Review of "The George C. Davis Site, Cherokee County, Texas." *American Anthropologist* 52:413-15

_____. 1952. "An Interpretation of the Place of Spiro in Southeastern Archaeology." In W. H. Hamilton, "The Spiro Mound." *Missouri Archaeologist* 14:89-106.

_____. 1961. "Relationships between the Caddoan Area and the Mississippi Valley." In "Symposium on Relationships between the Caddoan Area and Neighboring Groups," ed. E. M. Davis. *Bulletin of the Texas Archeological Society* 31:27-51.

GRIFFITH, W. J. 1954. "The Hasinai Indians of East Texas as Seen by Europeans, 1687-1772." Reprinted from Middle American Research Institute, Tulane University Publication no. 12. *Philological and Documentary Studies* 2 (3): 41-168.

HARRINGTON, M. R. 1920. "Certain Caddo Sites in Arkansas." Museum of the American Indian, Heye Foundation, Indian Notes and Monographs, Miscellaneous Series, no. 10.

HARRIS, R. K. 1953. "The Sam Kaufman Site, Red River County, Texas." *Bulletin of the Texas Archeological Society* 24:43-68.

HATCHER, M. A., trans. and ed. 1927. "Descriptions of the Texas or Asinai Indians I: Fray Francisco Casañas de Jesus Maria to the Viceroy of Mexico, August 15, 1691. *Southwestern Historical Quarterly* 30 (3): 206-18.

HOFFMAN, M. P. 1969. "Prehistoric Developments in Southwest Arkansas." *Bulletin of the Arkansas Archeological Society* 10 (1, 2, & 3): 37-49.

_____. 1970. "Archaeological and Historical Assessment of the Red River Basin in Arkansas." *Archeological and Historical Resources of the Red River Basin*, ed. H. A. Davis. Arkansas Archeological Survey, Publication on Archeology, Research Series, no. 1, pp. 135-94.

HRDLICKA, A. 1908. *Physiological and Medical Observations among Indians of Southwestern United States and Mexico.* Bureau of American Ethnology Bulletin no. 34

————. 1909. Report on an Additional Collection of Skeletal Remains, from Arkansas and Louisiana. In C. B. Moore, "Antiquities of the Ouachita Valley." *Journal of the Academy of Natural Sciences of Philadelphia* 14:171-249.

————. 1912. Report on Skeletal Remains from a Mound on Haley Place near Red River, Miller County, Arkansas. In C. B. Moore, "Some Aboriginal Sites on Red River." *Journal of the Academy of Natural Sciences of Philadelphia* 14, 2d ser., pt. 4, pp. 639-40.

————. 1927. "Catalogue of Human Crania in the United States National Museum Collection." *Proceedings of the United States National Museum*, vol. 69, art. 5.

————. 1940. "Catalog of Human Crania in the United States National Museum Collections: Indians of the Gulf States." *Proceedings of the United States National Museum* 87:315-464.

JACKSON, A. T. 1933. "Indian Pipes of East Texas." *Bulletin of the Texas Archeological and Paleontological Society* 5:69-86.

————. 1934. "Types of East Texas Pottery." *Bulletin of the Texas Archeological and Paleontological Society* 6:38-57.

————. 1935. "Ornaments of East Texas Indians." *Bulletin of the Texas Archeological and Paleontological Society* 7:11-28.

————. 1938. "Fire in East Texas Burial Rites." *Bulletin of the Texas Archeological and Paleontological Society* 10:77-113.

JELKS, E. B. 1961. *Excavations at Texarkana Reservoir, Sulphur River, Northeastern Texas.* Bureau of American Ethnology Bulletin no. 179; River Basin Survey Papers no. 21, nos. 1-78.

KEITH, K. D. 1973. "The Paleostomatology at the Moore Site (Lf-31), LeFlore County, Oklahoma." *Bulletin of the Oklahoma Anthropological Society* 22:149-57.

KELLER, J. E. 1974. "The Subsistence Paleoecology of the Middle Neches Region of Eastern Texas." Ph.D. dissertation, University of Texas, Austin.

KRIEGER, A. D. 1944. "Archaeological Horizons in the Caddo Area." In *El Norte de Mexico y el Sur de Estados Unidos,* pp. 154-56. Sociedad Mexicana de Anthropologia.

————. 1946. *Culture Complexes and Chronology in Northern Texas.* University of Texas Publication no. 4640.

————. 1947. "The First Symposium on the Caddoan Archaeological Area." *American Antiquity* 12 (3): 198-207.

66 TEXAS ARCHEOLOGY

LESSER, A., and WELTFISH, G. 1932. "Composition of the Caddoan Linguistic Stock." Smithsonian Miscellaneous Collections 87 (6): 1-5.

LONG, J. K. 1966. "A Test of Multiple-Discriminant Analysis as a Means of Determining Evolutionary Changes and Intergroup Relationships in Physical Anthropology." American Anthropologist 68 (2) pt. 1: 444-64.

MAPLES, W. R. 1962. "A Morphological Comparison of Skeletal Material from Sanders Focus and from Fulton Aspect." Master's thesis, University of Texas at Austin.

MARQUIS, A. 1974. A Guide to America's Indians. Norman: University of Oklahoma Press.

McCORMICK, O. F. III. 1973. The Archaeological Resources in the Lake Monticello Area of Titus County, Texas. Southern Methodist University Contributions in Anthropology, no. 8.

McKERN, W. C. 1939. "The Midwestern Taxonomic Method as an Aid to Archaeological Culture Study." American Antiquity 4 (4): 301-13.

MOONEY, J. 1896. "The Ghost-Dance Religion and the Sioux Outbreak of 1890." Annual Report of the Bureau of American Ethnology 14(2).

MOORE, C. B. 1908. "Certain Mounds of Arkansas and of Mississippi." Journal of the Academy of Natural Sciences of Philadelphia 13 (4).

————. 1909. "Antiquities of the Ouachita Valley." Journal of the Academy of Natural Sciences of Philadelphia 14 (1): 5-170.

————. 1912. "Some Aboriginal Sites on Red River." Journal of the Academy of Natural Sciences of Philadelphia 14, 2d ser. (4): 526-636.

NEUMAN, R. W. 1970. "Archaeological and Historical Assessment of the Red River Basin in Louisiana." Archeological and Historical Resources on the Red River Basin, ed. H. A. Davis. Arkansas Archeological Survey, Publications in Archeology, Research Series, no. 1, pp. 3-24.

————, and SIMMONS, L. A. 1969. A Bibliography Relative to Indians of the State of Louisiana. Department of Conservation, Louisiana Geological Survey, Anthropological Study no. 4.

NEUMANN, G. K. 1941. "Types of Artificial Cranial Deformation in the Eastern United States." (abstract). News Letter of the Southeastern Archaeological Conference 2 (4): 3-5.

————. 1952. "Archeology and Race in the American Indian." In Archeology of the Eastern United States, ed. J. B. Griffin, pp. 13-34. Chicago: University of Chicago Press.

————. 1954. "Measurements and Indices of American Indian Varieties." In Yearbook of Physical Anthropology 1952, ed. J. N. Spuhler, pp. 213-55. Wenner-Gren Foundation for Anthropological Research.

NEWCOMB, W. W., JR. 1961. The Indians of Texas, from Prehistoric to Modern Times. Austin: University of Texas Press.

NEWELL, H. P., and KRIEGER, A. D. 1949. The George C. Davis Site, Chero-

kee County, Texas. Memoirs of the Society for American Archaeology, no. 5.

ORR, K. G. 1941. "The Eufaula Mound: Contributions to the Spiro Focus." *Oklahoma Prehistorian* 4 (1): 2-15.

————. 1946. "The Archaeological Situation at Spiro, Oklahoma: A Preliminary Report." *American Antiquity* 11 (4): 228-56.

————. 1952. "Survey of Caddoan Area Archeology." In *Archaeology of Eastern United States,* ed. J. B. Griffin, pp. 239-55. Chicago: University of Chicago Press.

PARSONS, E. C. 1941. *Notes on the Caddo.* Memoirs of the American Anthropological Association, no. 57.

POWELL, J. W. 1966. *Linguistic Families of America North of Mexico.* Bureau of American Ethnology, 7th Annual Report, 1885-1886, ed. P. Holden, pp. 1-142. Lincoln: University of Nebraska Press, Bison Books. Reprint.

ROUSE, I. 1939. *Prehistory in Haiti: A Study in Method.* Yale University Publication in Anthropology no. 21.

SAPIR, E. 1929. "Central and North American Languages." *The Encyclopaedia Britannica,* 14th ed. 5: 138-40.

SCHAMBACH, F. n.d. "The Trans-Mississippi South: The Case for a New Natural Area West of the Lower Mississippi Valley and East of the Plains." Paper presented at the 1971 Caddo Conference, Balcones Research Center, Austin, Texas.

SHAFER, H. J. 1973. "Lithic Technology at the George C. Davis Site, Cherokee County, Texas." Ph.D. dissertation, University of Texas at Austin.

SHERZER, J. 1973. "Areal Linguistics in North America." In *Current Trends in Linguistics,* ed. T. A. Sebeok. *Linguistics in North America* 10: 749-95, New York: Mouton.

SIBLEY, J. 1922. *A Report from Natchitoches in 1807.* Edited, with an introduction, by A. H. Abel. Indian Notes and Monographs, Museum of the American Indian Heye Foundation.

SPIER, L. 1924. "Wichita and Caddo Relationships Terms." *American Anthropologist,* n.s. 26 (2): 258-63.

STEPHENSON, R. L. 1948. "Archaeological Survey of McGee Bend Reservoir: A Preliminary Report." *Bulletin of the Texas Archeological and Paleontological Society* 19:57-73.

STEWART, T. D. 1940. "Some Historical Implications of Physical Anthropology in North America." In *Essays in Historical Anthropology of North America* (published in honor of John R. Swanton). Smithsonian Miscellaneous Collections 100: 15-50.

————. 1941. "The Circular Type of Cranial Deformity in the United States." *American Journal of Physical Anthropology* 28:343-51.

STORY, D. A. 1972. "A Preliminary Report of the 1968, 1969, and 1970 Excavations at the George C. Davis Site, Cherokee County, Texas." Report of Field Research Conducted under National Science Foundation (GS-273 and 3200) and Interagency Contracts between The University of Texas at Austin and the Texas Building Commission and Texas Historical Survey Committee.

SUHM, D. A.; KRIEGER, A. D.; and JELKS, E. B. 1954. "An Introductory Handbook of Texas Archeology." *Bulletin of the Texas Archeological Society* 24:144-227.

SWANTON, J. R. 1931. "The Caddo Social Organization and Its Possible Historical Significance." *Journal of the Washington Academy of Sciences* 21:203-6.

————. 1942. *Source Material on the History and Ethnology of the Caddo Indians.* Bureau of American Ethnology Bulletin no. 132.

TAYLOR, A. R. 1963a. *The Classification of the Caddoan Languages.* Proceedings of the American Philosophical Society, vol. 107, pp. 51-59.

————. 1963b. "Comparative Caddoan." *International Journal of American Linguistics* 29 (2): 113-31.

TROIKE, R. C. 1957. "Tonkawa Prehistory: A Study in Method and Theory." Master's thesis, University of Texas at Austin.

WALKER, W. M. 1935. *A Caddo Burial Site at Natchitoches, Louisiana.* Smithsonian Miscellaneous Collections, vol. 94, no. 14.

WEBB, C. H. 1940. "House Types among the Caddo Indians." *Bulletin of the Texas Archeological and Paleontological Society* 12:49-75.

————. 1944. "Dental Abnormalities as Found in the American Indians." *American Journal of Orthodontics and Oral Surgery* 30 (9): 474-86.

————.1945. "A Second Historic Caddo Site at Natchitoches, Louisiana." *Bulletin of the Texas Archeological and Paleontological Society* 16:52-83.

WEBB, C. H., and DODD, M., JR. 1941. "Pottery Types from the Belcher Mound Site." *Bulletin of the Texas Archeological and Paleontological Society* 13:88-116.

WILLIAMS, S. 1964. "The Aboriginal Location of the Kadohadacho and Related Tribes." In *Explorations in Cultural Anthropology,* ed. W. H. Goodenough, pp. 545-70. New York: McGraw-Hill.

WOODALL, J. N. 1969. "Cultural Ecology of the Caddo." Ph.D. dissertation, Southern Methodist University.

WYCKOFF, D. G. 1970. "Archaeological and Historical Assessment of the Red River Basin in Oklahoma." In *Archeological and Historical Resources of the Red River Basin,* ed. H. A. Davis. Arkansas Archeological Survey, Publications in Archeology, Research Series, no. 1, pp. 67-134.

Historic Archeology in Texas

GERALD HUMPHREYS and WILLIAM SINGLETON

Definition and Theory

IT IS NOT SURPRISING that archeology and history, since both deal with the past, are found playing complementary roles in the discipline of historic archeology. It is easy to oversimplify the relationship by thinking of historic archeology as either the use of archeological methods to investigate historic sites or the use of historical documentation to interpret archeological remains. If this were true, the two studies would be independent. This, however, is not the case. Historic archeology is a legitimate field in its own right, one which combines the methods of both history and archeology.

Ivor Noel-Hume (1969, pp. 12-13), finding both the Webster and the Oxford English dictionaries inadequate, gives a general definition of archeology as "the study of the material remains of both the remote and recent past in relationship to documentary history and the stratigraphy of the ground in which they are found." That Noel-Hume's background is in history is obvious from this definition, which can also serve as a definition of historic archeology.

Prehistoric archeology is usually considered to entail the study of cultural remains for which there is no historical documentation. In his discussion, Noel-Hume pinpoints the major theoretical difference between historic and prehistoric archeology. Prehistoric archeology can tell us nothing about artifacts other than what is capable of being discovered from the artifacts and their spatial context. Historic archeology, on the other hand, employs historical documentation as another source of information, which helps in placing artifacts within a cultural context. Such documentation can sometimes reveal how, when, and where an artifact was manufactured, arrived at the site, was used at the site, and was discarded as trash. Also available to the historic archeologist is information on the social, religious, and economic functions and statuses associated with the artifacts. No such information is available to the prehistorian, except through artifact associations; i.e., from the archeological data themselves.

It is at the analytical level that historic and prehistoric archeology diverge and historical documentation enters. Archeological field methods are used to dissect a historic site, remove the artifacts, and record their stratigraphic and associational relationships. Historical methods are used in the analysis of the data to place them within a specific historical context. Thus, the theoretical interpretations of stratigraphic and associational relationships used in prehistoric archeology also apply to historic sites, but the methods and theories of prehistory, specifically typological and related analyses, have little or no meaning in historic archeology, except within a historically documented context. It is also obvious that all of the methods of historiography and historical documentation apply to the development of the historical context within which the artifacts and their spatial relationships are interpreted. The above discussion is not meant to suggest that archeological contexts cannot support new interpretations of historical documents, but simply to point out the extra dimension that documentary evidence adds to archeological interpretation.

A sharp dichotomy cannot be drawn between prehistoric and historic archeology, for there is a continuum in the thoroughness with which historic sites are documented. A historic site with little or no documentation would be treated in much the same way as a prehistoric site. At the other end of the spectrum are sites that are so well documented that an archeological investigation may not be necessary. Since most historic sites fall near the middle of this spectrum, some hybridization of the methods and techniques of history and anthropology is required.

Who then is to practice historic archeology? It seems reasonable that such a person needs training in both history and archeology, or that archeologists and historians should work together to obtain the best possible interpretation of the lives of the former occupants of a site.

At present it is rather hotly debated whether historic archeology is a sub-division of history or of anthropology. Most professional practitioners en-ter the field from one or the other discipline, although a few do trace their roots to architecture. This debate has resulted in the establishment of the Historical Archeology Forum and the publication of a considerable body of polemics, much of which is printed in that Forum.

Noel-Hume is perhaps the most able proponent of the historic posi-tion. His major contention is that anthropologically trained archeologists do not possess the historical acumen necessary to "know the documentary sources essential to the study of historical artifacts" (Noel-Hume, 1969, p. 13). He does not evade the fact that excavation techniques are not taught in history curricula, but feels that "digging can be readily learned by anyone, the only prerequisite being the possession of simple common sense—the ability to reason. . . . The excavator is, in theory, simply a technician who has mastered the art of taking the ground apart in such a way that it will give up its secrets" (Noel-Hume, 1969, p. 15). He seems unwilling to admit that historiography and the methods of his-tory are as easily learned, and he implies that entering historic archeology from history requires less preparation than entering from anthropology. Noel-Hume also implies that prehistoric archeology is a monolithic field with minor internal divisions. This is hardly the case, and few pre-historians would approach a new part of that field without preparation. Nor should they approach historic archeology without first acquiring knowledge and ability in historiography (or a competent historiog-rapher).

This is a far cry from saying that anthropological archeologists have no place in historic archeology, as two other more radical theorists, Clyde Dollar and Iain Walker, have done. Dollar's paper, presented to the 1967 Conference on Historic Site Archeology, prompted much of the current debate and precipitated the founding of the Historical Archaeology Forum (South, 1968). Dollar (1968, p. 11) states that when the anthropologist is faced with excavating a historic site, he is involved in a "whole new discipline, the problems relative to which he is probably not initially trained to understand or surmount." He presents ten theses to define what he feels are certain major methods, techniques, and limitations of historic archeology (Dollar, 1968, p.13). These theses can only be relevant to the contention that anthropologically trained archeologists are not qualified to conduct historic archeology if they are unique to the latter discipline.

Dollar's theses may be summarized as follows:

1. Historic archeology is very complex.

2. Seriation (which Dollar calls an extended field technique) does not produce distortion-free data.

3. Every artifact in a historic site has two dates, its date of manufacture and date of deposition.

4. The date of manufacture implies alpha and omega levels.

5. Historic sites have two periods, the historic period and the "alter" period.

6. Artifacts have two locations, horizontal and vertical.

7. An archeological artifact cannot be dated on the fact of its presence at a specific site, nor can a site be dated by the presence of a specific artifact.

8. Historic archeology is architectural in orientation and reconstructive in purpose and scope.

9. There is a basic dissimilarity between architectural evidence at a historic site versus a prehistoric site.

10. Historic sites must be identified and authenticated.

A quick consideration of the theses reveals that only the eighth is unique to historic archeology. If this thesis is strictly interpreted, however, only architects with a strong interest in the history of their field and some training in archeological field methods would be qualified to study historic sites.

Iain Walker (1968a, 1968b, 1970, esp. 1974) very firmly places himself in the historicists' camp when he states that "it is about time historical archeologists started doing history" (Walker, 1974, p. 180). Walker's major criticism is that "[Binford] and other [anthropologists] appear to never have tried to master historical data before entering the field of historical archeology" (Walker, 1974, p. 190). He sees the anthropologist doing historic archeology while ignoring history.

Other than "ignoring history" what have the anthropologically trained archeologists been doing? What has been their contribution to historic archeology? Most applications of anthropologically related concepts have centered on the technique of seriation. Although not invented by an anthropologist, this theoretical method has enjoyed considerable popularity among American prehistorians. Generally, most applications in historic archeology have involved tests of the seriation model (e.g., Deetz, 1965; Deetz and Dethlefsen, 1967) or attempts to use seriation as a predictive device (e.g., Binford, 1962; South, 1972,

1974). The extreme accuracy with which historic ceramics and especially tombstones can be dated offers invaluable opportunities for both types of applications.

Seriation, neither a causal nor an explanatory model, is a method of explicating nonrandom clusterings of certain cultural attributes across time and space and does not involve events or any historically important items. It is not surprising that novel applications appear to be foreign to historians practicing historic archeology. Why would the anthropologically oriented historic archeologists be so concerned with the method? They know that factors of hoarding, inefficient supply systems, or the "Doppler Effect" (Deetz and Dethlefsen, 1965) may invalidate the results of a seriation. However, this fact in itself points to one of the major values of historic archeology. A serious study of instances where the seriation method fails may result in the definition of causes of this breakdown.

This value of historic archeology may be generalized as follows: for behavioral models to be tested archeologically, they need not be derived by analogy, but can be developed directly from the historic record. Such homologous models should be considerably more rigorous and testable under more precise settings than prehistoric analogies. The degree to which these models can be applied to archeology should serve as a guideline to the applications of the analogous models of prehistory.

Schuyler (1971) points out that the aim of historic archeology should not simply be to describe the material remains of the past or to test the validity of certain historical models.

Anthropologists, once they have been trained in the use of documentary sources, can use these in their research but from a different point of view than *most* historians. Why cannot Historic Site Archaeologists, or anthropologists, investigate the broadest and most significant questions involved in American history, or any historic record for that matter [Schuyler, 1971, p. 86].

A start in this direction can be found in the words of Deetz (1963); Dethlefsen and Deetz (1968); Earle (1966); and Gilmore (1969, 1973). Deetz (1963) provides an example of the use of archeology in detecting change in the pattern of economic activities under one type of culture contact. Deetz (1965) also provides a test of the ability of archeological methods to detect changes in residence patterns among the protohistoric Arikara. Dethlefsen and Deetz (1968) and Earle

(1966) have likewise given an impetus to demographic studies in archeology, demonstrating the ability of skeletal studies to determine the true age/sex distribution of an archeological population. Gilmore (1969; 1973) provides an excellent example of simulation model-building to locate historic sites (cf. Morrow, 1971). This type of model could have great applicability to prehistoric archeology.

While these studies are only a beginning, they help demonstrate the feasibility of historic archeology as a testing place for archeological theory and as an area in which theory can be derived. Widespread uses of these purposes, however, do not seem to be forthcoming. It is unfortunate that such an opportunity should be wasted.

There is considerable debate among the practitioners of historic archeology as to who is best qualified to investigate historic sites. There are two broad purposes for doing these studies which seem to correlate with the two "schools" of historic archeologists. "Anthropological" historic archeologists want to test models applicable to cultural studies in general and "historical" historic archeologists want to use such sites for the interpretation of cultural heritage, especially for the general public's information. The latter persuasion has dominated historic archeology in Texas.

ETHNIC DIVERSITY AND HISTORIC PERIODS OF TEXAS

To realize the extent of the variety of ethnic influence throughout the history of Texas one need only visit the Institute of Texan Cultures in San Antonio. Such ethnic variety can be attributed to the geographical position of Texas, a state close to the concentration of Spanish colonies in Mexico proper, and one which attracted the English along the Atlantic seaboard and the French along the Mississippi and Red Rivers. In the early history of Texas we see efforts by both the French and Spanish to extend their influence over the area, with the Spanish being more successful. It was not until after the Anglo-American colonization, however, that peoples of great ethnic diversity came into Texas as settlers, which resulted in a rich and varied heritage within the state.

The following outline of Texas history serves as a framework for some of the important works in historic archeology in Texas (*Texas Almanac*, 1974-75).

I. Indian Era: Pre-European arrival in 1519

II. Conquest and Colonization (1519-1835):

A. Early exploration and missionaries (1519-1690)

ARCHEOLOGICAL INVESTIGATIONS (CONQUEST AND COLONIZATION)

The Indian Era defined above is not included in Noel-Hume's definition of historic archeology, for there is no documentation for these sites. Such a strict application of his definition, however, would exclude many sites that are considered historic. This definition should probably be interpreted to include any site that has a European component. This, of course, becomes an archeological definition based on the presence of items of European origin at the sites. There are various archeological complexes defined for the Historic Stage in Texas. A summary and evaluation of many of these are given by Suhm, Krieger, and Jelks (1954), Williams (1961, pp. 122-23), Jelks, E. M. Davis, and Sturgis, eds. (1960), Duffield and Jelks (1961), and H. A. Davis, ed. (1970). Such complexes are created by grouping sites containing similar assemblages.

It is often difficult, however, to determine which historically known Indian group can be associated with a given archeological complex. There is the possibility that archeologically grouped sites may not correlate with any historic Indian group, for the artifact inventories on which the groupings are based may crosscut ethnic groups. This is where historic records play a most important role in documenting the fact that a specific Indian group was occupying a certain site during a given time period. All of the archeological and historical data must be in agreement for an association to be accepted. A most systematic methodology for testing an archeological site against historic records has been developed by Gilmore (1969, 1973). Even when using this approach the problems are great and the documentation of a site may only be tentative. This explicitly stated approach, however, has not been applied to historic Indian sites.

Probably the best documented archeological complex is the Norteño Focus of North Central and Central Texas. Duffield and Jelks (1961) formalized the definition of this complex and associated the included sites with the southern group of the Wichita Indians. The archeological and historical investigations that culminated in the definition and continued investigation of the Norteño Focus can be found in the works of Bolton (1915, 1916), Witte (1938), Castañeda (1936-1958), Johnson and Jelks (1958), Stephenson (1947, 1970), Duffield and Jelks (1961), Harris and Harris (1961), Harris (1962), Harris et al. (1965), Jelks, ed. (1966), Bell et al. (1967), and Jelks (1970).

Other less well-documented Historic Stage complexes include the Allen and the Little River Foci, which have been defined for Northeast Texas and are associated with Caddoan groups. It is interesting that Williams (1961, p. 123) states that the Little River Phase is a tentative complex based on historic documentation, for, even though sites are known, none have evidently been excavated. Webb (1960, p. 53) points out that much work needs to be done to relate historic tribes to sites and to find more archeological sites at known historic locations. Williams discusses other Caddoan related phases (foci) but they are restricted to Louisiana and Arkansas.

In the coastal area of Texas the Rockport and Brownsville Foci are mainly of the Neo-American Stage, but continue into the Historic Stage (Suhm, Krieger, and Jelks, 1954; and Jelks et al., 1960). The Rockport Focus may be associated with the Karankawa Indians (Jelks et al., 1960, p. 170).

The Concepción and Conchos Foci have been defined in the Trans-Pecos area. Both of these complexes result from the contact of the Indians with Spanish colonists (Suhm, Krieger, and Jelks, 1954; and Jelks et al., 1960, p. 133). A similar contact situation existed in Southwest Texas along the Rio Grande from approximately A.D. 1600 to 1800. Here peoples of Coahuiltecan stock bitterly resisted the Spanish takeover until about 1800, after which they rapidly became extinct. Archeological sites of this period of mixed Indian and Spanish materials have been located in the Falcon Reservoir area, but no historic archeological complex has been defined for this area (Suhm, Krieger, and Jelks, 1954).

There are various isolated historic sites, such as burials (Kirkland, 1942; Newcomb, 1955; Suhm, 1962; Ray and Jelks, 1964; and Parsons, 1967), caches (Eagleton, 1955), and house sites (Hasskarl, 1957) found scattered over the state. It is difficult, if not impossible, to attribute these sites to definite Indian groups.

In summarizing the documentation of historic Indian occupations in Texas, one point is very clear: much work needs to be done. Known sites containing historic materials need to be excavated; other sites need to be located. The historical documents need to be more thoroughly investigated and models need to be developed and tested. Such models should not be restricted to the location and identification of sites, for much could be learned both from historical documents and from the archeological data about the nature of cultural contacts that occurred across Texas and the resulting change in aboriginal culture. Only then will the disciplines of history and anthropology be combined.

The most direct and intensive contact that occurred during this period between the Texas Indian and European cultures was largely the result of the Spanish mission efforts. This first Spanish mission in Texas was established in response to La Salle's building of Fort St. Louis on Matagorda Bay in 1685. In 1690 the expedition of Capt. Alonso de León (Governor of Coahuila) destroyed the abandoned remains of Fort St. Louis and continued to East Texas where the first Spanish missions, Nuestro Padre San Francisco de los Tejas and Santísimo Nombre de María, were established that same year. These missions were later abandoned as fear of French extension subsided (Gilmore, 1973, pp. 5-19; Latimer, 1973).

In 1714 the appearance of French explorer and trader Louis Juchereau de St. Denis at San Juan Bautista on the Rio Grande jolted the Spanish once again into reestablishing missions and settlements in Texas (Latimer, 1973, p. 15).

French trading activity along the Red River in the north was also motivating the Spanish. For example, Benard de la Harpe established the Nassonite Post in 1719 (Miroir et al., 1973). In 1716 a request to establish a mission at San Pedro Springs (San Antonio) was granted to Father Antonio de San Buenaventura Olivares. In 1718 the mission of San Antonio de Valero (the Alamo) was founded, but not at the present site. On May 5 the Villa de Béxar and the San Antonio de Béxar Presidio were founded (Schuetz, 1966, pp. 2-3). The founding of this mission and presidio was the beginning of the successful efforts of the Spanish to extend their influence, which lasted into the early part of the 1800s. Bolton (1915, 1916) and Castañeda (1936-58) give excellent discussions of the activities of Spain in Texas, and Scurlock (1973) has compiled a bibliography of source material related to Spanish activity in North America. At the Old Spanish Mission Research Library at San José Mission in San Antonio, there is now an active program for compiling documents concerning the Spanish colonial establishments in Texas (Leutenegger and Habig, 1973).

Some of these missions have been archeologically investigated. In 1950 excavations were conducted under the auspices of the Texas Memorial Museum at the site proposed by Bolton in 1924 to be the location of La Salle's colony of Fort St. Louis. Gilmore (1973), through an analysis of the artifacts recovered and the historical accounts, concluded that the site excavated was definitely that of Nuestra Señora de Loreto Presidio (1722-1726), and thus was also the site of Fort St. Louis. At the same time, Nuestra Señora del Espíritu Santo de Zuñiga Mission was established nearby. Both the presidio and mission were moved inland four years later. The site of the mission has not yet been located (Gilmore, 1973, p. 38).

Several of the mission complexes at San Antonio have been archeologically investigated. Excavations conducted include the missions of San Antonio de Valero (1718-1793) in 1966 (Schuetz, 1966; Tunnell, 1966; and Greer, 1967); San Juan Capistrano (1731-present) in 1967 (Schuetz, 1968 and 1969); San José (Schuetz, 1970, and Fox, 1970); and parts of the Acequia Madre, the water supply ditch for the mission complexes (Schuetz, 1970).

Other excavations of Spanish missions include the San Francisco Xavier missions and the associated presidio (1746-55) in Milam County, Texas (Gilmore, 1969); San Agustin de Ahumada Presidio (1756-66) in Chambers County, Texas (Shafer, 1966; Tunnel and Ambler, 1967), San Lorenzo de la Santa Cruz Mission (1762-1771) in Real County (Tunnell and Newcomb, 1969), and San Luis de las Amarillas de San Sabá Presidio (1757-1768) in Menard County (Gilmore, 1967). Work at the Nuestra Señora del Rosario Mission (1754-1831) in Goliad County has recently been completed (Gilmore, 1974).

Various reasons justify the excavations of these sites. Information for reconstruction was sought at the San Luis de las Amarillas Presidio, San Juan Capistrano Mission, and San Antonio de Valero Mission. More information on the aboriginal material culture of the Lipan-Apache Indians and of the Coahuiltecans was sought at the missions of San Lorenzo de la Santa Cruz and at San Juan Capistrano, respectively. Gilmore (1969), at the San Francisco Xavier missions and presidios of Nuestra Señora de Loreto and San Luis de las Amarillas, and Tunnell and Ambler (1967), at San Agustin de Ahumada Presidio, authenticated the geographical location of the sites. Skeletal remains of the Indian occupants at San Juan Capistrano Mission have been analyzed to determine demographic parameters, pathologies, epigenetic variation, and dental attributes (Humphreys, 1969, 1971). All sites contributed to the broadening of the data base of architecture, the plans of mission complexes, and the European material culture of this period in Texas. Such information can help provide a better understanding of the more mundane day-to-day activities that are rarely related in historical documents.

PERIODS OF THE REPUBLIC AND STATEHOOD

Following the secularization of most of the missions in Texas in 1793, Spanish influence began to decline. Miguel Hidalgo y Costilla (1753-1811) led a Mexican revolt against Spain in 1810, and Mexican independence was finally realized in 1821. The remainder of the missions were secularized in 1830. Meanwhile, the European population in Texas was also dwindling. To halt this decline the Mexican government allowed settlements by Anglo-American peoples from the United States and its territories.

Along with the introduction of Anglo-American colonists came conflict between the Mexican governmental administrative practices and the dissatisfied settlers, who sought to govern themselves. On March 2, 1836, Texas independence was declared at Washington-on-the-Brazos while the battle of the Alamo was in progress in San Antonio. Victory came at the battle of San Jacinto on April 21, 1836.

For the next ten years Texas existed as a Republic, and on December 29, 1845, it became the twenty-eighth state. During the years of the Republic and following, the Anglo-American influence became dominant in Texas, although the Mexican and Spanish influence will always be an integral part of the state's cultural heritage.

During the last two historic periods, economic, political, and demographic development and change have resulted in the founding and abandoning of townsites, communities, homesteads, and industrial complexes. Regardless of the ultimate outcome of the changes wrought by time, these remains can enrich public awareness of Texas's historic and cultural heritage. Some progress is being made through the efforts of the Texas Historical Commission, the Texas Park and Wildlife Department, and the the Texas Highway Department, each of which has an archeological staff and is attempting to preserve and interpret for the public both the historic and prehistoric resources of the state.

The Texas Historical Commission is the official agency for historic preservation in Texas and has a stated purpose: the "protection and development of this [historic] resource." (Latimer, 1973, 1:xi). *Historic Preservation in Texas* (Latimer, 1973) is a statement of the historic preservation plan for the state developed by the commission. This agency also administers the National Register of Historic Sites program and has compiled a comprehensive statewide inventory of historic sites in the state (Latimer, 1973, vol. 2).

It is mainly through the effort of the Office of State Archeologist, which is now a part of the Texas Historical Commission, but which was formerly with the State Building Commission, that the interpretive potential of these resources is being realized. The State Archeologist has actively employed both archeological excavations and historic documentation designed to develop these historic resources.

Some of the more important sites of this period are the early townsites, including Washington-on-the-Brazos. Part of this townsite is now administered as a state park by the Texas Parks and Wildlife Department, and future plans include complete reconstruction of the site. Some of the preliminary archeological and historical research has been completed (E. M. Davis and Corbin, 1967; Lorrain and Jackson, 1970; Shuffler, 1962 and 1965). Preliminary work has shown that there are abundant cultural material and architectural remains, and the potential for reconstructing the town will be limited only by the resourcefulness of the archeologists, architects, and historians, whose responsibility such work becomes.

Among other townsites studied are Gray Rock (1840-1881) in Franklin County (McCormick and Scott, 1971), Texana (1832-1883) in Jackson County (Wakefield, 1968), Velasco (1821-1875) in Brazoria County (Briggs, 1971), and Indianola (1844-1886) and Linnville (?-1840) in the Matagorda-Lavaca Bay area (Gilmore, 1973). Many other early towns passed into ruin after they had been damaged by hurricanes, bypassed by the railroad, destroyed by Indians, or deprived of their economic base.

The rural life of early Anglo-American Texas is also a rich archeological and historic source that has been investigated. At the Lyndon B. Johnson State Park three early homestead sites have been excavated

(Tunnell and Jensen, 1969; Ing, 1970). When reconstruction plans are completed, an interpretation of the Behrens, Sauer, and Danz homesites and related buildings will offer much to visitors.

Archeological work has also been conducted at the Carrington-Covert House (1850s-present) in Austin to provide interpretative data for one of the early Austinite families (Roberson, 1974). Similar work has been completed at the James S. Hogg birthplace in Rusk, Texas (Jensen, 1968).

Excavations of town homes and homesteads represent only the beginnings of the use of such resources to present to the Texas public and tourists an interpretation of the history of rural Texas. One needs only to consider a few of the archeological reports of the Texas Historical Commission, the Water Development Board, Texas Archaeological Salvage Program, Texas Archeological Research Laboratory, the SMU Archeological Research Program, the Witte Memorial Museum, and the Texas Parks and Wildlife Department to realize that there is a growing interest in this resource and an increasing realization of its potential. (See, for instance, Nunley, 1973; Bousman, 1974; Cliff et al., 1974; McGuff and Cox, 1973; Fox et al., 1974; Briggs, 1971; Mallouf et al., 1973; Scurlock, 1974; and Malone, 1970.)

Military sites (forts, battlegrounds, and encampments) and early industrial and shipwreck sites are also being investigated. During the late 1840s and the 1850s a chain of forts was constructed across Texas to protect settlers and travelers from Indian raids. Several of these forts have been excavated and are now open to the public. Fort Lancaster, located on the Pecos River at the confluence of Live Oak Creek in Crockett County, has been excavated for several seasons (Hays and Jelks, 1966; Clark, 1972). At present there is a visitor's center with a small museum area in the park. Most of the ruins around the parade grounds have been stabilized and are open to the public. Some other forts that have been excavated are Fort McKavett, Menard County (Pearson, 1973), Fort Griffin in Shackelford County (Olds, 1969), Fort Graham in Hill County (Alan Skinner, 1970: personal communication), and Fort Leaton in Presidio County (Ing and Kegley, 1971).

Other military sites that are known or have been approximately located include Camp Independence, the encampment of the First Army of the Republic (Wakefield, 1968; Mallouf et al., 1973); the last battle site of the Civil War at Palmito Ranch; Fort Brown; Fort Polk; the battle sites of Palo Alto and Resaca de la Palma of the Mexican

War, all in Cameron County (Briggs, 1971); and Old Velasco in Brazoria County, where the first battle of the Texas revolution was fought (Briggs, 1971).

Reported industrial sites include mills, brick factories, salt factories, and pottery kilns. Durrenberger (1965) reported the excavations at Anderson's Mill in Travis County. In 1974 the Texas Archeological Society held its field school at the McKinney Falls State Park in Travis County, where the McKinney homesite and mill were investigated. Work was continued at the mill and the turbine was found in place.

Skinner (1971) reports the excavation of a salt factory which operated from 1820 until 1870 at the Neches Saline in Smith County. Pottery kilns have been investigated by Sandra Myers (1970: personal communication) in Denton County, and others are reported by Nunley (1973) and Olin McCormick (1970: personal communication). Wakefield (1968) reports the location of the brick factory of the Blair Community.

Exciting shipwreck finds have been made in the southern shores along Padre Island, Texas. Scurlock (1974) summarizes this work, begun in 1967 by Platoro, Ltd. of Gary, Indiana. Texas state officials, realizing the potential of the sixteenth-century Spanish vessels, took legal steps to stop this work so that a state supported and controlled investigation and excavation of the resources could be initiated. In 1970 a magnetometer survey was made along sections of Padre Island (Hays and Herrin, 1970), and various "anomalies" were found and located relative to short reference points. Work has continued on these shipwrecks, and in the summer of 1973 a survey crew found the Spanish colonial camp on shore thought to belong either to the survivors or to salvagers.

A similar magnetometer survey has been conducted in Matagorda Bay during which sixteen anomalies were located (Briggs, 1971), some of which may relate to the two ships lost by La Salle in 1685 (Gilmore, 1973; Briggs, 1971). Recently the Texas Historical Survey Committee has compiled a list of ships known to have sunk along the Texas coast and within the bays (Briggs, 1971). Other shipwreck site reports include the possible location of the steamboat *Black Cloud*, which sank in the early 1870s (Prewitt, 1973), and the *Nassau* and the *Luzan* in the Brownsville area (Hall and Grombacher, 1974).

The above summary of some of the historic site research in Texas should provide a basis for suggesting what contribution historic archeology may make to the people of Texas, to the Texas visitor, to historic archeology as a discipline, and to both history and anthropology.

FUTURE AND RESEARCH POTENTIAL

Latimer (1973, p. xi) has stated:

The future of Texas is clearly linked to its past. What the state is—the outlooks and attitudes which characterize it—and what it will become in the future are the logical development from its roots and traditions. Historic preservation in Texas is an important part of the growing public awareness of and concern for our total environment, the state's historic patrimony is one of Texas' vital resources, equally as important as other natural and human resources.

This natural resource is currently falling before the bulldozers of progress and growth. It is not enough to let chance determine what aspects of our state heritage will or will not be preserved; an informed choice must be made with the help of a good plan evaluating future educational, intellectual, social, and recreational needs of Texans. This can best be done within the state administrative structure. But, to be most effective, this structure should be sensitive to and communicate with both internal subdivisions of the state and external agencies and organizations. The Historical Commission is so organized, for it is the liaison agency for the national historic preservation program and has within its organization communication lines open to the local and regional historical societies.

Cooperation also exists between the State Historical Commission and other state agencies, such as the Parks and Wildlife Department and the Water Development Board. Congruent with the development and continued reorganization of this state agency, a State Antiquities Code (Article 6145-9 of Vernon's Texas Civil Statutes) has been enacted to protect the historic and prehistoric resources of Texas. This act also created a state antiquities committee to control the excavation of sites on Texas public lands (Latimer, 1973). The Historic Commission is continually compiling a list of historic sites in Texas (Latimer, 1973).

The future for a strong and effective preservation program in Texas is promising. Historic archeology will be an integral part of this preservation plan, but the discipline has certain limitations that should be considered. First, it will be easy to assume that the listing of historic sites will contain all sites within an area to be surveyed. The listing should provide only background information for future archeological surveys.

It is also easy for bureaucratic agencies to become so involved in their own immediate concerns and programs, especially when financial resources become scarce, that lines of communication with other agencies are cut or impeded. Communication must be kept open to prevent unnecessary duplication of effort as well as unnecessary destruction of historical resources. Communication is imperative between the local and state personnel, for it is at the local level that most of the potential destruction of these resources can be identified and the necessary steps taken to prevent or to direct this destruction intelligently. It is imperative too that no agency be exempted from the antiquities code.

Thus, it is within the context of the preservation plan for Texas's historical resources that historic archeology has its greatest future. This is true at both the state level, where such investigations can provide part of the data for the interpretation of a state park, or at the local level, where archeology can aid the private individual or local society in the reconstruction of a historic building, or help provide material for local museum displays.

Historic archeology may make major contributions to the writing or even rewriting of Texas history. There is a great difference between stating that La Salle founded Fort St. Louis somewhere on the Texas coast in 1684 and locating and excavating the specific site. Historical documents can be used to postulate the location at which a given event occurred, but historic archeology can provide an independent data basis for testing that postulate using material culture, geography, physiography, and topography (Gilmore, 1969 and 1973).

Often the material context of the daily routine of the people who participated in a historical event is forgotten, for there are few historical documents that relate such information. The material remains at the survivors' camp of the 1553 shipwrecks on Padre Island can tell us much about how the predicament was faced by people of the era. Otherwise, such interpretations would be entirely left to the imagination. This is not proclaiming that archeological data do not have their limitations; that no one can deny. It does mean, however, that the historian can learn much from what lies covered in the ground. Such data can provide a unique visual and tactile experience with the past that historical documents cannot provide and, therefore, it should be used whenever possible to help interpret Texas's history.

What may anthropology in general gain from historic archeology? Undoubtedly, a major emphasis of anthropological archeology is the testing of inductively and deductively derived hypotheses. It is to be hoped that this will result in the construction of a body of laws of cultural process and change. It is from the resources of historic archeology that more rigorous behavior models can be developed from historical documentation. These hypotheses can then be independently tested using archeological data. As yet this approach has only been used to a limited extent and should not be confused with the use of ethnographic analogy.

It is within this context that historic archeology in Texas can make a great contribution to anthropology. Texas has many sites where an interaction of cultures occurred, especially during the period of conquest and colonization. These sites contain the archeological data necessary to test hypotheses developed from Spanish and French documents. Potential contributions are even greater, since the two interactions are unique, involving different sets of cultures of different natures. For example, the French maintained a trade relationship; the Spanish were introducing new religious concepts and a subsistence base. An expressed goal of the Spanish missionaries was to persuade the Indians to settle near missions and raise crops and cattle. The French were interested in furs and provided a means of exchange that would help the Indian obtain more furs than was possible with his own technology. This new technology would also enable him to pursue the hunting aspect of his subsistence more efficiently, without completely replacing it. Respective life styles would also change—from that of the wandering hunter-gatherer to a more settled and permanent life style for those influenced by the Spanish.

For others there may have been an actual increase in mobility and time devoted to hunting.

All of these are some of the systematic changes resulting from the two different cultural contacts that existed in Texas during the eighteenth and early nineteenth centuries, and they are potential sources of anthropologically oriented research. The new contact situation that developed during middle 1800s with the Anglo-American colonization of Texas has an equally great resource potential.

If this research field is utilized adequately, it will require the efforts of both historians and anthropologists, and it will produce a new researcher—the historical anthropologist——who uses the research methods of both anthropology and history.

BIBLIOGRAPHY

BELL, R. E.; JELKS, E. B.; and NEWCOMB, W. W., JR. 1967. *A Pilot Study of Wichita Indian Archeology and Ethnohistory.* Final report to the National Science Foundation for grant GS-964.

BINFORD, L. R. 1962. "A New Method for Calculating Dates from Kaolin Pipe Stem Fragments." *Southeastern Archaeological Conference Newsletter*, no. 9.

BOLTON, H. E. 1915. *Texas in the Middle Eighteenth Century.* Reprint. Austin: University of Texas Press, 1970.

————. 1916. *Spanish Exploration in the Southwest, 1542-1706.* Reprint. New York: Barnes and Noble, 1963.

BOUSMAN, C. B. 1974. *Archaeological Assessment of Lake Meredith Recreation Area.* Archaeological Research Program, Southern Methodist University, Dallas.

BRIGGS, A. K. 1971. *Archeological Resources in the Texas Coastal Lowlands and Littoral.* Texas Historical Survey Committee and Texas Water Development Board, Austin.

CASTAÑEDA, C. E. 1936-1958. *Our Catholic Heritage in Texas, 1519-1936.* 7 vols. Austin: Van Boeckmann-Jones Co.

CLARK, J. W., JR. 1972. *Archeological Investigations at Ft. Lancaster Historic Site, Crockett Co., Texas.* Texas Archeological Salvage Project Research Report no. 12, Austin.

CLIFF, M.; CARTER, C.; and VERRETT, L. 1974. *Archeological Survey of the Welsh Power Plant.* Archaeological Research Program, Southern Methodist University, Dallas.

DAVIS, E. M., ed. 1961. "Proceedings of the Fifth Conference on Caddoan Archeology." *Bulletin of the Texas Archeological Society* 31:77-143.

————, and CORBIN, J. E. 1967. *Archeological Investigations at Washington-on-Brazos State Park (1966).* State Building Commission Archeological Program Report no. 5, Austin.

DAVIS, H. A., ed. 1970. "Archeological and Historical Resources of the Red River Basin: Arkansas Archeological Survey Research Survey # 1." Publications in Archeology.

DEETZ, J. 1963. *Archaeological Investigations at La Purissima Mission.* UCLA Archaeological Survey Annual Report for 1962-63, pp. 165-241.

————. 1965. *The Dynamics of Stylistic Change in Arikara Ceramics.* Illinois Studies in Anthropology, no. 4.

————, and DETHLEFSEN, E. 1965. "The Doppler Effect in Archaeology: A Consideration of the Spatial Aspects of Seriation." *Southwestern Journal of Anthropology* 21:196-206.

————, and DETHLEFSEN, E. 1967. "Death's Head, Cherub, Urn and Willow." *Natural History* 76:29-37.

DETHLEFSEN, E., and DEETZ, J. 1968. "Eighteenth-Century Cemeteries: A Demographic View." *Historical Archaeology* 1:40-42.

DOLLAR, C. 1968. "Some Thoughts on Theory and Method in Historical Archaeology." The Conference on Historic Sites. *Archaeology* 2 (2): 3-30.

DUFFIELD, L., and JELKS, E. B. 1961. *The Pearson Site: A Historic Indian Site at Iron Bridge Reservoir, Rains Co., Texas.* University of Texas Anthropology Department Archeology Series, no. 4, Austin.

DURRENBERGER, E. P. 1965. "Anderson's Mill (41 TV 130): A Historical Site in Travis Co., Texas." *Bulletin of the Texas Archeological Society* 36:1-69.

EAGLETON, N. E. 1955. An Historic Indian Cache in Pecos Co., Texas. *Bulletin of the Texas Archeological Society* 26:200-217.

EARLE, T. 1966. "Chatham, Massachusetts: A Study in Death." Unpublished manuscript.

FOX, D. E. 1970. *Archeological Salvage at Mission San José, December, 1969, April and August 1970.* Texas Historical Survey Committee, Austin.

————; MALLOUF, R. J.; O'MALLEY, N.; and SORROW, W. M. 1974. *Archeological Resources of the Proposed Cuero I Reservoir, Dewitt and Gonzales Cos., Texas.* Texas Historical Survey Committee and Texas Water Development Board Report no. 12, Austin.

GILMORE, K. K. 1967. *A Documentary and Archeological Investigation of Presidio San Luis de las Amarillas and Mission Santa Cruz de San Saba, Menard Co., Texas.* State Building Commission Archeological Program Report no. 9, Austin.

————. 1969. *The San Xavier Missions: A Study in Historical Site Identification.* State Building Commission Archeological Program Report no. 16, Austin.

————. 1973. *The Keeran Site: The Probable Site of La Salle's Fort St. Louis in Texas.* Texas Historical Survey Committee Archeological Program Report no. 24, Austin.

————. 1974. *Mission Rosario Archeological Investigations 1973.* Texas Parks and Wildlife Dept. Archeological Reports, no. 14, pt. 1. Austin.

GLANDER, W. P. 1972. "History of the Aquilla Creek Watershed." In *The Natural and Cultural Environmental Resources of the Aquilla Creek Watershed,* edited by S. A. Skinner. Report submitted to the Corps of Engineering by the Institute for the Study of Earth and Man, Southern Methodist University, Dallas.

GREER, J. W. 1967. *A Description of the Stratigraphy, Excavations, and Artifacts from an Archeological Excavation at the Alamo.* State Building Commission Archeological Program Report no. 3, Austin.

HALL, S. D., and GROMBACHER, K. A. 1974. *An Assessment of the Archeology and Historical Resources to be Affected by the Brazos Island Waterway Project, Texas.* Texas Archeological Survey Research Report no. 30, Austin.

HARRIS, R. K. 1962. "Another Marker on the Trail of the Norteño: A Preliminary Report on the Gilbert Site." *The Record* 17(1).

————, and HARRIS, I. M. 1961. "Spanish Fort: A Historic Trade Site." *The Record* 16(1).

————; HARRIS, I. M.; BLAINE, J. C.; and BLAINE, J. 1965. "A Preliminary Archeological and Documentary Study of the Womack Site, Lamar Co., Texas." *Bulletin of the Texas Archeological Society* 36:287-364.

HASSKARL, R. A. 1957. "An Unusual Historic Indian House Site in Washington Co., Texas." *Bulletin of the Texas Archeological Society* 28: 232-40.

HAYS, T. R., and HERRIN, E. 1970. *Padre Island Project.* Report to the Antiquities Committee.

————, and JELKS, E. B. 1966. *Archeological Exploration at Ft. Lancaster in 1966: A Preliminary Report.* State Building Commission Archeological Program Report no. 4, Austin.

HUMPHREYS, S. B. 1969. "Human Skeletal Material from San Juan Capistrano Mission." In *The History and Archeology of Mission San Juan Capistrano, San Antonio, Texas* by M. K. Schuetz. State Building Commission Archeological Program Report no. 11, pp. 116-24, Austin.

————. 1971. "The Skeletal Biology of Eighteenth-Century Coahuiltecan Indians from San Juan Capistrano Mission, San Antonio, Texas." Master's thesis, Southern Methodist University.

ING, J. D. 1970. *Archeological Investigations at Lyndon B. Johnson State Park.* Texas Parks and Wildlife Department, Austin.

————, and KEGLEY, G. 1971. *Archeological Investigations at Ft. Leaton Historic Site, Presidio County, Texas.* Texas Parks and Wildlife Department, Austin.

JELKS, E. B. 1970. "Documentary Evidence of Indian Occupation at the Stansbury Site (41-39B1-1)." In "Archeological investigations in the Whitney Reservoir area, Central Texas," by R. L. Shephenson. *Bulletin of the Texas Archeological Society* 41:37-286.

————; DAVIS, E. M.; and STURGIS, H. F., eds. 1960. "A Review of Texas Archeology," pt. 29. *Bulletin of the Texas Archeological Society* 29.

————, ed. 1966. "The Gilbert Site." *Bulletin of the Texas Archeological Society* 37.

JENSEN, H. P. 1968. *Archeological Excavations at James S. Hogg Birthplace,*

Rusk, Texas. State Building Commission Archeological Program Report no. 14, Austin.

JOHNSON, LEROY, JR., and JELKS, E. B. 1958. "The Tawakoni-Yscani Village, 1760: A Study in Archeological Site Identification." *Texas Journal of Science* 10:405-22.

KIRKLAND, F. 1942. "Historic Material from Fielder Canyon Cave." *Bulletin of the Texas Archeological and Paleontological Society* 14:61-71.

LATIMER, T. 1973. *Historic Preservation in Texas,* vols. 1 and 2. Austin: Texas State Historical Commission.

LEUTENEGGER, B., and HABIG, M. A. 1973. *Excerpts from the* Libros de los Decretos *of the Missionary College of Zacatecas, 1707-1828, and a Biographical Dictionary.* Texas Historical Survey Committee Archeological Program Report no. 23, Austin.

LORRAIN, D., and JACKSON, M. 1970. *Archeological Investigations at Washington-on-the-Brazos.* RESAR.

McCORMICK, O. F. III, and SCOTT, M. L. 1971. *Lake Monticello Archeological Project: An Interim Report.* Archeological Research Program, Southern Methodist University, Dallas.

McGUFF, P. R., and COX, W. N. 1973. *A Survey of the Archeological and Historical Resources to be Affected by the Clear Creek Flood Control Project, Texas.* Texas Archeological Survey Program Report no. 28, Austin.

MALLOUF, R. J.; FOX, D. E.; and BRIGGS, A. K. 1973. *An Assessment of the Cultural Resources of Palmetto Bend Reservoir, Jackson Co., Texas.* Texas Historical Survey Committee and Texas Water Development Board Report no. 11, Austin.

MALONE, J. M. 1970. *Archeological Reconnaissance in the MacKenzie Reservoir Area of Tule Canyon.* Texas Historical Survey Committee and Texas Water Revelopment Board Report no. 8, Austin.

MIROIR, M. P.; HARRIS, R. K.; BLAINE, J. C.; and McVAY, J. 1973. "Benard de la Harpe and the Nassonite Post." *Bulletin of the Texas Archeological Society* 44:113-67.

MORROW, H. C. 1971. Review "The San Xavier Missions: A Study of Historic Site Identification," by K. K. Gilmore. *Historical Archaeology* 4:112-13.

NEWCOMB, W. W., Jr. 1955. "An Historical Burial from Yellowhouse Canyon, Lubbock Co., Texas." *Bulletin of the Texas Archeological Society* 26:186-99.

————. 1973. *The Indians of Texas.* Austin: University of Texas Press.

NOEL-HUME, I. 1969. *Historical Archaeology.* New York: Alfred A. Knopf, Inc.

NUNLEY, P. 1973. *An Assessment of Archeological Resources in the Vicinity of Garza-Little Elm Reservoir.* Richland Archeological Society Miscellaneous Papers, no. 1, Dallas.

OLDS, D. L. 1969. *Archeological Investigations at Ft. Griffin Military Post, Shakelford County, Texas.* Texas Archeological Research Laboratory, University of Texas, Austin.

PARSONS, M. L. 1967. *Archeological Investigation in Crosby and Dickens Cos., Texas.* State Building Commission Archeological Program Report no. 7, Austin.

PEARSON, E. L. 1973. *Archeological Investigations of Architectural Details of Structure M2, X, and VI at Ft. McKavett State Historic Site, Texas.* Texas Archeological Survey Program Report, Austin.

PREWITT, E. R. 1973. *An Archeological Reconnaissance of the Area to be Affected by the Louisiana Loop Pipeline, Cameron Parish, La., Jefferson and Liberty Cos., Texas.* Texas Archeological Survey Program Report no. 25, Austin.

RAY, C. N., and JELKS, E. B. 1964. "The W. H. Watson Site: A Historic Indian Burial in Fisher Co., Texas." *Bulletin of the Texas Archeological Society* 35:127-42.

ROBERSON, W. R. 1974. *The Carrington-Covert Archeological Investigation of a 19th Century Residence in Austin, Texas.* Texas Historical Survey Committee Archeological Program Report no. 25, Austin.

SCHUETZ, M. K. 1966. *Historical Background of the Mission San Antonio de Valero.* State Building Commission Archeological Program Report no. 1. Austin.

―――――. 1968. *The History and Archeology of Mission San Juan Capistrano, San Antonio, Texas,* vol. 1. State Building Commission Archeological Program Report no. 10, Austin.

―――――.1969. *The History and Archeology of Mission San Juan Capistrano, San Antonio, Texas,* (vol. 2. State Building Commission Archeological Program Report no. 11, Austin.

―――――. 1970. *Excavations of a Section of the Acequia Madre in Bexar Co., Texas and Archeological Investigations at Mission San Jose in April 1968.* Texas Historical Survey Committee Archeological Program Report no. 19, Austin.

SCHUYLER, R. L. 1971. "Historical and Historic Sites Archeology as Anthropology: Basic Definitions and Relationships," *Historical Archaeology* 4:83-89.

SCURLOCK, D. 1973. *Spain in North America.* Texas Historical Commission, Austin.

―――――. 1974. *An Assessment of the Archeological Resources of Padre Island National Seashore, Texas.* Texas Historical Commission Special Report no. 11, Austin.

SHAFER, H. J. 1966. *An Archeological Survey of Wallisville Reservoir, Chambers Co., Texas.* Texas Archeological Survey Program Report no. 2, Austin.

SHUFFLER, R. H. 1962. "The Signing of Texas' Declaration of Independence: Myth and Record." *Southwestern Historical Quarterly* 65:311-32.

————. 1965. "Washington-on-the-Brazos: Texas' Birthplace." *Texas Parade,* March 1965, pp. 46-50.

SKINNER, S. A. 1971. *Historical Archeology of the Neches Saline, Smith Co., Texas.* Texas Historical Survey Committee Archeological Program Report no. 12, Austin.

SOUTH, S. 1972. "Evolution and Horizon as Revealed in Ceramic Analysis in Historical Archaeology." *The Conference on Historic Site Archaeology* 6:71-116.

————. 1974. "The Horizon Concept Revealed in the Application of the Mean Ceramic Date Formula to Spanish Majolica in the New World." *The Conference on Historic Site Archaeology* 7:96-122.

————, ed. 1968. *The Conference on Historic Site Archaeology, 1967.*

STEPHENSON, R. L. 1947. "Archeology Survey of Whitney Basin: A Preliminary Report." *Bulletin of the Texas Archeological and Paleontological Society* 18:129-42.

————. 1970. "Archeological Investigations in the Whitney Reservoir Area, Central, Texas." *Bulletin of the Texas Archeological Society* 41: 37-286.

SUHM, D. A. 1962. "The White Site: An Historical Burial in Yoakum Co., Texas." *Bulletin of the Texas Archeological Society* 32:85-120.

————; KRIEGER, A. D.; and JELKS, E. B. 1954. *Introductory Handbook of Texas Archeology. Bulletin of Texas Archeological Society* 25, pt. 1.

TEXAS ALMANAC, THE. 1974-75, ed. Fred R. Pass. A. H. Belo Corporation, Dallas.

TUNNELL, C. D. 1966. *A Description of Enameled Earthenware from an Archeological Excavation at Mission San Antonio de Valero (the Alamo).* State Building Commission Archeological Program Report no. 2, Austin.

————, and AMBLER, J. R. 1967. *Archeological Excavations at Presidio San Agustin de Ahumada.* State Building Commission Archeological Program Report no. 6, Austin.

————, and JENSEN, H. P., JR. 1969. *Archeological Excavations in Lyndon B. Johnson State Park.* State Building Commission Archeological Program Report no. 17, Austin.

————, and NEWCOMB, W. W., JR. 1969. "A Lipan Apache Mission, San Lorenzo de la Santa Cruz, 1762-1771." *Texas Memorial Museum Bulletin* no. 14.

WAKEFIELD, W. H. 1968. Palmetto Bend and Choke Canyon Reservoirs, Texas. Texas Archeological Survey Program Report no. 5, Austin.

WALKER, I. C. 1968a. "Historic Archaeology: Methods and Principle." *Historical Archaeology* 1:23-33.

──────. 1968b. "Comment on Clyde Dollar's Paper." *The Conference on Historical Site Archaeology* 2 (2): 103-23.

──────. 1970. "The Crisis of Identity: History or Anthropology." *The Conference on Historic Site Archaeology* 3:62-69.

──────. 1974. "Binford, Science and History: The Probabilistic Variability of Explicated Epistemology and Nomothetic Paradigms in Historic Archaeology." *The Conference on Historic Site Archaeology* 7:159-201.

WEBB, C. H. 1960. "A Review of Northeast Texas Archeology." In "A Review of Texas Archeology," edited by Jelks et al. *Bulletin of the Texas Archeological Society* 29.

WILLIAMS, S. 1961. "Historic Sites in the Caddoan Area." In "Proceedings of the Fifth Conference on Caddoan Archeology," edited by E. M. Davis. *Buletin of the Texas Archeological Society* 31:78-143.

WITTE, A. H. 1938. "Spanish Fort: An Historic Wichita site." *Bulletin of the Texas Archeological and Paleontological Society* 10:234-44.

Faunal Analysis in Texas Archeological Sites

KURT D. HOUSE

IN THE HISTORY of archeology, faunal remains were probably the first nonartifactual material used in attempts to reconstruct the life-ways of prehistoric peoples. How strange it seems, then, that to amateurs and professionals alike, archeology has come to mean artifact analysis instead of a more generalized science of ancient peoples in their environment. To advance the development of faunal studies within Texas archeology this paper has the following objectives: (1) to impress upon archeologists the large potential of faunal analysis for their science, (2) to assess the quality of past faunal analyses in Texas archeological sites and to indicate, where necessary, ways of improvement, and (3) to develop an ecological approach appropriate and applicable to Texas archeology.

Only vertebrate remains, particularly those of mammals, will be discussed, because of my own familiarity with them and because such remains constitute the majority of vertebrate material in Texas sites.

What has been written for the archeologist interested in faunal analysis? Unfortunately, few general references are available for the Texas area, although, recently, specialists have been closing the gap. Flower (1876) offered perhaps the first usable identification manual, and Zeuner (1963) was one of the first to consider general issues of the field. In 1956, Cornwall wrote the first general reference for archeologists. He was followed by Ryder (1969a), who contributed a regional European work, then Chaplin (1971), whose study was also regional but contained basic recovery theory. Recently in this country, Daly (1969) and Grayson (1973) have reviewed faunal approaches, and Gilbert (1973) and Olsen (1961, 1973) have provided volumes which are of more interest to Texas archeologists. An economic approach was adopted by Higgs (1972), while Uerpman (1973) clarified the requirements for the reconstruction of paleo-economies as opposed to simple faunal analysis. The consensus that archeologists are commonly unqualified in the analysis of nonartifactual material led to a productive multidisciplinary conference (Taylor, 1957). Conversely, Wintemberg (1919) was one of the first to recognize that archeology could, in turn, make significant contributions to the study of fauna.

Too often the sources used by archeologists are regional identification manuals published in small numbers and thus not readily available. Consequently, it was difficult for amateur or professional archeologists to give proper consideration to fauna in their research. Some archeologists solved the problem with a false sense of confidence in their own ability, by assuming that with an identification manual they could accomplish the faunal analysis single-handedly from an easy chair. Actually, such species identification is only a first step, since it is the ecology of the species concerned that is necessary if the analysis is to be more than a species list.

This is not to say that vertebrate remains are the only remains worthy of study. On the contrary, Oberholser (1925), Tharp (1939), and others showed the importance of botanical studies in Texas to animal life. The evaluation and interpretation of invertebrate remains, especially the molluscs (Sparks, 1969; Meighan, 1969; Biggs, 1969), are also necessary when the archeologist uses the maximum information doctrine of his science. Strecker (1931), and later Cheatum and Fullington (1971), produced distributional studies of mussels in Texas, and Allen and Cheatum (1961) have written on gastropod molluscs in Texas archeological sites. Fish, amphibians, reptiles, and birds also compose a significant portion of prehistoric subsistence, but identifiable remains of these four groups are less imposing than are mammalian remains in Texas sites.

A pertinent question, therefore, is: Can or should the archeologist himself attempt analysis of these species? Differences of opinion reign. Ryder (1969a) believes it is the archeologist's responsibility to do so, but Chaplin (1971) is less clear, saying simply that the archeologist should "provide" for the analysis. Cornwall (1956), Slaughter (1974:

personal communication), Douglas (1969), and others believe that while the archeologist may follow the dictates of his own discipline, he should utilize competent zoologists, biologists, or paleontologists who are familiar with the ecology and diversity of animal life. Some recent innovative archeological work actively employs the multidisciplinary approach, engaging specialists in various fields of zoology to analyze different portions of the fauna. Such a situation, however, is the ideal, dependent on extensive financial support, and is a problem for few archeologists. But even when funds are available to pay zoologists for their expertise, these scientists are often unwilling to turn from their own research. Within salvage archeology, time is also a critical factor.

All of these circumstances have produced the present *status quo* of faunal analyses in Texas. From the following study of archeological reports, I agree with other professionals that few archeologists are qualified to make their own faunal analyses, and that the use of identification keys (which have been hailed as a panacea for species lists) is not enough. If maximal information is to be gained, a faunal analyst must be among those who write grant proposals, or an osteological specialist must be included. In salvage archeology, it is often possible to contract with the specialists engaged in assessing the value of other resources in the impact statement (cf. Sciscenti, 1972). For the archeologist who wishes guidance, the methods of planning and organization of bone studies are presented well in Chaplin (1971). Finally, the actual remains of animals in sites are only one medium for the discovery of the nature of exploitative strategies; there are other, less commonly used, techniques available to the archeologist.

Sources of Information and the Faunal Analyst

Ethnographic and Historical Sources

Krieger (1956a) was one of the first to realize that Texas archeologists have failed to use available documents to supplement their information on the hypothetical diets of groups. These documents contain reliable and detailed evidences of the foods eaten, methods of capture, hunting and gathering technology, and much other beneficial information. Gatchet (1891, p. 11), for example, in reporting on the Karankawas of the Texas coast, noted that "their food—venison, fish, oysters, turtles, etc., was always either boiled in rude earthen pots or roasted in the ashes of the fire."

Scatology

A wealth of information on Indian diet (e.g., Callen, 1969) is available from the analysis of human feces or coprolites (cf. Heizer, 1969) but this is also largely unused. The techniques of analysis are not difficult and require no elaborate equipment; paleo-feces are no doubt available from dry western Texas caves, as they are from those in adjacent Mexico (Taylor, 1956). Follett (1970) and Yarnell (1969) have shown the potential of coprolite analysis in other states, but only recently have any such studies been carried out in Texas (e.g., Bryant, 1974).

Other Indirect Methods

In some cases, pottery effigies (Scurlock, 1961) and other carvings and art forms are expressive of an intimate knowledge and exploitation of animals. Petroglyphs in western Texas (Crimmins, 1946) depicting rattlesnakes and other forms might similarly prove useful. Lithic, bone, and other tools also provide indirect evidence of fauna utilized. A bone tool is an unusual bipartite artifact; not only was it a part of functional technology, but it was also derived from some animal exploited—often a food animal. The relationship between tool material and technology is a complex one and cannot be explored in this paper. Where there are fleshers and scrapers, however, hides have been used; and where we find bone awls and needles, something has been punched and sewn.

Nonosteological Remains

Fur, hair, skin, and feathers are preserved most often in extremely arid regions; deerskin sandals, for example, were discovered in a dry West Texas cave (Schuetz, 1956, p. 131). In Texas, remains of this type have been found of bison and fox and of heron and other birds. Slaughter (1974: personal communication) inferred the ceremonial use of purple grackles from small deerskin bags full of their bones. Schorger (1961) discovered from a mummified specimen the plumage differences between wild turkeys (*Meleagris gallopavo merriami*) and domesticated turkeys, and also discovered what these same turkeys were fed by their Puebloan keepers (See Lange, 1950, and Leopold, 1948, on turkey domestication.)

One last caveat: not all the bones found in sites represent food remains, and the context in which bones are found may spell the difference between a reasonable reconstruction and a completely erroneous association.

AN ECOLOGICAL APPROACH

Perhaps the most helpful approach is an ecological one, stressing the behavior, distribution, and niche requirements of a species, as did the biotic province concept of Dice (1943), Blair (1950), and others. A Texas county map (fig. 1) was prepared, which not only allows site locations, but also facilitates faunal interpretation via the biotic province approach. This approach, which requires the viewing of the site within the harmony of animal and plant life now extant in the area, is wholly justifiable for Texas sites. The biotic approach, as defined by the cohesion of plant and animal communities, forces the integration of primary data and hypotheses with assumptions. The diversity of Texas habitats was early recognized as a haven for the naturalist interested in faunal variation, and a survey of biological resources began with Cope (1880) and Bailey (1905). This proceeded to the more integrated studies utilizing the biotic province concept in faunal surveys.

Figure 1 shows the biotic provinces of Texas, allowing any site to be plotted by county; reference to the fauna typical of that province permits an accurate prediction of the remains to be encountered during excavation. In the same way that one could predict with fair accuracy the biotic province where a faunal assemblage originated (with allowances for the intergradation of provinces), one can plot a site in its known location and predict accurately the archeological fauna which might be found. For example, the fact that an equivocal ungulate metapodial fragment is found in a site in the Austroriparian biotic province (fig. 1) means that it is more likely deer than antelope, and even further that it is more likely *Odocoileus virginianus* (white-tailed deer) than *O. hemionus* (mule deer).

In addition, one must take into consideration the method of accumulation, vertical features of landscape, sampling, and dating. Of these variables, dating is the most significant, since if the site is later than approximately 8000 B.P., as most Texas sites are, the animals present in the province today represent past fauna, with only a few exceptions. Slaughter (1969, p. 161) has found that present ranges indicate past ones, since there have been almost no shifts in niches since the approximate 8000-year B.P. threshold. This is true because of the indication that major climatic upheavals have not occurred since this time thresh-

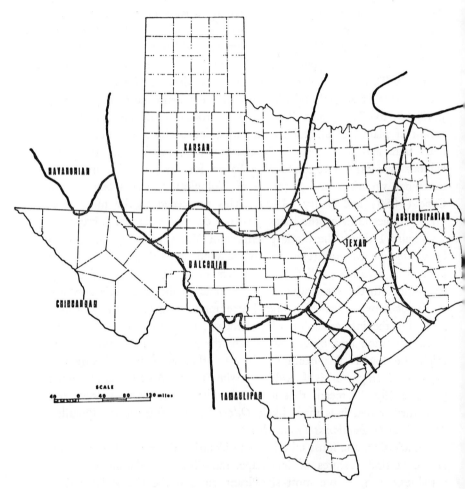

Fig. 1. Texas biotic provinces.

old; hence the length of occupation of an area by the present extant fauna dates back to the times of the establishment of an essentially modern climate. The province boundaries, moreover, are not separating boundaries in the strict sense; rather, the distribution of a species fades out gradually as biotic boundaries are crossed. While the provinces appear clear-cut, one must bear in mind that transitional zones exist both horizontally and vertically across space, especially where topography influences climate, as in the case in the Trans-Pecos region of the Chihuahuan province.

Considering the transitional nature of the biotic provinces of Texas on the one hand, and the cross-cutting nature of adaptive strategies of the humans who are responsible for the evidence on the other, it is hardly surprising that site reports reveal varying degrees of hunting mobility. The job of researchers would be simplified if faunal analyses of the earliest excavated sites had been more rigorous. Following the general notes on Texas vertebrates, table 1 has been developed to show the faunal distribution (since 8000 B.P.) in each province.*

General Comments on Texas Vertebrates

Fish

The percentage of total diet composed of fish determines the importance of analysis of these remains, and while the level in coastal province sites is high, the heavy dependence of inland groups living on major rivers (Word and Douglas, 1970) is less predictably so. Burr (1932) and Hubbs (1954, 1958) have published vital information on Texas fishes. Ryder (1969b) has published a general article, and Follett (1970) has shown that coprolite analysis can reveal which species have been exploited. The most common fish remains in Texas sites are of the genera *Ictalurus* (catfish) and *Lepidosteus* (gar), probably for reasons of availability and the relationship between group technology and the behavior of these genera. Carp and large-mouth bass are reported from Centipede and Damp Caves (Chihuahuan province), while Word and Douglas (1970) found that 33 percent of all faunal remains in Baker Cave (Chihuahuan province) were of fish. Catfish spines, being uncommonly durable, yield much information regarding age of the fish, species ecology, and climate. Fish scales, recently shown to be of important ecological value, and catfish spines have not deserved the neglect

*Tables are grouped at the end of the paper.

they have suffered in Texas faunal analysis. A fish-scale study in Texas, of the kind accomplished by Casteel (1974) for another area, offers tremendous potential.

Reptiles and Amphibians

Wright and Wright (1938), Brown (1950), and Smith and Sanders (1952) have reviewed amphibians and reptiles indigenous to Texas. These remains are uncommon in sites, undoubtedly because of differential bone survival. Rather than ignoring such remains or hastily concluding that amphibians and reptiles were unimportant, archeologists need to develop expertise in the recovery and identification of these lower vertebrates.

Birds

For three primary reasons, the study of bird remains offers much to Texas archeology: (1) the ecological tolerance of birds is narrow compared to mammals; (2) many species are migratory, thus of great value in seasonal dating; and (3) birds are among the best studied of groups in North America. While Dawson (1969) has provided an extensive bibliography, and Peterson (1960) is commonly used as a guide to extant Texas avifauna, bird bones are the most neglected of faunal remains in sites (Chaplin, 1971, p. 158). The food pellets of owls are composed to a large degree of rodent and small mammal bones, and are frequently a source of such bones in a site. This may explain the existence in some sites of exotic species not native to the province, since birds of prey are characterized by great mobility. Caves, where many birds roost, are commonly found along lines of drastic topographic change (e.g., the Balcones Escarpment), which are exactly the lines where two different environmental zones intersect (Slaughter, 1974: personal communication).

Mammals

Mammalian remains constitute the bulk of osteological remains; this is because of their relatively larger and denser bones and the greater quantity of bone in a medium-sized mammal as compared to that in the largest amphibian and reptile, and finally because there is evidence that there was a preference for these animals. The wide variety of habitat zones in Texas enables 137 native species of mammals to live throughout the state's mountains, grasslands, arid areas, forests, brushlands, waters, and skies. Davis (1966) has prepared a revised bulletin containing photographs, descriptions, and ranges of Texas mammals, although frequently the range maps are based on few sightings. The range maps are nevertheless a help to archeologists, since few Texas mammals have undergone distributional changes in the last several centuries, and even new range limits are available in the literature for most species.

Marine Mammals

Records of the Texas coast are extensive enough to lead one to expect some marine mammal remains in coastal sites. Although recent sightings have declined (Gunter, 1947), there is some evidence (Raun, 1964) that larger populations of some species were once available and exploited. Davis (1966, p. 10) records one genus of seal; the manatee; three genera of porpoises; and five genera of whales, although three of the five were cases of single individual whales stranded on beaches.

Bats

Whether and to what extent the twenty-six species of indigenous Texas bats were utilized by aboriginal groups is an intriguing problem on which little work has been done. Cave evidence is often equivocal, since bats could have existed in habitation caves simultaneously with humans, but without predator-prey interaction.

Terrestrial Mammals

At least four species, the gray wolf, Bighorn sheep, bison, and elk, which occur in archeological sites have become extinct in Texas, the first three in historical times. It is not known when the southwestern subspecies of elk (*Cervus canadensis merriami*) disappeared (Gilmore, 1947), but it was probably during Spanish times. In addition to these indigenous species, the red wolf, margay cat, and grizzly bear, all once native, may now be considered extinct in the state. All of these mammals are important to archeologists, however, since recent information indicates a much wider distribution in the past. In Orange County (Austroriparian province) fossil margay dating to a few thousand years ago (Davis, 1966, p. 117) has been found, and preempts the later decline of the original seven native cats of the state (Russell, 1971). The ursid population in East Texas and the Guadalupe Mountains was also probably quite significant at one time, the black bear lasting until after the turn of the century in the Big Thicket.

Conversely, there are five species of non-native mammals whose ranges have expanded since their introduction: Barbary sheep, two species of rats, the house mouse, and the nutria. The significant range expansion of these five species in recent times may serve the historical archeologist especially well, while the large number of imported species such as European suids (Krieger, 1956b), African antelopes, and Asian deer promise unique challenges to future archeologists, since some have been known to hybridize with native species. Some native species have been studied well enough for distributional data to be especially useful; these include the gray squirrel (Goodrum, 1964), porcupine (Best and Kennedy, 1972), and armadillo (Kalmbach, 1943). The red fox, *Vulpes fulva*, is an example of a final category, since zoological opinion is divided on whether or not the species was native to Texas. Red foxes have been reported, however, in Pleistocene deposits of Schulze Cave in the Balconian province (Dalquest et al., 1969).

When the last date of occurrence is known for a species, it is included in parentheses—for example, *Felis onca* (jaguar)-Tex,T,B,(1903),C (1962). Fish and birds are not listed, because of range modifications and other limitations necessarily imposed in this paper. The common names of mammals were included in the first listing of a given species.

FAUNA REPORTED FROM TEXAS ARCHEOLOGICAL SITES

What does the record of excavation actually show? In using the testing procedure of matching site record against available faunal data, the following should be considered:

1. Sites as tabulated are the result of archeological choosing, sometimes under the stress of salvage. Increasingly, excavations are located where the archeologist considers problems to lie, not where preservation and other factors are optimal.

2. Ideally, the study of bones from a site should begin at the site itself; this allows *in situ* information which can be critical. This is rarely accomplished in Texas sites, however, and in few cases was the fauna analyzed in a systematic way.

Theoretically, each site report would contain an integrated faunal analysis performed by an expert zoo-archeologist or other specialist. The deductions of this faunal report would contribute directly to the conclusions of the site report. Too frequently in Texas sites, however, even when faunal analysis is done, the information is not integrated into the final report. Moreover, archeologists frequently present syntheses of group life and subsistence patterns without any faunal data whatsoever!

While most Texas site reports lack an adequate faunal analysis (noted also recently by Dillehay, 1973), notable exceptions do exist, such as the 1968 report of Dibble and Lorrain and that of Word and Douglas (1970), both studies done in Val Verde County. A compromise with time and resources has been made by some archeologists who, while they may not accomplish an optimal analysis, attempt to understand faunal resources by including a small section on the present fauna of the site. In this category are the Lake Monticello (McCormick, 1973), Holdsworth and Stewart (Hester and Hill, 1972), and Upper Neches River (Anderson et al., 1974) sites.

In contrast, some of the "new" archeology has neglected faunal remains in deference to hypothetical schemes involving less substantive evidence (e.g., Devil's Hollow site, Collins, 1972). Since nutritional requirements (White, 1952, 1953a & b, 1954, 1955), food resources, food preferences, technological level, population size, and a host of other variables are uncontrolled, faunal speculation added to numerous other assumptions makes such a post-event reconstruction worth less than even meager energy devoted to any remains.

To assess the quality of faunal analyses done in Texas archeological sites, a sample of site reports was compiled (table 2) from almost four decades of the *Bulletin of the Texas Archeological Society*, in addition to random publications issued by other agencies (denoted by asterisks), chosen mainly on the basis of accessibility of the report. The sites from the *Bulletin* are too numerous to list in the bibliography, but each reference in the table notes the author, publication year, and biotic province. These sites may be taken as representative of all reports accomplished in the state during the same period. While not all excavations result in published reports, there is no evidence that this fault is related to site location, or that it hampers the representative nature of my sample. When more than one report on a site exists, the one containing the most faunal information follows the site name. The fauna were not placed at temporal levels, even though this may have been done in the original report, as for example in the Scharbauer, where several species are obviously Pleistocene, not Holocene. No correlation with human artifacts has been implied or changed from the original report; Hester (1971) has illustrated one way in which the reported association of artifacts and fauna can go awry. NFR means "no fauna reported"; it does not, however, always mean "no fauna encountered," and even in cases where fauna were reported few were analyzed. In some sites where fauna were obviously present (e.g., Bone Implement Burial), the specific fauna were not reported. Most such reports were omitted, however, unless other information in the report was redeeming for purposes of this paper.

CONCLUSION

On the one hand, there are poignant deficiencies in realization of the potential of fauna in Texas studies; on the other, one can see the positive effects of newer theory stressing reconstructive ecology. On the positive side are the Baker Cave (Word and Douglas, 1970) and Bonfire Shelter (Dibble and Lorrain, 1968) reports; in the latter, for example, the method of kill, butchering techniques, season of occupation, and even human behavior are hypothetically reconstructed.

Of the 11,527 reported sites in the state (Spock, 1974: personal communication), our knowledge is based only on an unknown total number of archeological reports; 72 percent of our sample reported fauna, about 20 percent could generously be termed analyses, with less than 5 percent judged adequate by Chaplin's criteria (1971, p. 61). Moreover, this knowledge is unevenly distributed throughout the state, as can be seen in table 3. It is clear from the data presented in this table not only that we have a much better idea of which fauna were exploited biologically in the Texan province (twenty-four sites as opposed to one Navahonian), but also that groups in the Texan, Austroriparian, and Balconian form the bulk of our ideas of exploitative strategies and cultural stages of native cultures. Since cultural stages are defined in terms of types and the diversity of resources exploited and methods used (i.e., technology), this is a critical consideration. What this all means is that we have a vague idea of prehistoric Texas Indian behavior mostly from those who lived in the eastern third of the state (Texan, Austroriparian, and Balconian provinces), and we grow less sure as we proceed westward. This bias optimizes neither the archeological reconstruction of cultures nor good synthetic theory.

Broadly speaking, two categories of site fauna are seen. On the one hand, there are sites where we see the remains of species that are not present in the area today (e.g., beaver at Centipede and Damp Caves); on the other hand, there are sites which do not produce the fauna in the area today. While the former species case is undoubtedly explainable in terms of range restriction due to climatic changes, the latter case is more mysterious. The extant species which presumably were also extant in the site area in former times (to ca. 8000 B.P.), but which are not discovered in site fauna, are conspicuous. For example, in the Tamaulipan three common vulnerable species, the roadrunner (*Geococcyx californianus*), land tortoise (*Gopherus* sp.), and alligator (*A. mississippiensis*), are expected (table 1), and while the latter two are identified in similar climates (Neill et al., 1956), they are rare or absent in Texas sites (see table 2). Two simple explanations are plausible. Either these species were present and not exploited or the animals were not present and therefore their present ranges are recently established because of climatic or other changes.

While the time period required for such extensive range expansion may seem longer than that available, we need only observe the rapid historical range expansion of the armadillo (Kalmbach, 1943) to remain open-minded to this proposition for other species. This might also be the explanation for the paucity of peccary remains in southern Texas sites, since Lundelius and Slaughter (1971, p. 23) note that the occurrence of peccary (*Pecari* or *Tayassu tajacu*) or pocket gopher (*Thomomys*) indicates a recent geological deposit. Contrariwise, the seal remains from the Tamaulipan (Raun, 1956) are unexpected on the basis of present range. They serve to remind us that much of the range-shifting may have been very recent, and in many cases it is left to the shrewd faunal analyst to elicit information from collections already analyzed. An understanding of the level of exploitation of marine resources possessed by coastal natives is lacking in Texas archeology. Much more research is needed. Quick reference to table 1, for example, tells the casual observer that several species of whales and porpoises, the manatee, and even seals must have been available to coastal natives, even though these species are now rarely seen on the Texas coast. Likewise, remains of the bullfrog (*Rana catesbeiana*), although some are recorded in table 1, are rare in Austroriparian and Texan sites, but the scarcity of amphibian and reptilian remains in these humid areas, and to a lesser extent in other areas of the state, is probably more the result of differential preservation than of any other single factor.

Table 1 also shows that the majority of amphibians in Texas are in the eastern third of the state (Austroriparian and Texan), where it is comparatively more humid; and, conversely, that the majority of reptilian species, especially lizards, are adapted to the western two-thirds of the state. Indian groups in eastern Texas, therefore, could be expected to have had a diet composed to a greater extent of amphibians; in the western, mainly Chihuahuan, portion, the dietary void caused by the paucity of amphibians may have been filled by reptiles, especially lizards. The reader is encouraged to make similar conclusions by comparing table 1 to table 2. Unfortunately, these specific cases cannot all be discussed in this paper; it is appropriate here to try to discover generalizations which summarize the faunal case histories in the archeology of Texas.

Generalizations regarding the distribution of prehistoric fauna are difficult to find in archeological literature, with the following few exceptions. Lundelius (1967) has stated that no central Texas archeological site has yielded peccary bones, and Slaughter (quoted in Dalquest et al., 1969) says that the ringtail (*Bassariscus*) is present in most late Recent archeological faunas he has examined. There is unpublished evidence for the consumption of the brains of small mammals as well as for the common occurrence of bears (*Ursus americanus*) in northeastern Texan Caddoan sites. From table 1, it is clear that the bulk of faunal material is derived from large herbivores, especially deer. This supports the most yield/least effort hypothesis, but we cannot but wonder how they were captured and killed. Moreover, most of the Archaic sites present an economic picture of what Jarman (1972) has called deer economies, which suggests that a comparison of European Mesolithic deer economies with such groups in the New World might have interesting results. Because of their availability in the past, ideas of exploited fauna in Texas are biased in favor of mammals; this is aided by the fact that less is known of the worldwide exploitation of reptilian, amphibian, and avian species. Similarly, while Hibbard (1958) has shown microfauna to be sensitive to climatic changes, his work has been ignored in archeology.

Our anthropological goal is the reconstruction of exploitative behavior. We assume that a spectrum of fauna and flora was extracted by a certain band from its territory by hunting the mobile vertebrates and gathering the relatively immobile plants and invertebrates as a part of their total behavioral pattern. To this end, Elder (1965) has attempted to reconstruct hunting pressures, and Nunley (1972) has proposed a generalized model which allows the interrelation of technology, social organization, settlement pattern, and other aspects of a living and breathing society.

In summarizing faunal studies in Texas, the following weaknesses should be noted:

1. The overwhelming proportion of sites have been excavated and

reported within a nonecological framework, much of the information having been lost during excavation. Unique *in situ* data in the form of fly pupae, for example, enabled Gilbert and Bass (1967) to detect the seasonality of burial at a site in another state.

2. Qualified osteological specialists for archeology do not exist in significant numbers in Texas, nor are they likely to appear soon unless changes occur in present training programs.

3. Archeologists have proven largely unsuccessful in their own attempts at faunal analysis; some cases of species determination are difficult even for the zoologist. (E.g., see Howard, 1949, for separation of dog from coyote and Olsen, 1960, for separation of bison from cattle.)

4. Inadequate use is made of ethnographic, biologic, ecologic, and other sources of information outside the archeologist's own field. For example: a paleontological expedition once made the initial discovery of an early-man kill site (Suhm, 1961, p. 207); unexpected remains of domestic dog and human teeth appeared in 11,000-year-old fauna of Schulze Cave, Balconian province (Dalquest et al., 1969, p. 225); a remarkably sophisticated antler tool was encountered by paleontologists in the Sulphur River Formation in the Texan province (Slaughter and Hoover, 1963, pp. 146-47); and Frank (1964) noted in a speleological report that *Spermophilus* existed in four Chihuahuan archeological sites.

5. Not only is the population approach necessary, but the percentages of unidentifiable remains must be stated; as Uerpman (1973) has noted, the reconstruction of the economy in the report may be based on only a very small portion of the total available bone.

6. We have as yet no balanced view of prehistoric economies in Texas, thus little chance for a holistic formulation of cultural stages based on behavioral differences.

Given these weaknesses in methodology, it is understandable that faunal studies in Texas archeology are so few. The inevitable fragmentary nature of the bones found and the only partial representation of food remains in sites are limitations we must work with, but we may benefit by making innovative data interpretations which are warranted. A hypothesis which suggests that cave sites approach the ideal of total representation more closely than do open sites is more valuable than mere speculation, simply because it can be tested. Similarly, we may test the hypothesis that states: "The number of different species in a mountainous site will be larger due to the exploitation of several vertical biotic zones available within short lateral distances, compared to the number of species exploited by a group living on terrain with virtually no relief." We can then build on the above case the theory that the second Indian culture, which exploited fewer species, may have covered more area in doing so, although the biomass obtained would not significantly differ *per capita.*

That most of the present and nearly all of the early archeology of Texas was accomplished by amateurs is laudable; it carries with it, however, a sobering warning. The amateur frequently lacks not only a grounding in the maximal-information philosophy of archeology, but also the equipment and means to achieve it even if he shares the philosophy. Some subtle signs, however, indicate that the situation may be improving in Texas, through field schools and other ways in which the theory of archeology is reaching the community.

Today, few archeologists are satisfied with a sterile analysis of site remains via a species list; rather, they want to reconstruct ancient economies in order to reconstruct past behavior accurately. European faunal analyses long ago confronted this goal, but only recently has a somewhat differently evolving New World fauna analysis tradition reorganized in the adoption of an ecological approach toward the reconstruction of human behavior. The preoccupation with domestication criteria in the Old World was paralleled in the New World by the urge to use fauna only for climatological indicators and to ascertain the degree of exploitation (see Martin and Wright, 1967, on overexploitation). The evidence that the entry of man in the New World coincided with severe climatic fluctuations and drastic range changes and extinctions of animals makes it clear that we must not rely on single-cause explanations but must resign ourselves to a system of many variables which we can only seek continually to control.

From different approaches, archeologists have chosen to deemphasize, ignore, or concentrate on those aspects of faunal analysis which offer the most potential for a particular problem. Most Old World researchers, for example, consider the engagement of a qualified faunal expert a necessary part of preliminary excavation planning. Chaplin (1971) has stated that from the beginning the organization of proposed archeological research should include: (1) provision of a bone specialist and staff; (2) specification of type of site work to be done by the specialist; (3) field routines and requirements for recording, collecting, preserving, and transporting the bones; and (4) financing of the field and laboratory analyses. Researchers have agreed that comparing bones found in sites to bones of complete skeletons from museums or other collections is advisable, and House (1970) has suggested a suitable methodology adapted to academic archeological programs.

Because zoologists are difficult to recruit and most archeologists realize their own limitations, a middle-ground hybrid, the professional zoo-archeologist, has been welcomed. Still, until specialists in zoo-archeology become available or archeologists themselves take the initiative in developing proper faunal and paleoeconomic studies in Texas, the great promise of this field will not be realized. A solution may lie in the training of amateurs to do faunal analyses—a permissible plan if whoever does the training is primarily interested in the relationship of man and animals interacting in the environment. In salvage operations, especially in Texas where governmental assistance is spread over such a large area, a sensible plan is for the archeologist in charge of the contract to utilize a paleontologist to assay the faunal resources and to write in a portion of grant support for that purpose (cf. Gillete and Thurmond, 1972, and Gillette, 1974). Invariably, the paleontologist is more aware of sophisticated techniques for recovering animal remains and methods of reconstruction than is the archeologist. Streuver (1974) has estimated, for example, that as much as 45 percent of faunal remains may escape detection in standard archeological recovery operations. The rewards to the faunal specialist exist also in the fact that by noting ancient ranges of fauna, he may make contributions to ecology as did Guilday and Parmalee (1965).

Of the various assumptions commonly employed by faunal investigators, some have been shown tenuous at best, some misleading, but a few innovative. If his analysis is to remain objective, the zoo-archeologist must beware of archeological preconceptions, e.g., accepting the existence of a cultural level which might bias ideas of exploited fauna (Payne, 1972). However, in contrast to a position of absolute independence of types of evidence, Payne (1972, p. 81) also rightfully warned: "No aspect of a site can be viewed meaningfully in isolation, and the work of the different specialists should become an integrated approach in which each makes full use of the information provided by the others." Undoubtedly, better utilization of faunal remains in Texas sites would allow a more accurate re-creation of the behavior of ancient Texas groups. In Texas, cultural phases such as the Lerma have been defined in terms of a "hunting phase," with others as "pre-ceramic hunting and gathering" and "Paleo-Indian big game economies." In Florida, Percy (1974) was able to correlate types of fauna with sites of known cultural and temporal contexts. The same could be attempted in Texas to evaluate these traditional concepts. Overall faunal analysis, including techniques for recovery of microvertebrates, would clarify the accuracy of many time-space cultural concepts. We have all heard the query, "How long was the Archaic and where did it extend?" Even a computerized data bank is feasible, allowing one to request and have supplied in seconds data correlating exploited fauna with cultural phase.

In conclusion, it seems that the main reason for the minimal contribution of faunal analyses to archeology in Texas is a lack of understanding of its potential. Faunal research offers a challenging part of ecological reconstruction to the amateur or professional who espouses maximum-information orientation during the necessarily destructive excavation. The archeologist who considers the modern principles of biology and ecology will provide a well-organized faunal analysis, and in so doing will not only enhance the profile of his field in science, but also maximize the return of his research.

TABLE 1

DISTRIBUTION OF TEXAS FAUNA BY PROVINCES

Provinces occupied are indicated by the following letter codes after the species name:

A = Austroriparian   T = Tamaulipan   K = Kansan
Tex = Texan   B = Balconian   C = Chihuahuan
                          N = Navahonian

† = Recent introduction   ! = Historical demise
                  ? = Probable but unconfirmed occurrence

(Note: In some cases, the last reported occurrence is noted by year in parentheses.)

FAUNA AND PROVINCE	FAUNA AND PROVINCE
AMPHIBIANS	*Hyla versicolor*, A, Tex, B
FROGS AND TOADS	*Hypopachus carcus*, B
Acris gryllus, A, Tex, T, B, K	*cuneus*, T, B
Bufo cognatus, K, N	*Leptodactylus labialis*, T
compactilis, T, B, K, C, N	*Microhyla carolinensis*, A, Tex
debilis, B, K, C, N	*olivacea*, Tex, T, B, C
marinus, T	*Pseudacris clarkii*, Tex, T, B
punctatus, B, K, C, N	*negrita*, A, Tex
valliceps, A, Tex, T, B	*streckeri*, Tex, T, B
woodhousi, A, Tex, B, K, N	*Rana calamitans*, A
Eleutherodactylus latrans, B, C	*catesbeiana*, A, Tex, T, B (bullfrog)
Hyla arenicolor, C, N	*palustris*, A
baudinii, T	*pipiens*, Tex, T, B, C, N
cinerea, Tex	*Scaphiopus couchii*, Tex, T, B, C, K, N
crucifer, A, Tex	*hammondii*, C, K, N
femoralis, A	*holbrooki*, A, Tex, T
squirrella, A	

FAUNA AND PROVINCE	FAUNA AND PROVINCE

Syrrhophus campi, T
    marnocki, B, C

REPTILES

  TURTLES AND TORTOISES

Gopherus berlanderi, Tex, T
Terrapene carolina (box turtle), A,
    Tex
    ornata, Tex, A, T, B, K, C,
    N?
Trionyx sp. T, C, A

  SALAMANDERS, NEWTS

Ambystoma maculatum, A
    opacum, A
    talpoideum, A
    texanum, Tex
    trigrinum, Tex, T, B, K,
    C, N
Amphiuma means, A
Desmognathus fuscus, A
Eurycea latitans, B
    longicausa, A
    nana, B
    neotenes, B
    pterophila, B
Manculus quadridigitatus, A
Necturus beyeri, A
Plethodon glutinosus, A, B
Siren intermedia, A, Tex, T
Triturus meridionalis, T
Typhlomoge rathbuni, B

  LIZARDS, ETC.

Anolis carolinensis, A, Tex
Cnemidorphorus gularis, T, B, K, C
    sexlineatus, A, B, K
    grahamii, C
    perplexus, C
    tesselatus, C
Coleonyx brevis, T, B, C
Crotaphytus collaris, Tex, B, K, C, N
    reticulatus, T
Eumeces gaigei, N
    laticeps, A
    multivirgatus, N
    obsoletus, Tex, B, K, N
    taylori, N
    tetragrammeus, T
Gambelia wislizeni, C
Gerrhonotus liocephalus, C
Holbrooki maculata, B, K, C
    propinqua, T
    texana, B, K, C, N

Leiolopisma laterale, A, Tex, B
Ophiosaurus ventralis, A, Tex, B
Phrynosma cornutum (Horned Liz-
    ard), Tex, K, T, B, C,
    N
    douglasii, C
    molestum, K, C
Sceloporus magister, C
    merriami, C
    olivaceous, Tex, B
    poinsettii, B, C, N
    undulatus, A, Tex, K, C
Urosaurus ornatus, B, C, N, T?
Alligator mississippiensis, A, Tex, T

  SNAKES

Agkistrodon mokasen, A, Tex, T, B
    (water moccasin),
    piscivorus, B
Arizona elegans, Tex, T, B, K
Carphophis amoena, A
Coluber constrictor, A, Tex, B
    flagellum, A, Tex, T, B, K, C
    taeniatus, C, B
Coniophanes imperialis, T
Crotalus atrox (diamondback rattle-
    snake), Tex, T, B, K, C
    cutulatus, C
    horridus, A, Tex
    lepidus, C
    molossus, B, C
    viridis, K
Diadophis punctatus, A, B
    regalis, C
Drymarchon corais, T
Drymobius margaritferus, T
Elaphe laeta, A, T
    obsoleta, A, Tex, B
    subocularis, C
Ficimia cana, B, C
    streckeri, T
Haldea striatula, A, B
    valeriae, A, B
Heterodon contortrix, A, B
Hypsiglena ochrorhyncha, B
Lampropeltis alterna, C
    getulus, A, Tex
Leptodeira septentrionalis, T
Leptotyphlops dulcis, B, K
Micrurus fulvius, A, B, Tex
Natrix erythrogaster, A, Tex, T, B, K
    hateri, K
    rhombifera, A, Tex, T, B
    rigida, A

| FAUNA AND PROVINCE | FAUNA AND PROVINCE |

Natrix sipedon, A
Opheodrys aestivus, A, B, Tex
Pituophis catenifer, Tex, K, C
Rhinocheilus lecontei, K
Salvadora grahami, C, N
    hexalepis, C, N
    lineata, B
Sonora episcopa, B
    semiannulata, C
    taylori, T
Storeria dekayi, A, B, Tex
Tantilla atriceps, C, N?
    nigriceps, K
Thamnophis eques, C
    marcianus, K, Tex, T, B
    C
    sauritus, A, Tex, T, K
    sirtalis, K, B

MAMMALS

BATS

Antrozous pallidus, T, B, K, C
Dasypterus floridanus, A, Tex, T
Eptesicus fuscus, A, Tex, T, B, K, C, N
Eumops penotis, C
Lasionycteris noctivagans, B
Lasiurus borealis, A, Tex, T, B, K, C, N
    intermedius, A
    seminolus, A, Tex
Mormoops megalophylla, T, B, C
Myotis californicus, C
    lucifugus, C
    subulatus, C
    thysanodes, C
    velifer, T, B, K, N
    volans, C
    yumanensis, C
Nycticeius humeralis, A, Tex, T, B
Pipistrellus hesperus, C
    subflavus, A, Tex, T, B, K
Plecotus townsendi, K, C, N
Tadarida cynocephala, A, Tex
    macrotis, C
    mexicana, C, Tex, T, B, K, N

CARNIVORES

Bassariscus astutus (ringtail), A, Tex, T, B, K, C, N
Canis latrans (coyote), A, Tex, T, B, K, C, N
    lupus (wolf), B (Dalquest et al., 1969), C, N?

Canis niger (red wolf), A?, Tex, T?, B?
Conepatus leuconotus (hog-nosed skunk), T
    mesoleucus, A, Tex, T, B, K, C, N
Felis concolor (puma), A, Tex, B (1958), K, C, N, T
    onca (jaguar), Tex, T, B (1903), C (1962)
    pardalis (ocelot), A, Tex, T (1902), C
    weidii (margay), T, C
    yagouaroundi (jaguarundi), T, C
Lutra canadensis (otter), A, Tex
Lynx rufus (bobcat), A, Tex, T, B, K, C, N
Mephitis macroura (hooded skunk), C, N
    mephitis (striped skunk), A, Tex, T, B, K, C, N
Mustela frenata (weasel), A, Tex, T, B, C, N
    nigripes (ferret), B, K, C
    vison (mink), A, Tex, T, B, K, C
Nasua narica (coati-mundi), T, C
Procyon lotor (raccoon), A, Tex, T, B, K, C, N
Spilogale putorius (spotted skunk), A, Tex, T, B, K, C, N
Taxidea taxus (badger), A, Tex, T, B, K, C, N
Urocyon cinereoargenteus (gray fox), A, Tex, T, B, K, C, N
Ursus americanus (black bear), A?, Tex!, T!, B!, C (1977), N?
    horribilis (grizzly), B!, Tex! (Dalquest et al., 1969), C!, N
Vulpes fulva (red fox), A, Tex
    macrotis (desert fox), C
    velox (swift fox), K

INSECTIVORES

Blarina brevicauda (short-tailed shrew), A, Tex, T
Cryptotis parva (little short-tailed shrew), A, Tex, T, B, K
Notiosorex crawfordi (Crawford shrew), Tex, T, B, K, C, N
Scalopus aquaticus (mole), A, Tex, T, B, K, C

FAUNA AND PROVINCE	FAUNA AND PROVINCE

RODENTS

Amnospermophilus interpres (antelope ground squirrel), C

Baiomys taylori (pygmy mouse), A, Tex, T, B

Castor canadensis (beaver), A, Tex, T?, B

Citellus interpres, C, N
    mexicanus (Mexican ground squirrel), T, B, C
    spilosoma (spotted ground squirrel), K, B, T, C, N
    tridecemlineatus (thirteen-lined ground squirrel), Tex
    variegatus (rock squirrel), T, B, C, N

Cratogeomys castanops (chesnut-faced pocket gopher), B, K, N

Cynomys ludovicianus (prairie dog), B, K, C, N

Dipodomys elator (Loring kangaroo rat), Tex, K
    merriami (Merriam kangaroo rat), C, N
    ordi (Ord kangaroo rat), T, B, K, C, N
    spectabilis (banner-tailed kangaroo rat), C, N

Erethizon dorsatum (porcupine), B, C, N

Eutamias canipes (chipmunk), C, N

Geomys arenarius (New Mexican pocket gopher), C, N
    bursarius (Plains pocket gopher), A, Tex, T, B, K
    personatus (South Texas pocket gopher), T

Glaucomys volans (flying squirrel), A, Tex

Liomys irroratus (spiny mouse), T

Microtus mexicanus (Mexican meadow mouse), N, Tex (*ochrogaster?* Blair, 1950)

Mus musculus† (house mouse), A, Tex, T, B, K, C, N

Myocastor coypus† (nutria), A, Tex, T, B, K

Neotoma albigula (wood rat), B, K, C, N
    floridana, A, Tex, T, B
    mexicana, C
    micropus, T, B, K, C, N

Ondatra zibethicus (muskrat), A, Tex, K, C

Onychomys corridus (short-tailed grasshopper mouse), C
    leucogaster, T, B, K, C

Oryzomys couesi (rice rat), T
    palustris, A, Tex, T

Pedomys ludovicianus (meadow mouse), Tex (Blair, 1950)
    ochrogaster, A

Perognathus apache (pocket mouse), C
    flavus, K
    hispidus, A, Tex, T, B, K, C, N
    intermedius, C, N
    merriami, T, B, K, C
    nelsoni, C
    pencillatus, C

Peromyscus boylii (brush mouse), B, K, C, N
    eremicus (desert white-footed mouse), C
    gossypinus (cotton mouse), A, Tex
    leucopus (white-footed mouse), A, Tex, T, B, K, C, N
    maniculatus (deer mouse), A, Tex, T, K, C, N
    nasutus (long-nosed white-footed mouse), K
    nattalli (golden mouse), A, Tex
    pectoralis (encinal mouse), B, K, C, N

Pitimys pinetorum (pine vole), A, Tex, B

Rattus norvegicus† (Norway rat), A, Tex, T, B, K, C, N
    rattus† (roof rat), A, Tex, T, B, K, C, N

Reithrodontomys fulvescens (long-tailed harvest mouse), A, Tex, T, K
    humulis (dwarf harvest mouse), A
    megalotis (desert harvest mouse), C
    montanus (gray harvest mouse), Tex, B, K, N

Sciurus carolinensis (Eastern gray

FAUNA AND PROVINCE	FAUNA AND PROVINCE

squirrel), A, Tex
niger, A, Tex, T, B, K
Sigmodon hispidus (Hispid cotton
rat), A, Tex, T, B, K, C,
N
 ochrognathus (yellow-nosed
cotton rat), C, N
Thomomys baileyi (Bailey pocket
gopher), C
 bottae (Botta pocket
gopher), B, C, N
Zapus hudsonicus (jumping mouse),
Tex (Blair 1950), K

OTHER MAMMALS

Amnotragus lervia† (Aoudad sheep),
K, C, B, N?
Antilocapra americana (pronghorn
antelope), K, C, N, T!
Balaenoptera musculus (blue whale),
A (1939), T?
 physalus (common fin-
back whale), A
(1951), T?
Bison bison (buffalo), B!, K!, C!, N!,
T!, Tex!
Cervus canadensis merriami (elk), C
(Gilmore, 1947), N!
Dasypus novemcinctus (armadillo), A,
Tex, T, B, K, C?, N?
Didelphis marsupialis (opossum), A,
Tex, T, B, K, C, N
 mesamericana, T, C
Globicephala melaena (blackfish por-
poise), T (1945)

Kogia breviceps (pygmy sperm whale),
A!, Tex?, T!
Lepus californicus (jack rabbit), A?,
Tex, T, B, K, C, N
Mesoplodon europaeus (beaked whale),
T (1946)
Monachus tropicalis (West Indian
seal), T!
Odocoileus hemionus (mule deer), B,
K, C, N
 virginianus (white-tailed
deer), A, Tex, T, B, K, C
Ovis canadensis (bighorn sheep), N?
(subspecies *nelsoni*, desert bighorn
in C)
Pecari tajacu (peccary), A, Tex, T, B,
K!, C, N?
Physeter catodon (sperm whale), A
(1910), T?
Stenella pernettyi (spotted long-nose
porpoise), A, Tex?, T
Sylvilagus aquaticus (swamp rabbit),
A, Tex
 auduboni (Audubon cottontail), K, C
 floridanus (eastern cottontail), A, Tex, T, B, K
 robustus (Davis Mountains
cottontail), C, N
Trichechus manatus (manatee), A,
Tex, T
Tursiops truncatus (bottled-nosed porpoise), A, Tex, T

TABLE 2

FAUNAL REMAINS IN SITES AS REPORTED

Asterisk following author indicates source other than *Bulletin of the Texas Archeological Society.* NFR indicates no fauna reported.

SITE, AUTHOR, AND BIOTIC PROVINCE	FAUNAL REMAINS
Acton (Blaine et al., 1968) Texan	NFR
Albert George (Walley, 1955) Austroriparian	*B. bison, Odocoileus virginianus*

SITE, AUTHOR, AND BIOTIC PROVINCE	FAUNAL REMAINS

Arroyo los Olmos
(Newton, 1968)
Tamaulipan

NFR

Ayala
(Hester & Ruecking, 1969)
Tamaulipan

Turtle, snake: *Geomys* sp., *Canis latrans,*
O. virginianus

Baker Cave
Word & Douglas, 1970)
Chihuahuan

Fish: *Ictalurus punctatus* (channel catfish)

Reptiles: snakes, *Testudinata*; lizards including
Phrynosoma cornutum, P. douglassi

Birds: *Meleagris gallopavo* (turkey)

Rodents: *A. interpres, Castor canadensis,
Cratogeomys castanops, Erethizon dorsatum,
Geomys* sp., *Neotoma,* sp., *N. albigula, N.
mexicana, N. micropus, Ondatra zibethicus,
Perognathus* sp., *P. hispidus, Peromyscus* sp.,
Sigmodon hispidus, Spermophilus sp., *S.
mexicanus, S. variegatus, Thomomys* sp.

Carnivores: *Bassariscus astutus, Canis latrans,
Conepatus mesoleucus, Procyon lotor, Spilogale
putorius, Urocyon cinereoargenteus, Vulpes velox*

Other: *Antilocapra americana, Lepus* sp.,
Odocoileus sp., *Odocoileus virginianus,
Sylvilagus* sp.

Beidleman Ranch
(Suhm, 1961)
Kansan

Bison antiquus (?)

Belton Reservoir
(Miller & Jelks, 1952)
Texan

Bison sp., *Odocoileus virginianus*

Berclair
(Hester & Parker, 1970)
Texan

B. bison, Odocoileus sp.

Blackburn Crossing Reservoir
(Johnson, 1961)
Texan

NFR

Blackwater Locality #1
(Hester et al., 1972*)
Kansan

Reptiles: *Terrapene ornata, agassiz,* and
canaliculata

Bird bones

Rodents: *Cynomys* sp., *Ondatra zibethicus,
Microtus pennsylvanicus*

Carnivores: *Aenocyon dirus, Canis latrans,
C. lupus, Smilodon californicus, Vulpes velox*

Site, Author, and Biotic Province	Faunal Remains
Blackwater Locality # 1 (cont'd)	Other: *Bison* sp., *B. antiquus, Camelops, Cervus* sp., *Equus* (3 sp.), *Mammoth* sp., *Parelephas, Platygonus* sp., *Tanupolama macrocephala*
Blum Rockshelter (Jelks, 1953) Texan	Small mammals, *Odocoileus virginianus*
Blue Mountain Rockshelter (Holden, 1938) Kansan	Bird (?), rodents, carnivores Other: *Antilocapra americana, B. Bison, Equus* sp.
Boggy Creek (Hasskarl, 1961) Texan	*Antilocapra* sp. (?), *Odocoileus* sp.
Bone Implement Burial (Harris, 1945) Texan	*Bison* sp.
Bonfire Shelter (Dibble & Lorrain, 1968*) Chihuahuan	Unidentified remains: fish, snake, bat Rodents: *Citellus mexicanus, C. variegatus, Cratogeomys* sp., *Geomys* sp., *Neotoma* sp., *Onychomys* sp., *Perognathus* sp., *Peromyscus* sp., *Reithrodontomys* sp., *Sigmodon* sp., *Thomomys* sp. Carnivores: *Urocyon cinereoargenteus* Other: *Camelops* sp., *Elephas* sp., *Equus* sp., *Lepus* sp., *Odocoileus* sp., *Sylvilagus* sp.
Boy Scout Rockshelter (Pollard et al., 1963) Balconian	Fish, turtles, snakes, birds, small mammals, *B. bison, Odocoileus* sp.
Brawley's Cave (Olds, 1963) Texan	Birds, *B. bison, O. virginianus*
Burnt-Rock Midden (Sturgis, 1956) Texan	NFR
Buried Midden (Riggs, 1968) Balconian	NFR
Buzzard, Little Buzzard, and Forrester Caves (Long, 1961) Texan	Fish: *Ictalurus* Reptiles: turtle Birds: "eagle, heron, or goose" (?) Other: *Conepatus* or *Mephitis* sp., *Didelphis, Odocoileus virginianus, Sylvilagus aquaticus*

Site, Author, and Biotic Province	Faunal Remains
Cedar Bayou (Ambler, 1967) Austroriparian	Fish: gar, drum Reptiles: turtle, alligator Rodents: *Sciurus* sp., "gopher," *Sigmodon* sp. Carnivores: *Procyon lotor* Other: *B. bison, Didelphis marsupialis, O. virginianus, Sylvilagus* sp.
Cedar Creek Reservoir (Story, 1965) Texan	Fish: *Lepidosteus* and other unidentified Reptiles: *Terrapene* sp., snake Birds: *Meleagris gallopavo* and other unidentified Rodents: *Castor canadensis, Geomys* sp., *Sciurus* sp. Carnivores: *Canis familiaris* (domestic dog), *C. latrans, Procyon lotor, spilogale putorius* Other: *B. bison, Didelphis virginianus, Dasypus novemcinctus, Lepus* sp., *O. virginianus, Sylvilagus* sp.
Centipede and Damp Caves (Epstein, 1962) Chihuahuan	Fish: *Lepidosteus* sp.(?), *Ictalurus furcatus* (blue catfish), *Carpoides carpio, Pilodectus olivaria* (flathead catfish), *Micropterus salmoides* (large-mouthed bass) Reptiles: lizards, including *Gehrronotus* sp., *Phrynosoma* sp., snakes, and *Trionyx* sp. (soft-shelled turtle) Birds Bats: *Eumops perotis* Rodents: *Castor canadensis, Citellus mexicana, C. spilosoma, C. variegatus, C. leucurus, Erethizon dorsatum, Geomys* sp., *Neotoma albigula, N. mexicana, Onadatra zibethicus, Sigmodon hispidus, S. ochrogaster* Carnivores: *Bassariscus astutus, Canis latrans, Conepatus mesoleucus, Mephitis mephitis, Procyon lotor, Spilogale putorius, Urocyon cinereoargenteus* Other: *Bison* or *Bos, Equus, O. virginianus, Ovis* sp. (domestic)
Clark (Watt, 1965) Texan	Reptiles: land tortoise "Rodents" Other: *Odocoileus virginianus*
Collins (Suhm, 1955) Texan	*Odocoileus virginianus*

SITE, AUTHOR, AND BIOTIC PROVINCE	FAUNAL REMAINS
Corpus Christi Bay (Corbin, 1963) Tamaulipan	Fish, rodents Other: *Odocoileus* sp.
Crumley (Kelly, 1961) Balconian	Carnivores: *Canis familiaris* or *lupus* or *latrans* Other: *B. bison, Odocoileus virginianus*
Culpepper (Scurlock, 1962) Austroriparian	NFR (*Canis* sp. effigy)
DeCordova Bend (Skinner, 1971) Texan	Fish: fresh water drum Reptiles: *Terrapene* Other: *P. lotor, O. virginianus*
Deep Archeological Site (Jackson, 1939) Texan	Birds: *Meleagris gallopavo* Other: *B. bison, Odocoileus* sp.
Devil's Mouth (Johnson, 1961, 1964*) Chihuahuan	Fish: *Ictalurus, Lepidosteus, Carpoides*, misc. others Reptiles: *Trionyx* sp., snakes Birds Rodents: *Citellus variegatus, Geomys bursarius, Neotoma micropus, Sigmodon hispidus, Thomomys umbrinus* Carnivores: *Canis latrans, Urocyon cinereoargenteus* Other: *Lepus californicus, Odocoileus virginianus Sylvilagus auduboni*
Devil's Hollow (Collins, 1972) Balconian	*Odocoileus virginianus*
Dunlap Complex (Word, 1971) Balconian	Bird, small mammals, *O. virginianus*
Falcon Reservoir (Cason, 1952) Tamaulipan	Mammoth (not associated), bird, *Odocoileus virginianus*
Field Ranch (Jensen, 1968) Texan	NFR

Site, Author, and Biotic Province	Faunal Remains
Fingerprint Caves (Quinn & Holden, 1949) Kansan	Fish Reptiles: turtle, lizards Birds Rodents Other: *Antilocapra americana, Bison bison,* *Odocoileus virginianus*
Floyd Morris (Collins et al., 1969) Tamaulipan	Fish: shark Carnivores: Canis latrans Other: *Pecari tajacu*
Fullen (O'Brien, 1971) Austroriparian	Fish: *Lepidosteus* Reptiles, turtle Rodents: *Cricetidae* Other: *Bison bison, Odocoileus virginianus*
Galena (Ring, 1961) Austroriparian	NFR
Garza (Runkles, 1964) Kansan	Reptiles: land tortoise, *Crotalus* sp. (rattlesnake) Rodent Carnivores: *Canis lupus* Other: *B. bison*
Gilbert (Lorrain, 1967) Austroriparian	Fish: *Aplodinotis grunniens, Lepidosteus* sp., *L. osseus, Ictalurus* sp. Amphibia: frog Reptiles: snake, *Terrapene carolinensis* (box turtle), *Graptemys pseudogeographica,* *Macroclemys temmicki, Kinosternon* sp., *Pseudemys* sp. Birds: *Meleagris gallopavo,* other birds Rodents: *Geomys bursarius, Sciuris carolinensis* Carnivores: *Bassariscus astutus,* or fox, *Canis* sp., *Felis concolor, Lynx rufus, Mephitis mephitis,* *Procyon lotor, Spilogale putorius, Ursus* *americanus* Other: *Bison* or *Bos, Equus* (domestic?), *Didelphis virginianus, Lepus californicus,* *Odocoileus virginianus, Sylvilagus* sp.

SITE, AUTHOR, AND BIOTIC PROVINCE	FAUNAL REMAINS

Grace Creek
(Jones, 1957)
Austroriparian

Small mammals, *Odocoileus virginianus*

Granite Beach
(Crawford, 1965)
Balconian

NFR

Ham Creek
(Forrester, 1964*)
Texan

Bison bison, Odocoileus sp.

Happy Patch
(Green, 1971)
Balconian

NFR

Harroun
(Jelks & Tunnell, 1959*)
Austroriparian

NFR

High Bluff
(Flinn, 1968)
Kansan

Reptiles: turtle

"Bird or small mammals"

Rodents: *Sciurus* sp.

Other: *Odocoileus virginianus*

Hitzfelder Cave
(Givens, 1968)
Balconian

Carnivores: *Canis* sp.

Other: *Odocoleus virginianus*

Holdsworth & Stewart
(Hester, Hill, Holdsworth,
   and Gilbow, 1972)
Tamaulipan

Reptiles: *Gopherus* sp. (land tortoise)

Rodents: *Neotoma micropus, Sigmodon hispidus*

Other: *Bison bison, Lepus californicus, Odocoileus
   texanus, Sylvilagus* (auduboni?)

Jake Martin
(Davis & Davis, 1960*)
Austroriparian

NFR

Jim Arnold
(Tunnell, 1964)
Kansan

Odocoileus sp.

Johnson
(Campbell, 1947)
Tamaulipan

Fish: *Chaetodipterus, Balistes* (marine fish)

Reptiles: turtles—*Terrapene, Chelydra*

Birds: *Anas platyrhynchos* (mallard duck), *Anas
   acuta* (pintail), *Anas americana* (widgeon),
   Buteo sp. (hawk), *Gavia immer* (common
   loon), *Spatula clypeata* (shoveler)

Rodents: *Thomomys*

SITE, AUTHOR, AND BIOTIC PROVINCE	FAUNAL REMAINS
Johnson (*cont'd*)	Carnivores: *Canis* sp. (*latrans?*), *Procyon lotor*
	Other: *Bison bison, Lepus californicus, Odocoileus, Pecari tajacu,* porpoise or manatee
Kyle (Jelks, 1962*) Texan (western limit)	Fish: *Lepidosteus, Carpoides, Ictalurus* sp., crayfish, misc.
	Amphibia: frogs
	Reptiles: snakes, turtles
	Birds
	Carnivores: *Canis* sp., *C. latrans, Conepatus mesoleucus, Procyon lotor, Taxidea taxus*
	Rodents: *Castor canadensis, Citellus* sp., *Cricetines, Geomys* sp., *Microtus (Pitimys) pinetorum, Neotoma* sp., *Onychomys leucogaster, Perognathus hispidus, Sciurus niger, Sigmodon hispidus*
	Insectivores: *Cryptotis parva* (shrew), *Scalopus aquaticus* (mole)
	Other: *Bison bison, Antilocapra americana, Odocoileus virginianus, Sylvilagus* sp.
Laguna Madre (Campbell, 1956) Tamaulipan	Fish: *Lepidosteus*
	Birds
	Other: *Odocoileus virginianus*
La Jita (Hester & Riskind, 1971) Balconian	Reptiles: turtles: *Chelydra serpentina* (snapping), *Terrapene ornata, Trionyx* sp.
	Small mammals: *Sigmodon hispidus, Sylvilagus floridanus, S. auduboni* Carnivores: *Canis* sp. Other: *Antilocapra americana, Bison bison, Odocoileus virginianus*
Lake Creek (Hughes, 1962) Kansan	Birds
	Reptiles: *Terrapene* sp.
	Small mammals: *Lepus californicus,* rodents, other unidentified fragments
	Other: *Bison bison, Odocoileus* sp. (possibly some antelope)
Lake Palestine and Upper Neches River (Anderson et al., 1974*) Austroriparian	Fish: *Ictalurus* sp., misc. other
	Amphibia: *Rana catesbiana* (bullfrog)
	Reptiles: turtles: *Pseudemys* sp., *Terrapene carolina, Trionyx* sp., unidentified snakes
	Birds: *Meleagris gallopavo,* owl

SITE, AUTHOR, AND BIOTIC PROVINCE	FAUNAL REMAINS
Lake Palestine and Upper Neches River (*cont'd*)	Small mammals: *Neotoma* sp., *Sciuris* sp., *Sylvilagus* sp. Carnivores: *Bassariscus astutus, Mephitis* or *Spilogale, Procyon lotor, Urocyon* or *Vulpes* Other: *Didelphis virginianus, Odocoileus virginianus* (*O. virginianus* = 90% of remains)
Langtry Creek Burial Cave (Greek & Benfer, 1963) Chihuahuan	Rodents
La Perdida (Weir, 1956) Tamaulipan	NFR
Lehman Rock Shelter (Kelly, 1947) Balconian	*Bison bison*
Limerick (Duffield, 1961) Texan	Rodents: *Castor canadensis* Carnivores: *Procyon lotor* Other: *Didelphis virginianus, Odocoileus virginianus*
Little Sunday (Hughes, 1958) Kansan	NFR
McCann (Preston, 1969) Balconian	*Bison bison, Odocoileus virginianus*
McGee Reservoir (Tunnell, 1961) Austroriparian	NFR
Merrell (Campbell, 1948) Balconian	NFR
Midden Circle (Greer, 1968) Chihuahuan	NFR
Obshner (Crook & Harris, 1955) Texan	NFR
Panhandle Aspect Sites (Duffield, 1964) Kansan	*Antilocapra americana* (?), *Bison bison, Odocoileus* sp.

SITE, AUTHOR, AND BIOTIC PROVINCE	FAUNAL REMAINS

Pearson
(Duffield & Jelks, 1961*)
Texan

NFR

Plainview
(Sellards et al., 1947*)
Kansan

Bison taylori, Canis occidentalis

Proctor Reservoir
(Prewitt, 1964)
Balconian

Reptiles: *Terrapene*

Unidentified small mammals

Other: *Bison bison, Odocoileus* sp.

Rancho Diexmero and Goliad
(Raun, 1964)
Tamaulipan

Monachus tropocalis (West Indian seal)

Reagan Canyon
(Kelly & Smith, 1963)
Chihuahuan

NFR

Resch
(Webb et al., 1969)
Austroriparian

Birds

Odocoileus sp., (probably *hemionus*)

Roark Cave
(Kelly, 1963)
Chihuahuan

Odocoileus sp. (probably *hemionus*)

Sam Kaufman
(Harris, 1953; Skinner
et al., 1969*)
Austroriparian

Small mammals
Other: *Odocoileus virginianus, Ursus* sp.

San Miguel
(Hester, 1968)
Tamaulipan (surface survey)

NFR

Scharbauer
(Wendorf et al., 1955*)
Kansan

Reptiles: turtle

Small mammals: *Cricetidae* sp., *Citellus* sp.,
   Cynomys ludovicianus, Geomys arenarius or
   bursarius, Lepus sp., *Neotoma* sp., *Sylvilagus* sp.

Carnivores: *Canis* sp. (*dirus* or *ayersi*)

Other: *Bison* sp. and *B. bison, Camelops* sp.,
   Cervidae (deer or elk), *Capromeryx* or *Mazama?*
   (extinct antelope), mammoth, *Platygonus* sp.,
   sloth, *Equus*

Tortuga Flat
(Hill & Hester, 1973)
Tamaulipan

Fish, turtles, snakes

Small mammals: *Geomys bursarius, Lepus
   californicus, Marmota flaviventex, Neotoma
   micropus, sigmodon hispidus*

SITE, AUTHOR, AND BIOTIC PROVINCE	FAUNAL REMAINS

Tortuga Flat (*cont'd*)

Carnivores: *Canis latrans, Urocyon cinereoargenteus*

Other: *Antilocapra americana, Bison bison, Odocoileus virginianus*

Twelve Room House
(Moore, 1947)
Chihuahuan

NFR

Twin Buttes
(Green, 1961)
Balconian

Unidentified bones

Val Verde Cave
(Schuetz, 1961)
Chihuahuan

Fish, birds, reptiles (*Crotalus* sp.), rodents

Other: *Odocoileus* sp.

W. A. Myatt
(Wheat, 1947)
Kansan

NFR

Whitney Reservoir
(Stephenson & Jelks, 1970)
Texan

Fish: *Lepidosteus*

Birds: goose (?), waterfowl, and wading birds

Small mammals: rabbit

Other: *Bison bison, Odocoileus* sp.

Williams Cave
(Ayer, 1936*)
Navahonian

Reptiles: *Iguanidae* (lizard)

Birds: *Meleagris gallopavo*

Small mammals: *Citellus variegatus* or *grammurus*, *Cratogeomys castanops, Cynomys gunnusoni, Erethizon epixanthum epixanthum, Lepus californicus, Neotoma albigula albigula, Perognathus intermedius, Sylvilagus auduboni*

Carnivores: *Canis dirus, Felis concolor (oregonensis), Lynx rufus, Urocyon cinereoargenteus, Ursus horribilis*

Other: *Antilocapra americana, Equus semiplicatus, Notrotherium shastense* (extinct ground sloth dung), *Odocoileus hemionus, virginianus, Ovis canadensis*

Williamson County Mounds
(Schuetz, 1957)
Texan

Birds: goose (?), waterfowl, and wading birds

Wolfshead
(Duffield, 1963)
Austroriparian

NFR

Womack
(Harris et al., 1965)
Austroriparian

NFR

SITE, AUTHOR, AND BIOTIC PROVINCE	FAUNAL REMAINS
Yarbrough & Miller (Johnson, 1962) Texan	Fish; birds (turkey?) Small mammals: *Lepus californicus, Sylvilagus* sp. Carnivores: *Canis familiaris* (articulated skelton), *Conepatus, Mephitis* or *Spilogale, Mustela* sp., *Procyon lotor* Other: *Didelphis virginianus, Odocoileus virginianus*
Youngsport (Shafer, 1963) Balconian	*Odocoileus* sp., other bone
Zavonian Spring (Davis & Horn, 1964) Austroriparian	Unidentified bone, probably deer

TABLE 3

DISTRIBUTION OF SAMPLE SITES

BIOTIC PROVINCE	CONTAINS FAUNAL ANALYSIS	LACKS FAUNAL ANALYSIS	TOTAL
Austroriparian	3	13	16
Texan	4	20	24
Tamaulipan	3	8	11
Kansas	2	12	14
Balconian	1	14	15
Chihuahuan	4	6	10
Navahonian	1	0	1
Totals	18	73	91

BIBLIOGRAPHY

ALLEN, D. C., and CHEATUM, E. P. 1961. "Ecological Implications of Fresh-water and Land Gastropods in Texas Archeological Studies." *Bulletin of the Texas Archeological Society* 31:291-316.

ANDERSON, K. M.; GILMORE, K.; McCORMICK, O. F. III; and MORENON, E. P. 1974. *Archeological Investigations at Lake Palestine, Texas.* Southern Methodist University Contributions in Anthropology, no. 11.

BAILEY, V. 1905. "Biological Survey of Texas." *North American Fauna* 25:1-222.

BEST, T. L., and KENNEDY, M. 1972. "The Porcupine (*Erethizon dorsatum*) in the Texas Panhandle and Adjacent New Mexico and Oklahoma." *Texas Journal of Science* 24 (3): 351.

BIGGS, E. J. 1969. "Molluscs from Human Habitation Sites and the Problem of Ethnological Interpretation." In *Science in Archaeology*, ed. Don Brothwell and Eric Higgs, pp. 423-28. London: Thames & Hudson.

BLAIR, W. F. 1950. "The Biotic Provinces of Texas." *Texas Journal of Science* 2:93-117.

BROWN, B. 1950. *An Annotated Check List of the Reptiles and Amphibians of Texas*. Waco, Texas: Baylor University Press.

BRYANT, V. M. 1974. "The Role of Coprolite Analysis in Archeology." *Bulletin of the Texas Archeological Society* 45:1-28.

BURR, J. G. 1932. *Fishes of Texas*. Texas Game, Fish, and Oyster Commission Bulletin no. 5.

CALLEN, E. O. 1969. "Diet as Revealed by Coprolites." In *Science in Archaeology*, ed. Don Brothwell and Eric Higgs, pp. 235-43. London: Thames & Hudson.

CASTEEL, R. 1974. "On the Remains of Fish Scales from Archeological Sites." *American Antiquity* 39 (4): 557-81.

CHAPLIN, R. E. 1971. *The Study of Animal Bones from Archaeological Sites*. New York: Seminar Press.

CHEATUM, E. P., and FULLINGTON, R. W. 1971. *The Aquatic and Land Mollusca of Texas: Part 1, The Recent and Pleistocene Members of the Gastropod Family Polygyridae in Texas*. Dallas: Dallas Museum of Natural History.

COLLINS, M. 1972. "The Devil's Hollow Site: A Stratified Archaic Campsite in Central Texas." *Bulletin of the Texas Archeological Society* 43:77-100.

COPE, E. D. 1880. "On the Zoological Position of Texas." *Bulletin of the U.S. National Museum* 17:1-51.

CORNWALL, I. W. 1956. *Bones for the Archeologist*. New York: Macmillan Co.

CRIMMINS, M. L. 1946. "The Rattlesnake in the Art and Life of the American Indian." *Bulletin of the Texas Archeological Society* 17:28-41.

DALQUEST, W. W.; ROTH, E.; and JUDD, F. 1969. "The Mammal Fauna of Schulze Cave, Edwards County, Texas." *Bulletin of the Florida State Museum* 13 (4): 1-276.

DALY, P. 1969. "Approaches to Faunal Analysis in Archeology." *American Antiquity* 34 (2): 131-45.

DAVIS, W. A., and DAVIS, E. M. 1960. *The Jake Martin Site*. University of Texas Anthropology Department Archeology Series, no. 4, Austin.

DAVIS, W. B. 1966. *The Mammals of Texas*. Texas Parks and Wildlife Department Bulletin no. 41.

DAWSON, E. W. 1969. "Bird Remains in Archaeology." In *Science in Archaeology*, ed. Don Brothwell and Eric Higgs, pp. 359-75. London: Thames & Hudson.

DIBBLE, D., and LORRAIN, D. 1968. *Bonfire Shelter: A Stratified Bison Kill Site in Val Verde County, Texas.* Miscellaneous Papers no. 1, Texas Memorial Museum, Austin.

DICE, L. R. 1943. *The Biotic Provinces of North America.* Ann Arbor: University of Michigan Press.

DILLEHAY, T. D. 1973. "Toward a More Complete Ascertainment of Animal Bones from Archeological Sites." *Texas Archeology* 17 (1): 12-13.

DOUGLAS, C. 1969. "Catfish Spines from Archeological Sites in Texas." *Bulletin of the Texas Archeological Society* '40:263-65.

DUFFIELD, L., and JELKS, E. B. 1961. *The Pearson Site: A Historic Indian Site at Iron Bridge Reservoir, Rains Co., Texas.* University of Texas Anthropology Department Archeology Series, no. 4, Austin.

ELDER, W. H. 1965. "Primaeval Deer Hunting Pressures Revealed by Remains from American Indian Middens." *Journal of Wildlife Management* 29:366-70.

FLOWER, W. H. 1876. *Osteology of the Mammalia.* London: Macmillan & Co.

FOLLETT, W. I. 1970. *Fish Remains from Human Coprolites and Midden Deposits Obtained during 1968 and 1969 at Lovelock Cave, Churchill County, Nevada,* ed. Robert F. Heizer and Louis K. Napton. Contributions of the University of California Archeological Facility, vol. 10, pp. 163-75.

FORRESTER, R. E. 1964. *The Ham Creek Site.* Fort Worth: Tarrant County Archeological Society.

FRANK, R. M. 1964. *The Vertebrate Paleontology of Texas Caves.* Publications of the Texas Speleological Association, vol. 2, no. 3, pp. 1-43.

GATCHET, A. S. 1891. *The Karankawa Indians, the Coast People of Texas.* Archaeological and Ethnological Papers of the Peabody Museum, Harvard University, vol. 1, no. 2.

GILBERT, B. M. 1973. *Mammalian Osteo-Archeology: North America.* Columbia, Missouri: Missouri Archeological Society.

――――, and BASS, W. M. 1967. "A Seasonal Dating of Burials from the Presence of Fly Pupae." *American Antiquity* 32 (4): 534-35.

GILLETTE, D. 1974. Appendix II: Animal Bone, in *Archeological Investigations at Lake Palestine, Texas.* Southern Methodist University Contributions in Anthropology, no. 11.

――――, and THURMOND, J. 1972. "Literature Survey of the Paleontological Resources of the Trinity River Basin." In *Environmental and Cultural Resources within the Trinity River Basin,* compiled by James V. Sciscenti. Archeology Research Program, Southern Methodist University.

GILMORE, R. M. 1947. "Report on a Collection of Mammalian Bones from Archeological Cave Sites in Coahuila, Mexico." *Journal of Mammalogy* 28:147-65.

GOODRUM, P. D. 1964. *The Gray Squirrel in Texas.* Texas Parks and Wild-life Department Bulletin no. 42.

GRAYSON, D. K. 1973. "On the Methodology of Faunal Analysis." *American Antiquity* 38 (4): 432-39.

GUILDAY, J. E., and PARMALEE, P. W. 1965. "Animal Remains from the Sheep Rock Shelter (36 Hu 1), Huntington County, Pennsylvania." *Pennsylvania Archaeologist* 35 (1): 34-49.

GUNTER, G. 1947. "Sight Records of the West Indian Seal, *Monachus tropicalis* (Gray) from the Texas Coast." *Journal of Mammalogy* 28: 289-90.

HEIZER, R. F. 1969. "The Anthropology of Prehistoric Great Basin Human Coprolites." In *Science in Archaeology*, ed. Don Brothwell and Eric Higgs, pp. 244-50. London: Thames & Hudson.

HESTER, T. R. 1971. "An Eolith from Lower Pleistocene Deposits of South-ern Texas." *Bulletin of the Texas Archeological Society* 42:367-71.

————, and HILL, T. C., JR. 1972. "Prehistoric Occupation at the Holds-worth and Stewart Sites of the Rio Grande Plain of Texas." Appendixes by Holdsworth and Gilbow. *Bulletin of the Texas Archeological Society* 43:33-75.

HIBBARD, C. W. 1958. "Summary of North American Pleistocene Mammalian Local Faunas." *Papers of the Michigan Academy of Science, Arts, and Letters* 43:3-32.

HIGGS, E., ed. 1972. *Papers in Economic Prehistory.* Cambridge: Cambridge University Press.

HOUSE, K. D. 1970. "Preparation of Faunal Specimens for Archeological Purposes." Unpublished manuscript.

HOWARD, W. E. 1949. "A Means to Distinguish Skulls of Coyotes and Do-mestic Dogs." *Journal of Mammalogy* 30 (2): 169-71.

HUBBS, C. 1954. "Corrected Distributional Records for Texas Fresh-water Fishes." *Texas Journal of Science* 6 (3): 277-91.

————. 1958. *A Checklist of Texas Fresh-water Fishes.* Texas Game and Fish Commission, IF Series, no. 3.

JARMAN, M. R. 1972. "European Deer Economies and the Advent of the Neolithic." In *Papers in Economic Prehistory*, ed. E. S. Higgs, pp. 125-48. Cambridge: Cambridge University Press.

JELKS, E. 1962. *The Kyle Site.* University of Texas Anthropology Depart-ment Archeology Series, no. 5, Austin.

————, and TUNNELL, C. 1959. *The Harroun Site.* University of Texas Anthropology Department Archeology Series, no. 2, Austin.

JOHNSON, L. 1961. *The Devil's Mouth Site.* University of Texas Anthro-pology Department Archeology Series, no. 6, Austin.

KALMBACH, E. R. 1943. *The Armadillo: Its Relation to Agriculture and Game*. Austin: Texas Game, Fish, and Oyster Commission.

KRIEGER, A. D. 1956a. "Food Habits of Texas Coastal Indians in the Early Sixteenth Century." *Bulletin of the Texas Archeological Society* 27:47-58.

_____. 1956b. "Historical Survival of the Atlatl in the Lower Mississippi Region." *Bulletin of the Texas Archeological Society* 27:195-205.

LANGE, C. H. 1950. "Notes on the Use of Turkeys by Pueblo Indians." *El Palacio* 57 (7): 204-9.

LEOPOLD, A. S. 1948. "The Wild Turkeys of Mexico." *Transactions of the 13th North American Wildlife Conference*, pp. 393-400.

LUNDELIUS, E. L. JR. 1967. "Late Pleistocene and Holocene Faunal History of Central Texas." In *Pleistocene Extinctions: The Search for a Cause*, ed. P. S. Martin and H. E. Wright, pp. 287-319. New Haven: Yale University Press.

_____, and SLAUGHTER, B. 1971. "Fossil Vertebrate Remains in Texas Caves." In *Natural History of Texas Caves*, ed. E. L. Lundelius and Bob Slaughter, pp. 15-27. Dallas: Gulf Natural History.

MCCORMICK, O. F. III. 1973. *Archeological Resources in the Lake Monticello Area of Titus County, Texas*. Southern Methodist University Contributions in Anthropology, no. 8.

MARTIN, P. S., and WRIGHT, H. E., eds. 1967. *Pleistocene Extinctions: The Search for a Cause*. New Haven: Yale University Press.

MEIGHAN, C. E. 1969. "Molluscs as Food Remains in Archaeological Sites." In *Science in Archaeology*, ed. Don Brothwell and Eric Higgs, pp. 415-22. London: Thames & Hudson.

NEILL, W. T.; GUT, H. J.; and BRODKORB, P. 1956. "Animal Remains from Four Preceramic Sites in Florida." *American Antiquity* 21 (4): 383-95.

NUNLEY, P. 1972. "Toward a General Model of Hunting and Gathering Societies." *Bulletin of the Texas Archeological Society* 43:13-31.

OBERHOLSER, H. C. 1925. "The Relations of Vegetation to Bird Life in Texas." *American Midland Naturalist* 9 (11): 564-94.

OLDS, D. 1965. "Report on Material from Brawley's Cave, Bosque County, Texas." *Bulletin of the Texas Archeological Society* 36:111-52.

OLSEN, S. J. 1960. *Post Cranial Skeletal Characters of Bison and Bos*. Papers of the Peabody Museum of American Archaeology and Ethnology 35 (4): 1-61. Cambridge, Mass.: Harvard University.

_____. 1961. "A Basic Annotated Bibliography to Facilitate the Identification of Vertebrate Remains from Archeological Sites." *Bulletin of the Texas Archeological Society* 30:217-22.

_____. 1973. *Mammal Remains from Archaeological Sites. Part 1— South-*

eastern and Southwestern United States. Papers of the Peabody Museum of Archaeology and Ethnology, Harvard University.

PAYNE, S. 1972. "On the Interpretation of Bone Samples from Archaeological Sites." In *Papers in Economic Prehistory*, ed. E. S. Higgs, pp. 65-81. Cambridge: Cambridge University Press.

PERCY, G. 1974. "A Review of Evidence for Prehistoric Indians' Use of Animals in Northwest Florida." *Bureau of Historic Sites and Properties Bulletin* no. 4, pp. 65-93. Florida, Department of State.

PETERSON, R. T. 1960. *A Field Guide to the Birds of Texas.* Boston: Houghton Mifflin.

RAUN, G. G. 1956. *A Bibliography of Recent Texas Mammals.* Bulletins of the Texas Memorial Museum, no. 3.

————. 1964. "West Indian Seal Remains from Two Historic Sites in Coastal South Texas." *Bulletin of the Texas Archeological Society* 35: 189-92.

RUSSELL, D. 1971. "Texas Cats." *Texas Parks and Wildlife* 29 (10): 25-27.

RYDER, M. 1969a. *Animal Bones in Archaeology.* London: Blackwell Scientific Publishers.

————. 1969b. "Remains of Fishes and Other Aquatic Animals." In *Science in Archaeology*, ed. Don Brothwell and Eric Higgs, pp. 376-94. London: Thames & Hudson.

SCHORGER, A. W. 1961. "An Ancient Pueblo Turkey." *Auk* 78 (2): 138-44.

SCHUETZ, M. K. 1956. "An Analysis of Val Verde County Cave Material." *Bulletin of the Texas Archeological Society* 27:129-60.

SCISCENTI, J. V., comp. 1972. *Environmental and Cultural Resources within the Trinity River Basin.* Archeology Research Program, Southern Methodist University.

SCURLOCK, J. D. 1961. "The Culpepper Site, a Late Fulton Aspect Site in Northeast Texas." *Bulletin of the Texas Archeological Society* 32:285-316.

SLAUGHTER, B. H. 1969. "Animal Ranges as a Clue to Late-Pleistocene Extinction." In *Pleistocene Extinctions: The Search for a Cause*, ed. P. S. Martin and H. E. Wright, pp. 155-67. New Haven: Yale University Press.

————, and HOOVER, B. R. 1963. "Sulphur River Formation and the Pleistocene Mammals of the Ben Franklin Local Fauna." *Journal of the Graduate Research Center* 31 (3): 132-48.

SMITH, H. M., and SANDERS, O. 1952. "Distributional Data on Texas Amphibians and Reptiles." *Texas Journal of Science* 4 (2): 204-19.

SPARKS, B. W. 1969. "Non-marine Mollusca and Archaeology." In *Science in Archaeology*, ed. Don Brothwell and Eric Higgs, pp. 395-406. London: Thames & Hudson.

STRECKER, J. K. 1931. *The Distribution of the Naides or Pearly Fresh-water Mussels of Texas*. Baylor University Special Bulletin no. 2.

STRUEVER, S. 1974. Address, Texas Archeological Society meeting, Dallas.

SUHM, D. A. 1961. "The White Site: An Historical Burial in Yoakum County, Texas." *Bulletin of the Texas Archeological Society* 32:85-120.

TAYLOR, W. W. 1956. "Some Interpretations of the Carbon 14 Dates from a Cave in Coahuila, Mexico." *Bulletin of the Texas Archeological Society* 27:215-34.

———, ed. 1957. *The Identification of Non-artifactual Archeological Materials*. Washington, D.C.: National Academy of Science, National Research Council.

THARP, B. C. 1939. *The Vegetation of Texas*. Texas Academy of Science. Natural History: Non-technical Series no. 1.

UERPMAN, H. P. 1973. "Animal Bone Finds and Economic Archeology: A Critical Study of the 'Osteo-archeological' Method." *World Archeology* 4 (3): 307-22.

WENDORF, F.; KRIEGER, A.; ALBRITTON, C.; and STEWART, T. D. 1955. *The Midland Discovery*. Austin: University of Texas Press.

WHITE, T. E. 1952. "Observations on the Butchering Techniques of Some Aboriginal Peoples," no. 1. *American Antiquity* 17 (4): 337-38.

———. 1953a. "Observations on the Butchering Techniques of Some Aboriginal Peoples," no. 2. *American Antiquity* 18 (2): 160-64.

———. 1953b. "A Method of Calculating the Dietary Percentage of Various Food Animals Utilized by Aboriginal Peoples." *American Antiquity* 18 (4): 396-98.

———. 1954. "Observations of the Butchering Techniques of Some Aboriginal Peoples," no. 4. *American Antiquity* 19 (3): 254-64.

———. 1955. "Observations on the Butchering Techniques of Some Aboriginal Peoples," no. 9. *American Antiquity* 21 (2): 170-78.

WINTEMBERG, W. J. 1919. "Archaeology as an Aid to Zoology." *Canadian Field Naturalist* 33:63-72.

WORD, J., and DOUGLAS, C. 1970. *The Archeology of Baker Cave*. Bulletins of the Texas Memorial Museum, no. 16.

WRIGHT, A. H., and WRIGHT, A. A. 1938. "Amphibians of Texas." *Transactions of the Texas Academy of Science* 21:5-35.

YARNELL, R. A. 1969. "Contents of Human Paleofeces." In *The Prehistory of Salts Cave, Kentucky*, ed. P. J. Watson, pp. 41-54. Illinois State Museum Reports of Investigations, no. 16.

ZEUNER, F. E. 1963. *A History of Domesticated Animals*. New York: Harper & Row.

Spanish Colonial Settlements in Texas

KATHLEEN GILMORE

Introduction

THE UNDERSTANDING OF THE ARCHEOLOGY of Spanish Colonial settlements is based on the historical background of those settlements and their role in the total milieu of the time. Therefore, I have included a section dealing with a historical overview of these settlements in Texas, followed by a discussion of their archeology and related problems. The settlements of the El Paso area are not included, as their history is more closely related to that of New Mexico.

In 1976 the United States commemorated the bicentennial of the Declaration of Independence of thirteen colonies from Great Britain. English colonization had started at Jamestown, Virginia, in 1607 and at Plymouth, Massachusetts, in 1620. Because many histories of the United States emphasize British colonization and the expansion of English-speaking people toward the west, it is not generally realized that Spanish exploration and colonization had started about a hundred years earlier in what is now the continental United States, giving, especially to the Southwest and Texas, an enduring Spanish flavor. Spanish settlements in Texas, exclusive of the El Paso area, began in 1690 with the settlement of two missions in eastern Texas (see fig. 1).

Scholars of Texas history, such as Herbert E. Bolton (1914, 1915, 1917), W. E. Dunn (1917), Castañeda (1936-1958), and many others, have long studied this period, obtaining for the archives at the University of Texas transcripts of documents from Spain and other areas. But this era of Texas history was neglected by archeologists until recent years. Consequently, irretrievable information has been lost; but much more can be recovered by careful study, excavation, and analysis.

Much of the excavation done in the 1930s served as a means of solving architectural problems for archeologists who did not realize that additional information could be obtained. The discovery of architectural information is, however, no longer the sole aim of the excavation of a Spanish Colonial site. Not only can well-planned excavation provide information on architecture; it can also expand our knowledge of interaction between Spanish and Indian, substantiate, refute, or supplement information obtained from documents, and offer a testing of hypotheses generated from documentary, ethnological, and prehistoric data. To gain this additional information, however, a site often has to be reexcavated, and the prior excavations are a problem to the excavator because the methods of recording information were not as standardized in the thirties as they have become in recent years. Thus the archeology of Spanish Colonial settlements is by its nature interdisciplinary, with historical and documentary studies, in addition to natural science studies, forming the basis for designing archeological research and generating hypotheses to further the understanding of human behavior and cultural change.

In essence, however, this approach is not new. It was noted by Brew in 1949, when he wrote in *Franciscan Awatovi* (p. xx):

One of the primary aims of archaeology is to reconstruct conjecturally not only the buildings and industries and arts of a bygone time but also the way of life of the builders of those buildings and the practicers of those arts. Why did they build as they did? Why did they draw certain designs and not others? What did they think as they stood on the doorstep and surveyed their environs, as they sat talking with their neighbors, as they read in the privacy of their own rooms and made plans for the activities of the morrow? It is in such speculation that archaeology and anthropology meet and it is by answering these questions that archaeologists justify their labors.

HISTORICAL OVERVIEW

The colonial area from Florida, around the Gulf Coast, through the Southwest, and to California was the northern frontier of the Spanish Empire. It began with Ponce de León's exploration of the coastline of Florida in 1513. Piñeda explored the entire Gulf Coast in 1519, one

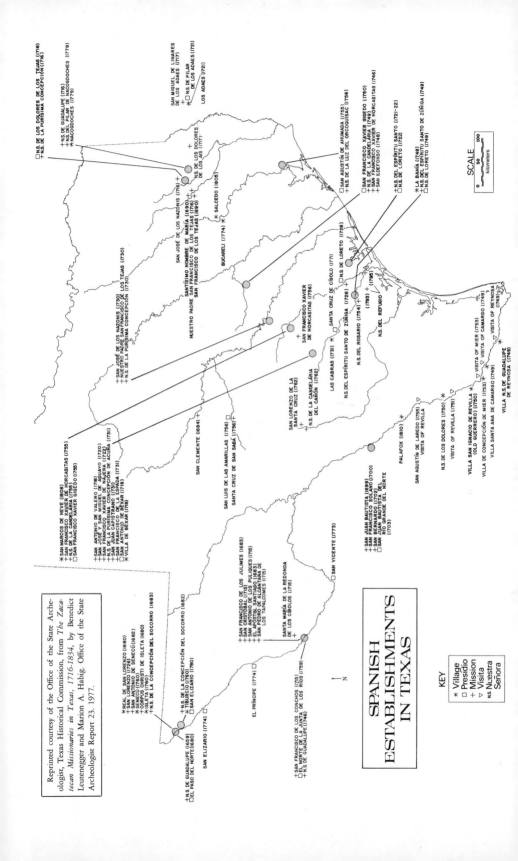

SPANISH ESTABLISHMENTS IN TEXAS

KEY

* Village
□ Presidio
+ Mission
▽ Visita
NS Nuestra Señora

SCALE
0 50 100
Kilometers

Reprinted courtesy of the Office of the State Archeologist, Texas Historical Commission, from *The Zacatecan Missionaries in Texas, 1716-1834*, by Benedict Leutenegger and Marion A. Habig, Office of the State Archeologist Report 23. 1977.

hundred years before the Pilgrims stepped ashore in Massachusetts. Cabeza de Vaca was shipwrecked on the Texas coast in 1528, eighty years before John Smith landed at Jamestown. Coronado explored the Southwest and the Central Plains in 1540, and the De Soto expedition traveled through the Southeast and came into eastern Texas in the same years.

The Spanish explorers and conquistadores came from the south—from the Caribbean and Mexico—and the history of the United States actually had its origins in that area, with expansion and colonization toward the north. That is, the first movement of Europeans into what is now the United States was toward the north instead of toward the west, as is generally thought. As Thomas (1971, p. 3) states, "This advance continued over two and a half centuries, but it was overlaid by the later westward movement which blotted out the colonial history of Florida, the Gulf Coast and the West."

Conquistadores found not a vacant wilderness, but a land populated with people whose ancestors had first arrived in North America some ten thousand years before. Without help from these natives and their agricultural products, sometimes obtained at sword point, the Spanish explorers might not have returned to their homeland. Nor was the later westward movement of Anglo-Americans into a rank wilderness; rather, the explorers found well-developed Spanish towns, institutions, and attitudes with which they clashed, as the Spanish had clashed with the populations they had encountered years before.

The French were exploring Canada and the Great Lakes at about the time British subjects were landing on the Atlantic seaboard. By the late 1600s the explorer La Salle had proposed his great scheme for colonizing the Mississippi River valley, beginning with a settlement at its mouth. Alfred B. Thomas (1971, p. 3), writing on Gulf Coast colonial history, comments that La Salle's conception represented one of the few original ideas of the colonial period. Apparently La Salle's plan was that Louisiana would connect Canada and the agricultural resources of the Mississippi valley with the tropical products of Santo Domingo; it would be a buffer against the British on the Atlantic seaboard, would give France control of the Gulf Coast by splitting Florida from Mexico, and thus would open the way for the seizure of Mexican silver mines by the French.

La Salle left France in 1685 (Joutel, 1714) for the purpose of establishing the first colony at the mouth of the Mississippi, but he passed the mouth of the Mississippi and landed in Matagorda Bay on the Texas coast. Some researchers (e.g., Parkman, 1963) believe this was no accident, but was by design, to be nearer the silver mines. In view of the later history of this settlement, however, it does appear La Salle had mistakenly sailed past the mouth of the Mississippi River. As his specific plans were never revealed (Joutel, 1714), an element of doubt will always remain as to whether he was truly lost.

The Spanish quickly became cognizant of the French plan to settle in the south and claim the lands drained by the Mississippi River, and they immediately instigated a search for the French colony. It took twelve expeditions by land and by sea to discover the settlement (Weddle, 1973), and when it was finally found by Alonso de León (Bolton, 1963), it had been destroyed by the Indians.

The French threat reawakened the Spanish interest in the deserted Gulf Coast and the Mississippi Valley. The expeditions sent to search for La Salle necessarily explored the Gulf Coast and, to reinforce Spain's claim to the area, de León was sent to look for further French activity, to burn La Salle's village, and to establish two missions in "Tejas country." *Tejas*, as used by the Spanish, indicated a geographic area where the Hasinai Indians lived. The term was used by the Indians probably to mean "friend" or "ally," and Bolton (1908) suggested it was mistaken by the Spanish for the Indian tribal name. The two missions established in 1690 were San Francisco de los Tejas and Santísimo Nombre de María (see fig. 1). Because of sickness, the distance from supplies, the lack of cooperation of the Indians, and, more importantly, the subsistence of the French threat, these two missions were abandoned in 1693.

French interest on the Gulf Coast, however, was far from abandoned. The French had established a post at Biloxi in 1698, but moved to Mobile Bay in 1702. To strengthen their hold westward, Louis Juchereau de St. Denis was sent up the Red River in 1713. He established a post at Natchitoches on the river, and proceeded on across Texas to the Spanish post of San Juan Bautista on the Rio Grande. The outcome of this expedition had far-reaching consequences. The French were again threatening Spanish interests on the northern frontier, and, to protect the eastern border, a presidio and four missions were established in the Tejas country, another near what is now Robeline, Louisiana, and one about midway between the easternmost mission of the Tejas country and the one near Robeline.

The presidio, Nuestra Señora de los Dolóres de los Tejas, was placed on the west side of the Neches River, but later moved. Mission San Francisco de los Tejas was placed across the Neches about a league; Mission Nuestra Señora de la Purísima Concepción was located about six leagues to the northwest, east of the Angelina River; Mission San José de los Nazonis was northeast of Purísima Concepción; Nuestra Señora de Guadalupe was in the village of the Nacogdoches Indians. The mission near Robeline was San Miguel de Linares de los Adaes, and the midway mission was Nuestra Señora de los Dolóres de los Aís (Tous, 1930; Bolton, 1908).

It soon became apparent that the distance between the Tejas area and Presidio San Juan Bautista on the Rio Grande was too great without a way station. The San Antonio River had been known for a long time as a desirable area, and Mission San Antonio de Valero—to become known as the Alamo—and Presidio San Antonio de Béxar were established on the river in 1718 (Hoffman, 1935).

Again in 1719 Texas was caught in the network of international intrigue. While France and Spain were jockeying over possessions in Europe, the French on the Gulf Coast captured Pensacola from the Spanish, which scared the Spanish of East Texas into panic and retreat. At the same time, the French established a post on the Red River near present Texarkana (Miroir, Harris et al., 1973). Once more East Texas was abandoned by the Spanish (Bannon, 1970).

It took the peace between France and Spain and the largest and last Spanish expedition of its kind to reopen the area. This expedition was led by the Marqués de San Miguel de Aguayo in 1721 and 1722 and consisted of about five hundred men, almost three thousand horses, six hundred head of cattle, nine hundred sheep, and almost eight hundred mules, six hundred of which had loads of clothing, arms, munitions, and supplies (Forrestal, 1934). Not only were the missions reestablished, but a presidio was built near the mission of the Adaes (Louisiana). This presidio, Nuestra Señora de Pilar de los Adaes, was the capital of Spanish Texas until 1772.

Another presidio with a nearby mission was established by the Aguayo expedition near Espíritu Santo Bay (now Matagorda Bay). This presidio, Nuestra Señora de Loreto de la Bahía, was built on the exact spot of La Salle's ill-fated village (Gilmore, 1973), following the pattern used so often by the Spanish of building atop sites of those they wished to subdue. Archeological analysis established that this presidio and La Salle's Fort St. Louis were located on Garcitas Creek, which flows into Lavaca Bay, the northern extension of Matagorda Bay (Gilmore, 1973).

Presidio Loreto de la Bahía and Mission Espíritu Santo de Zuñiga were moved to the Guadalupe River after about four years; and later, in 1749, they were moved to the San Antonio River near what is now Goliad, Texas. In 1731 the three missions of East Texas were moved to the San Antonio area, and the presidio in East Texas was closed (see fig. 1).

Thus, during the first third of the eighteenth century a line of missions and forts had been established to hold the northern frontier for Spain. These establishments stretched from the Rio Grande to an area across the Sabine River and nearly to the Red River. It was during this time that the last of the thirteen British colonies, Georgia, was being founded. Not only did the Spanish forts and soldiers act as frontier agents, but the missions and missionaries also were an integral part of the frontier system, a fact which was well recognized by the government. This was well expressed by Bolton (1917, p. 10):

The value of the missionaries as frontier agents was . . . clearly recognized, and their services were thus consciously utilized by the government. In the first place, they were often the most useful of explorers and diplomatic agents. The unattended missionary could sometimes go unmolested, and without arousing suspicion and hostility, into districts where the soldier was not welcome, while by their education and their trained habits of thought they were the class best fitted to record what they saw and to report what should be done.

The years following 1731 saw little expansion of the Spanish frontier system, but beginning about 1745 there was a very real danger from the Apaches who were raiding along almost the entire frontier. There was still the real or imagined danger from the French, and the realization by the missionaries that new Indian converts were needed. The last factor, but certainly not the least, was the desire of the government to extend and strengthen the frontier, not only with missions and presidios but also with colonists in settled villages.

To fulfill part of these needs, a presidio and three missions for the Tonkawa, Attacapa, and Karankawa Indians were established near what is now Rockdale on the San Xavier (now the San Gabriel) River (Gilmore, 1969). A town was proposed but was never developed. These missions and presidios were abandoned in less than ten years. The Indians would congregate for brief periods and leave, and a priest and a civilian were murdered. All this, together with severe drought and attacks by the Apaches, combined to force removal.

In 1746, José de Escandón explored the Gulf Coast and the interior from the Guadalupe River to the Rio Grande. He proposed sites for the founding of towns and a few missions. By 1756 the settlements of Laredo, Revilla, Mier, Camargo, and Reynosa, as well as large cattle ranches, had been established on both sides of the Rio Grande.

The Karankawa and the Apache continued to give the Spanish trouble, but a group of Karankawa at last expressed their desire to enter mission life, and in 1754 Mission Nuestra Señora del Rosario was established on the San Antonio River about three miles from Presidio La Bahía and Mission Espíritu Santo (see fig. 1). Irrigation was not possible in the area, but soon large herds of cattle developed and cattle could be traded for agricultural products in San Antonio. It was here in the San Antonio and Rio Grande river valleys that the great cattle industry of Texas and the western United States had its beginnings. These Spanish cattle were the progenitors of the wild herds of Texas longhorns (Dobie, 1941) which were rounded up and driven to northern markets in the late nineteenth century.

In the vain hope of making peaceful converts of the nomadic Apaches, another presidio, San Luís de las Amarillas, and a mission, San Sabá de la Santa Cruz, were established in 1757 on the San Sabá River near what is now Menard. The Apaches failed to assemble at the mission, but other Indians, enemies of the Apaches, being unaware of this, attacked and burned the mission nine months after it was founded, killing two priests (Weddle, 1964). It was never rebuilt, and the exact location has never been found (Gilmore, 1967). Comanche and other northern Indians continued raiding the nearby presidio until it had to be abandoned, the captain retreating to Mission San Lorenzo, which had been founded for the Lipan Apache in 1762 on the Nueces River. Mission San Lorenzo de la Santa Cruz (Tunnell and Newcomb, 1969) had meager results as far as the Lipan Apache were concerned, and continuing Comanche raids forced its abandonment after about seven years.

Almost simultaneously with the settlements on the Rio Grande and the missions for the Karankawa and Apache, the southeastern border was threatened by the discovery of French traders on the Trinity River near the coast. This led in 1756 to the establishment on the lower Trinity of Presidio San Agustín de Ahumada and Mission Nuestra Señora de la Luz for the Orcoquisa Indians. A village was also planned for the area, but it never materialized. The internal conflict between the military and clergy, and the swampy, unhealthy nature of the area, in combination with the lack of cooperation of the Indians, rendered the complex ineffective for almost its entire existence. It was abandoned in 1771 (Tunnell and Ambler, 1967).

The international situation again had consequences felt in Texas. The Seven Years War in Europe, known as the French and Indian War in America, came to a close in 1763. France surrendered Canada to England, and to keep England from getting Louisiana also, ceded the area west of the Mississippi River and New Orleans to Spain. This gave Spain the Mississippi as her eastern frontier, and the defenses in eastern Texas were no longer needed. But as England had acquired Florida at the same time, Spain's North American colonies were now endangered by English encroachments from the east by land and by water from the Gulf. Spain's worries in the northern colonies were indeed just beginning (Bannon, 1970; Dibble and Newton, 1971), and reorganization was necessary. With this in mind, a tour of inspection was made by the Marquis de Rubi (Kinnaird, 1958).

The results of this inspection were the withdrawal or closing of all East Texas establishments, including those on the lower Trinity; the San Sabá presidio was to be moved, as well as Mission San Lorenzo. By the end of 1772 most of this had been accomplished.

Apaches were continuing to raid the settlements, and, to protect travelers and ranchers, a satellite fort of Presidio San Antonio de Béxar at San Antonio was established in 1771 about half way between Béxar and La Bahía on Cibola Creek. It was named Santa Cruz del Cibolo (Bolton, 1914, 2:123).

As a result of the closing of the East Texas settlements, civilians living in the area of Presidio los Adaes were ordered to leave that area also and move to San Antonio, but they requested and were granted permission to settle nearer their old homes. Consequently, the civil settlement of Nuestra Señora del Pilar de Bucareli was founded in 1774 on the Trinity River at the crossing of El Camino Real. An epidemic, floods, and Comanche raids forced its abandonment in 1779, and the settlers went to the old mission area at Nacogdoches. The site of the village of Bucareli has never been precisely identified.

Mission Rosario in southern Texas (see fig. 1) was also completely abandoned by the Indians and finally by the priests in 1780. It was reoccupied and rebuilt beginning in 1789 in another attempt to control the Karankawa. The Karankawa, however, were not easy to satisfy, and wanted a mission nearer the coast, even closer to their homes (Gilmore, 1974.) In a final attempt to control the unmanageable Karankawa, the last mission to be built in Texas, Nuestra Señora del Refugio, was established in 1794. Its final location was at the present town of Refugio (Obereste, 1942).

Secularization was ordered for Texas missions in 1794. This meant the mission land was given to the Indians and they were to run their own affairs. But the Indians at Rosario, Refugio, and Espíritu Santo, it was believed, were not ready to accept this responsibility; these missions were not secularized until 1831 (Walters, 1951), although few Indians were left in the missions at that time. Rosario, for example, had been abandoned in 1805.

In 1821 Mexico gained independence from Spain, and the Spanish Colonial period ended. Politically, the American Revolution had affected Texas very little during the time it was taking place, but with the acquisition of Louisiana by the United States in 1803, Texas offered a new frontier and a new challenge in another country, and English-speaking entrepreneurs coming into Texas found viable settlements with a different set of laws, ideologies, and life styles; and they clashed.

The Archeology of Spanish Colonial Settlements

In dealing with the archeology of Spanish Colonial sites, the archeologist approaches the project with several questions in mind: (1) is this the location of a particular settlement? (2) what was the life style or behavior of the inhabitants? (3) what were the cultural changes taking place, that is, what kinds of interactions were taking place among the inhabitants? and (4) will documentary and excavated data coincide? These questions form the basis of establishing a research design for excavating a specific site. This research design must include provision for an archival search for primary or firsthand accounts concerning the settlement, and a careful analysis and screening of these documents for evidence of the geography, topography, physiography, and structures pertaining to the site, as well as clues to social and kinship relationships. As a result of this analysis, models are formed from which hypotheses are posed for testing.

Each of the foregoing questions is also concerned with certain problems that must be taken into consideration. One of these is that the precise location of many of the Spanish Colonial settlements is unknown.

Many had structures of wood plastered with mud; these have fallen and decayed and are no longer evident on the surface. To demonstrate the exact location of a settlement, not only must the geography agree with documentary evidence, but the artifacts found at a site must be those of the time period and cultural traditions of the settlement (Gilmore, 1969).

A serious problem with finding specific sites is that some have been destroyed. A borrow pit for gravel and shell and a pipeline took nearly all of the presidio site on the lower Trinity River. Leveling and mill operations took much of a mission site in East Texas. An East Texas town is probably on top of another historic mission.

Other problems are involved with testing for life style, interaction, and acculturation. In Texas, the "direct historical approach" (Strong, 1940) cannot be used, since there are no Indians living in the same areas they occupied during the time Texas was a Spanish colony, and many of the Indian groups mentioned in historical accounts either are no longer extant or have had much of their life style and world view diluted since that time by reservation life and intermarriage. In other words, detailed ethnography of the Indians of Texas is virtually nonexistent (see Newcomb, 1961), and many propositions involving archeological material cannot be checked by using extant groups. It is entirely possible, however, that much additional ethnographic material remains in unexplored archives. This problem may be partly resolved by using for analogy other groups who live in similar climatic conditions and who have made what are assumed to be similar cultural adaptations.

Another set of problems has been created by previous excavations of many of the sites. This, of course, further biases the information, and the archeologist must test an additional proposition on how much disturbance has taken place. This has been termed "the archeology of archeologists."

These excavations in Texas may conveniently be divided into three categories: (1) those by trained persons whose notes are on record; (2) those by trained persons whose notes are not on record and cannot be found; and (3) those by untrained persons who keep no notes. If notes and maps are available, previous excavations can be found in the ground and remapped. If notes and maps cannot be found, then former excavations have to be delimited by the consistent size of trenches or evcavated areas, and by refill material. Excavations necessarily leave back dirt, some of which may have contained artifacts, that is placed on a surface which was not excavated. The disposal of back dirt, whether by trained or untrained persons, may become an important factor in the interpretation and explanation of a site. If a thin layer of black dirt containing artifacts is left on the surface, then excavations below the "plow zone" are more likely to yield valid information.

If excavations are backfilled with excavated material, and if the colors of soil zones are not markedly different, it may be virtually impossible to delimit those excavations at a later time. Backfill of clean river sand is easy to detect and to reexcavate.

Excavations and collections of artifacts by untrained persons, aided unfortunately by metal detectors, are continually taking place at Spanish Colonial sites. They are usually based on the lure of Spanish artifacts, sometimes thought to be gold. Most Spanish settlements in Texas, however, being frontier settlements, had few articles of precious metals, and where they were present, they were not left behind when the settlement was abandoned.

These kinds of excavations are usually evidenced by their lack of preciseness—the holes are usually round—and by the lack of complete backfilling. The artifacts found may be sold or kept, but regardless of the disposal of the artifacts, no records are made to indicate where they came from in the site, and in some cases no record of the site itself is made. Irretrievable information, which would aid the archeologist in reconstructing past human behavior, is lost.

Documentary information also may be deceptive in that the writers were culturally biased and were not always objective in their reporting. In addition, subtleties and original meaning may be lost in translation by changes in syntax and the meaning of words. Yet most missionaries were excellent observers, as noted by Bolton (1917), and their observations should not be discounted without valid evidence.

BIBLIOGRAPHY

BANNON, J. F. 1970. *The Spanish Borderlands Frontier, 1513-1821.* New York: Holt, Rinehart and Winston.

BOLTON, H. E. 1908. "The Native Tribes about the East Texas Missions." *Texas State Historical Association Quarterly* 11 (4): 249-76.

———. 1914. *Athanase de Mézières and the Louisiana-Texas Frontier, 1768-1780.* 2 vols. Cleveland: Arthur H. Clark Co.

———. 1915. *Texas in the Middle-Eighteenth Century.* Reprint. New York: Russell and Russell, 1962.

_____. 1917. *The Mission as a Frontier Institution in the Spanish-American Colonies*. Academic Reprints. El Paso: Texas Western College Press, 1962.

_____. 1963. *Spanish Exploration in the Southwest, 1542-1706*. Reprint. New York: Barnes and Noble.

BREW, J. O., and MONTGOMERY, W. S. 1949. *Franciscan Awatovi*. Peabody Museum, Harvard University Report no 3. Cambridge.

CASTAÑEDA, C. E. 1936-58. *Our Catholic Heritage in Texas, 1519-1936*. Vols. 1, 2, 3, and 4 (of 7 vols.). Austin: Van Boeckmann-Jones Co.

DIBBLE, E. F., and NEWTON, E. W. 1971. *Spain and Her Rivals on the Gulf Coast*. Pensacola, Florida: Historic Pensacola Preservation.

DOBIE, J. F. 1941. *The Longhorns*. Reprint. New York: Grosset's Universal Library, 1971.

DUNN, W. E. 1917. *Spanish and French Rivalry in the Gulf Region of the United States, 1678-1702*. University of Texas Bulletin 1705. Austin.

FORRESTAL, P. P., trans. 1934. *Peña's Diary of the Aguayo Expedition*. Preliminary Studies of the Texas Catholic Historical Society, vol. 2, no. 7. Austin.

GILMORE, K. 1967. *A Documentary and Archeological Investigation of Presidio San Luis de las Amarillas and Mission Santa Cruz de San Sabá, Menard County, Texas*. State Building Commission Archeological Program Reports, no. 9. Austin.

_____. 1969. *The San Xavier Missions: A Study in Historical Site Identification*. State Building Commission Archeology Program Reports, no. 16. Austin.

_____. 1973. *The Keeran Site: The Probable Site of La Salle's Fort St. Louis in Texas*. Texas Historical Commission Office of the State Archeologist Reports, no 24. Austin.

_____. 1974. *Mission Rosario Archeological Investigations 1973*. Texas Parks and Wildlife Dept. Archeological Reports, no. 14, pt. 1. Austin.

HOFFMAN, F. L., trans. 1935. *Diary of the Alarcon Expedition into Texas, 1718-1719*. Quivera Society Publications, vol. 5. Los Angeles.

JOUTEL, H. 1714. *A Journal of La Salle's Last Voyage*. Reprint. New York: Corinth Books, 1962.

KINNAIRD, L., trans. 1958. *The Frontiers of New Spain: Nicolas de La Foro's Description, 1766-1768*. Berkeley: The Quivera Society.

MIROIR, M. P.; HARRIS, R. K.; BLAINE, J. C.; MCVAY, J.; BOOK, D. C.; CIGAINERO, F.; MCVAY, R.; ROFFAELLI, J. B., JR.; and SCHOEN, P. E. 1973. "Bernard de la Harpe and the Nassonite Post." *Bulletin of the Texas Archeological Society* 44.

NEWCOMB, W. W., JR. 1961. *The Indians of Texas*. Austin: University of Texas Press.

OBERESTE, W. H. 1942. *History of Refugio Mission.* Refugio, Texas.

PARKMAN, F. 1963. *La Salle and the Discovery of the Great West.* New York: Signet Books.

STRONG, W. D. 1940. "From History to Prehistory in the Northern Great Plains." In *Essays in Historical Anthropology of North America.* Smithsonian Miscellaneous Collections, vol. 100, pp. 353-94. Washington, D.C.

THOMAS, A. B. 1971. *Gulf Coast History: An Overview.* In E. F. Dibble and E. W. Newton, eds., *Spain and Her Rivals on the Gulf Coast.* Pensacola: Historic Pensacola Preservation.

TOUS, G., trans. 1930. *Ramon Expedition: Espinosa's Diary of 1716.* Preliminary Studies of the Texas Catholic Historical Society, vol. 1, no. 4. Austin.

TUNNELL, C. D., and AMBLER, J. R. 1967. *Archeological Excavations at Presidio San Agustin de Ahumada.* State Building Commission Archeological Program Report no. 6. Austin.

————, and NEWCOMB, W. W., JR. 1969. "A Lipan Apache Mission, San Lorenzo de la Santa Cruz, 1762-1771." *Texas Memorial Museum Bulletin* no. 14.

WALTERS, P. H. 1951. "Secularization of the La Bahía Missions." *Southwestern Historical Quarterly* 54 (3): 287-300.

WEDDLE, R. S. 1964. *The San Sabá Mission: Spanish Pivot in Texas.* Austin: University of Texas Press.

————. 1973. *Wilderness Manhunt.* Austin: University of Texas Press.

A Historic Tunica Burial at the Coulee des Grues Site in Avoyelles Parish, Louisiana

H. F. GREGORY

INTRODUCTION

IN AUGUST, 1960, the chief of the Tunica-Biloxi tribe, the late Joseph Alcide Pierite, Sr., with the help of his brother, Percy, now also deceased, and a neighbor, Michel Smith, uncovered a grave in a field along the Coulee des Grues which was farmed by the Pierites. The land had been allotted them, in traditional Tunica-Biloxi fashion, by the chief, Horace Pierite, Sr., and the Pierites farmed it communally as had their ancestors (fig. 1). The burial, like others in the vicinity, had eroded from an older, abandoned Tunica-Biloxi burial ground. Unlike other tribal cemeteries, this area had not been kept out of cultivation. Further, none of the older Tunica-Biloxi could link this area to specific families, and it was apparently a very old burial.

Joseph Pierite, Sr., then tribal sub-chief, sought help from the Louisiana State Parks Commission, and four archeology students were dispatched to him from the Department of Geography and Anthropology at Louisiana State University in Baton Rouge. They were to record the burial, already partially cleared by Michel Smith, who had gained some knowledge of field techniques at the Colfax Ferry Site excavations directed by Clarence H. Webb (Gregory and Webb, 1965). The remains and artifacts had been left *in situ*. The local sheriff assigned deputies to guard the burial, and a mortician provided a funeral tent to protect both burial and deputies from the hot Louisiana sun.

146

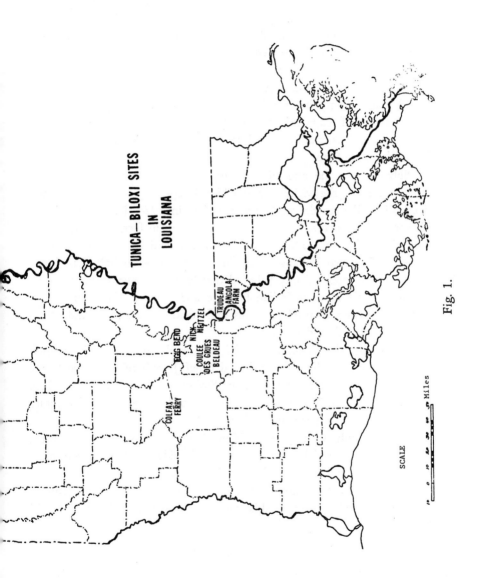

TUNICA—BILOXI SITES IN LOUISIANA

COLFAX FERRY

EGG BEND

NICK. MEITZEL

COULEE DES GRUES BELDEAU

TRUDEAU ANGOLA FARM

SCALE

Miles

Fig. 1.

Newspaper and radio reporters got wind of the find, and soon the airwaves crackled with the news that Indians near Marksville, Louisiana, had found and dug up the remains of none other than Hernando de Soto. For two days the news releases, in English and French, attracted visitors to the site. Tunica-Biloxi protestations that the grave was one of their own did little to deter the news media, and excavation and photography went on in the midst of a crowd of awestricken onlookers, angry Tunica-Biloxi, and tired deputies. Chief Joseph Pierite later recalled that his only interest in the burial had been to substantiate the long presence of his people on their Coulee des Grues lands and to learn more about their traditions, while local non-Indians only wanted to know about De Soto.

Subsequently, he and his brother, Percy, uncovered a number of other graves in the vicinity, and Chief Joseph explained that he was magically called to do so. In an interview in 1974, he explained that his people had been able to speak to their dead; in fact, as a boy he had heard his father and other elders do so. He used the owls—feared by many Southeastern Indians as harbingers of death—to help him locate graves. Chief Joseph firmly believed that he was chosen to fight for his people's claims to their Indian heritage and identity. His venture into archeology was a by-product of his traditional belief system and of the need to affirm tribal identity.

Eventually, the skeletal material was exhibited for a brief period; but tribal traditionalists objected, and Chief Joseph reburied the bones. The artifacts, except for a few in the Smithsonian collection, were kept for a tribal exhibit. That exhibit is now planned for the new tribal center which is (1978) under construction.

Unfortunately, Chief Joseph did not live to see the end of his vision. Even his own funeral became archeological evidence of tribal continuity (Brain, 1976) and this probably would not have surprised him.

This burial, then, became one more piece of the evidence the Tunica-Biloxi tribe needed to prove, like most Indian communities, that it still lives.

ETHNOHISTORICAL BACKGROUND

The end of the French and Indian War resulted in a number of awkward situations for Louisiana Indians. Most had been French allies, and some of those groups found themselves on English territory. By the 1760s, tribes of such former French allies had begun shifting west.

Alabama, Biloxi, and others began moving toward the Spanish lands west of the Mississippi.

By the early eighteenth century the Tunica and Ofo had shifted to the bluffs opposite the mouth of Red River (Brain, 1977); Swanton places them there as early as 1706 (Swanton, 1911). The Tunica lived on the east bank of the Mississippi River, while the Ofo settled across and upstream from them. Their villages were still occupied in 1778 (Hutchins, 1784). Brain (1977) suggests that they were moving west before the end of the 1700s.

In 1779 the Ofo, Biloxi, and Tunica attacked a British convoy moving toward the Illinois post; they were apparently entering a pantribal association by about that time (Downs, 1976).

By the 1790s the Tunica, some Ofo, and the Biloxi were settled on the Coulee des Grues. The Biloxi lived south of the stream, while the Tunica were on the north bank. The Ofo had already absorbed the Avoyels, and a band of Choctaw eventually moved in southwest of them. Some Choctaw remain, intermarried with the tribe.

Another group of Tunica had settled on Bayou Rouge, and these had also mingled with Ofo and Biloxi. According to Downs (1976), the Bayou Rouge group also moved into the Coulee des Grues area after whites usurped their lands in the 1840s.

These shifts were not without conflict. One group of Biloxi, under Tatamplavec and Bossebout, sold their land along the Coulee and moved up Red River near the Pascagoula and Apalachee-Tensa (Saucier, 1941; Gregory and Webb, 1965). However, Biloxi and Tunica continued to intermarry and to work together. As late as the 1920s the Biloxi and some Choctaw actually elected a Tunica chief for a unified group (Downs, 1976). This echoed Perruquier, an Ofo, who had served as chief of the groups in the late eighteenth century (Downs, 1976). The Tunica-Biloxi remain a unified tribe. At any rate, the Coulee des Grues area became, after guarantees from the Spanish governors Miro and de Galvez (Downs, 1976), the major village of the combined groups. About 1804 there were nearly fifty houses there.

In the 1840s, conflict between non-Indians and the tribal people led to violence, and the Tunica chief, Melacon, was killed by a white. Three Indian women filed charges, and the tribe retained their land (Downs, 1976).

The Indian people at Coulee des Grues were eventually confined to their acreage, once surrounded—under Spanish rule—by a square league (6.2 square miles) of land. The tribe has gradually been encircled by the non-Indian community, but it remains a separate, sovereign socio-political unit.

A number of families have lived on the tribal land for generations, each with a piece of land allotted them by their chief. All the land was farmed, except for a number of cemeteries and ball ground/dance ground areas. Families maintained separate burial areas, seven of which have been left out of cultivation. Five of these have been used since 1930, and three are still in use in the 1970s. Roughly, these can be correlated with the Barbry, Chiki, Pierite, Castete, Constin, Wiha, and Yuchigant families (fig. 2). A Choctaw burial area was nearby at the Nick Site (Ford, 1936), an Ofo cemetery was destroyed by the Marksville City Pool, and the Neitzel site was Biloxi.

Tunica-Biloxi religion stresses deep respect for their dead. Also there are deep-rooted ghost beliefs, and care has been taken never to disturb other burials.

The burial we are discussing was found on the Pierite allotment, and probably represents a family now extinct. The Pierite family maintains another cemetery nearby, and an Ofo lady was also buried on their land.

The Barbry, Pierite, and Jackson families also maintain two other cemeteries. No burials have been investigated in any of these other areas.

Traditional burial practices seem to have changed somewhat over the centuries. Biloxi influences, and possibly also Ofo and Choctaw influences, have come into play. One of the earliest descriptions of traditional burial practices was left by a nun at the local convent who noted that the nuns helped get a coffin for the burial of a chief in the 1850s (Mc-Cants, 1970).

Volsin Chiki, a chief and a strong proponent of tribal religion, described, in the middle nineteenth century, Tunica burial practices (Swanton, 1911, p. 325):

The body of the dead person was kept for one day and then interred, many persons making speeches on the occasion. The corpse was laid with its head toward the east, which the Tunica chief told the writer was simply their way of burying, the reason having apparently been forgotten.

Chiki did not note coffins, but it seems likely that they were still in use. The late chief Joseph Pierite also noted that a fire must be lighted near the grave for four days and nights so that the deceased could travel.

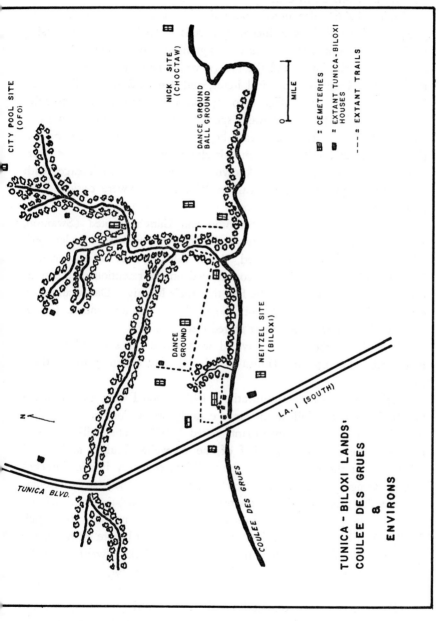

TUNICA - BILOXI LANDS:
COULEE DES GRUES
&
ENVIRONS

Fig. 2.

His daughter, Ana Mae Juneau, later spoke of that custom to Brain (1976) as it related to Chief Joseph's burial.

Brain (1976) also noted continuity between Chief Joseph's grave goods and those of eighteenth-century burials at the Trudeau Site. Missing in Brain's account was the cultural significance of several items: the eagle feather, the knife, and the fire (a votive lamp was substituted for the latter). These were magical items, and Tunica-Biloxi traditionalists insist on their privacy. Suffice it to say that each item had a nonsecular function and that placement was a special part of the burial ceremony.

Tribal religionists have always kept curiosity seekers, including anthropologists, at arm's length. Burials should not be disturbed or interrupted, and even the mystics—known to have come from lineages with the power to manipulate or "call back" the dead—were criticized for their actions by others in the tribe.

It is not likely, then, as Swanton and Gatschet noted (Swanton, 1911), that the orientation toward the east was no longer understood. All marked, and most unmarked, Tunica-Biloxi graves are so oriented. Haas (1942, pp. 531-35) has commented on the retention of the solar myth by the Tunica, and on the fact that their Midnight Dance and corn ceremonials (Fête du Blé) both honored the sun and moon. Consequently, the east was their most sacred direction.

After death, the person traveled west across the sky and found a new land. Contemporary Tunica-Biloxi still have a firm grip on these things.

Brain (personal communication, 1974) noted that the Trudeau Site burials did not follow the strict easterly orientation, nor were they on "hills," as Swanton's informants noted (1911). The "hills" seem a relative thing on the low relief of the Avoyelles Prairie, and burial orientation at the Colfax Ferry Site, a Biloxi cemetery in Natchitoches Parish (Gregory and Webb, 1965), suggests that these strict orientations are due more to Biloxi influence than to any Christian conversion.

Annually, food was placed on the graves by young boys from each family. Each boy was dispatched to his family's area before dawn on the day of the Fête du Blé to "feed the dead." Volsin Chiki (Swanton, 1911) stated that this custom was still observed in his day for both new corn and beans.

Ghosts "live" in the cemeteries and can be heard quarreling on gray, wet winter days, according to the traditionalists (personal communication, Clementine Broussard, 1976).

Thus it can be seen that graveyards are among the most sacred precincts of the Tunica-Biloxi geography. When recent tribal development began, the elders took steps to delineate older cemeteries and to emphasize their importance. The first request the tribal council made was for money to fence in their cemeteries; roads and housing were next on their list of priorities. No further excavations are to be permitted on tribal land, and future development has been carefully scheduled to avoid disturbance.

The Tunica-Biloxi, in spite of recent anthropological observations to the contrary (Brain, 1977, p. 19), have retained much of their traditional culture. Their "mental culture" (Brain, 1977) seems to have been maintained in an almost continuous flow from the 1690s to the present. No place in Tunica-Biloxi life lacks some continuity, and religion, magic, and myth have persisted strongly; and, though the maintenance mechanisms are poorly understood, the "deep structures" of their culture seem remarkably intact.

THE BURIAL

The burial (fig. 3) was a supine male with its head to the northeast. After having been uncovered by the original discoverers, it had been left *in situ.*

The remains had been located in a fallow plot, or corn field. Smith and the Pierites had only partially exposed the burial, which was in a shallow pit, not more than four feet deep. At the time of excavation, the tops of associated kettles were less than a foot from the present surface. The fact that the burial lay in a road track had undoubtedly prevented its disturbance by plowing. Rows of cornstalks ran up to the very edge of the tracks. The whole field showed evidence of extensive sheet erosion, with wash into the coulee.

Further excavation revealed evidence of a crude box of rough cypress boards or bark nailed with square-cut nails at four corners. Into this coffin was placed the corpse in ceremonial dress, accompanied by two muskets and two long knives. The muskets were placed, stocks at the pelvis, along each side of the body. The two knives were crossed at the upper right of the head.

The corpse had worn a shirt of red-green paisley, fragments of which survived. Upon this were sewn four large silver armbands. Three very large silver crescents were suspended across the chest. Evidently

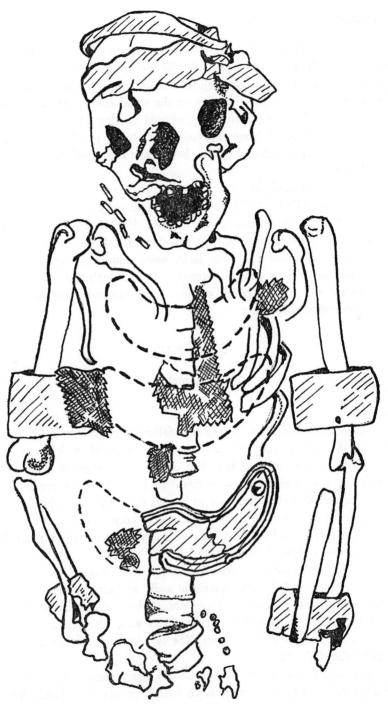

Fig. 3. Tunica man: burial in Pierite allotment, Coulee des Grues site.

the salts of these silver ornaments preserved the fabric underneath; in fact, many of the ribs were stained a dull blue color from contact with the silver.

Just below the waist, a band of white doughnut-shaped glass "seed" beads was located *in situ* and obviously marked a bead border, either of the shirt or, possibly, a breechcloth. This band of beads, somewhat disturbed in the original excavation, seemed to extend across the front of the burial. No evidence of associated fabric could be found. It is the author's contention that these beads represent a border on the shirt, or else a beaded cloth band.

Two beautifully made silver headbands had been carefully placed around the forehead of the individual. Adhering to the backs of these bands were small fragments of white linen, obviously part of a headpiece composed of the silver bands (fig. 3) and the fabric.

Around the neck were, *in situ*, a string of large (approximately 1 cm. long) tubular beads of black, red, and white striped glass. No other indications of dress, other than four buckles found near the knees, were present.

A cache of hardware—three iron kettles, an ax, a pewter cup, an adz, a harpoon, a hoe, a set of stirrups, a spike, and two bridle bits— was on the top of the coffin. Strips of cypress bark found under the kettles indicated a lid or liner between these heavy iron artifacts and the corpse.

At the feet was another cache of burial furniture. Included were four vessels of polychrome floral pattern dinnerware: a plate, two bowls, and a bowl with a lid. Two other vessels, a dish and a small deep bowl, were of the ware commonly known as blue feather edge of Leed's ware. A single deep bowl of a mocha-colored banded ware bearing dendritic patterns completed the ceramic deposit. These vessels were arranged into two neat stacks, capped by the deep bowls, both inverted. Also in this cache were a brass chain, a scattering of black and white doughnut-shaped seed beads, and a tin-wood chest, rusted almost solid, with an ornate curved brass handle.

The chest contained a brass stock plate which fitted one of the rifles, an iron spoon, a mass of small straight pins, a bone-handled clasp knife, a brass spring object, a mass of fine rouge, a mass of black and white seed beads, a brass powder horn, two badly crushed silver bracelets, and five silver mill dollars. The coins, covering the period between 1760 and 1803, were of French, Spanish, and American mint.

INTERPRETATION

This burial provides a substantial view of the Tunica in the early nineteenth century. The 1803 American coin provides a secure minimal date for the burial and places the events some time between the Spanish and American periods of Louisiana history. The mixed European-Indian nature of the grave recalls a comment about the Tunica by a nineteenth-century traveler (Darby, 1818): "It would puzzle Montesquieu himself as to who has influenced who the most."

By this time the Tunica and the Biloxi, who settled across the Coulee at the Neitzel Site (Williams, 1962, p. 56), had been living in the area for nearly eighteen years. The Poste des Avoyelles had been established in 1780, ostensibly to "protect Indian lands" (Saucier, 1941, p. 15), so the Tunica had been in constant contact with their European neighbors. Roman Catholic missions were established for the Tunica as early as 1704 to 1706 (Swanton, 1911, pp. 308-9), and the missionaries were still baptizing children at the Mississippi River village (the Trudeau Site) as late as the 1770s (Baudier, 1939).

Yet traditional burial practices do not seem to have waned. As Brain (1976) has pointed out, Tunica mourners still place special grave goods with their dead, and in spite of Christian influence, metal detectors have confirmed such items in unmarked nineteenth-century burials at Coulee des Grues. Traditional Native American traditions have persisted into the present. The last corn dance (*fête du blé*) was held by the Tunica and Biloxi at Old River in the 1940s (personal communication, Chief Joseph Pierite, 1969), and traditionalists frequently mention "bringing it back soon." Marriages were still made by Tunica chiefs or "medicine doctors" well into the 1930s and 1940s.

Some slight changes crept in, such as the strict eastern orientation of graves, fairly well-defined "family" burial concentrations, and a preference for slight rises in the terrain—for example, the "hill" mentioned by Volsin Chiki to Swanton in 1911. Brain (1974) reports that earlier burials occur in both "highs" and "lows" at the Trudeau Site. However, these practices seem related more to cultural influence from continuing Biloxi and Tunica interaction than to outside pressure. At the Colfax Ferry Site (Webb, 1962; Gregory and Webb, 1965) a documented Pascagoula-Biloxi cemetery was placed on a low hill, and at least one other Pascagoula cemetery also fits that pattern.

The Biloxi influence also seems more likely than French or Spanish influence because of the well-documented Tunica resistance to European religion (Swanton, 1911, pp. 308-9). Catholic influence was probably less intense at Coulee des Grues than at the earlier sites nearer the Mississippi, because there was no church in the area until 1796, when the Church of Nuestra Señora del Carmen was established at the post (Saucier, 1941, p. 49). Resistance to missionaries may have actually been another, less well-documented factor which influenced the Tunica, Ofo, and Biloxi to move from their earlier communities nearer the older French settlement at Pointe Coupee.

Not only was the placement of grave goods retained, but the associated artifacts give clear insight into the multiple roles of a nineteenth-century Tunica man. The muskets, knives, and harpoon suggest that a strong emphasis remained on hunting and fishing. Also of some interest here is the presence of a hoe blade in the cache (fig. 4). Brain (1973) has commented on the fact that among all the Lower Valley tribes only the Tunica men were described as tilling their crops, a point he and one of his students (Brown, 1974) felt was indicative of a patrilineal society. Apparently the men at Coulee des Grues were still maintaining that traditional structural pose. Linguistic and ethnographic data suggest a matrilineal, ranked clan structure rather than a patrilineage. However, the hoeing remained a man's job too.

Another set of tools, the ax and adz, suggest carpentry—most likely house carpentry—because of the nature of the adz, a heavy foot adz used for squaring beams. Smaller adzes, known in Louisiana as round adzes or *tilles rondes*, are noticeably absent. These are widely used in making dugout canoes or pirogues.

Similarly, the presence of stirrups and bridles is very interesting. A preoccupation with livestock seems to have continued well into the 1800s. Their move from the Tunica hills does not carry the Tunica away from the main avenue to the Caddo, namely the Red River. Their old horse trade with the Natchitoches and Avoyels seems to have predisposed their preference for another village on the Red, but near the mouth of the stream, actually on land next to the Avoyel.

The dress was unmistakably Indian: beadwork, silver ornaments, headdress with silver headbands, and long paisley shirt or jacket. Although made entirely of European materials—silver, fabric, beads—the outfit most clearly denoted the ethnic identity of the man. Individually, the artifacts could have fit any European household, but worked into silver headbands, beaded onto the hem of a shirt, worn as a "turban" under two delicate silver headbands, they signify "Indian identity."

Fig. 4. Artifacts found with remains in Coulee des Grues Tunica burial.

The ceramics were not expected. These culinary artifacts are surprising in a man's grave, especially that of a man who rode horseback, hunted, harpooned, and carpentered. Since all these are male roles, the placement of ceramics and cook pots is especially striking. Brain (1974) has pointed out that at the Trudeau Site, an apparent eighteenth-century locality, such items seem associated with women, not with men. On the other hand, at both Coulee des Grues and the Colfax Ferry Site (Gregory and Webb, 1965), kitchen items were not associated only with women; nearly every grave had some ceramics and kettles. Since the Colfax Ferry Site has been linked to the Tunica (the Biloxi-Pascagoula actually had also lived on Coulee des Grues), this variation may again be viewed as due to the influence of these migrants. Evidently the close proximity of the Biloxi to the Tunica, both on the Mississippi and at Coulee des Grues, had a strong effect. These tribal acculturative patterns seem more important in terms of culture change than was the almost wholesale switch to European technology.

Mary Haas (1950) points out that her informant, the Tunica chief Sesosterie Yuchigant, noted that there were villages on Bayou Clair (actually Bayou Clear), under a chief he called Mingo (Choctaw for chief), that had once been located across the coulee from their village. These clearly are the Colfax Ferry Site concentrations. Thus the traditional interaction was so much a part of oral tradition that knowledge of these upstream village details persisted until as late as the 1930s. Chief Joseph Pierite (personal communication, 1965) explained that the bands argued over some game. The Biloxi apparently left in 1804, about the date of this burial.

Another point worth mentioning here is that all guns found at Coulee des Grues, the two muskets from this burial and several others found subsequently, lacked locks and lock plates. At Colfax Ferry all the guns lacked barrels (personal communications, Clarence H. Webb, 1965). This mutilation of weapons is so ubiquitous at these sites as to suggest intentional "killing" of the pieces. The practice of artifact mutilation was apparently not extended to other artifacts at either site, but the male-associated guns had all been worked over. Again, this seems a post-Mississippi River village trait, since Ford's excavations at Angola Farm yielded whole muskets, some still loaded, and a pistol (Ford, 1936). If the Biloxi village mentioned by Hutchins (1784, pp. 63, 65) as located near the Tunica on the Mississippi River can be found, perhaps the influence of this group can be more accurately charted. Speculative though these observations are, they reinforce the close interaction between the two tribes.

The small chest found with the Coulee des Grues burial is of considerable interest. It was obviously one of the small chests frequently inventoried in European households in Louisiana in the eighteenth century (Parish Archives: Natchitoches Parish and Avoyelles Parish, Louisiana). This chest not only resembled those of the Tunica's European neighbors, but contained personal items as theirs usually did. The contents of the chest were not, however, the same as those usually listed for contemporary Europeans. A stack of five silver coins of French, Spanish, and American mint (1773-1803) filled one corner. The razor makes the use of the springs as tweezers unlikely, but they could have been used to handle heated objects, and the coins were probably destined to become jewelry (several dozen coin brooches were later found at Coulee des Grues). The Biloxi term for silver ornaments was *axisahi* (Swanton and Dorsey, 1912, p. 313), the same term they used for money. The Tunica term, *laspi*, meant metal of money, and Mary Haas considered it a loan from the French *l'espèce* (Haas, 1953, p. 230). Still, the term was the base which was modified to *laspitapachu* or metal "adorners," the circular brooches wrought from European coins. To date these coin-derived brooches have been found at Coulee des Grues, Colfax Ferry, the Nick Site (near Coulee des Grues) (Jimmy Durham, 1973: personal communication), and at a site attributed to the Alabama-Coushatta in Eastern Texas (Hsu, 1969). At all sites some brooches still bore evidence of the original coin on the interior face. Several Tunica still have such brooches, as do the Louisian-Coushatta and Choctaw. They are generally worn pinned to ribbons, a tradition dating from the French Revolution.

Silver headbands, virtually identical to those from Coulee des Grues, again occurred at Colfax Ferry (Webb, 1962), and one is in the possession of Chief Emile Stouf of the Chitimacha tribe. He attributed his to the grave of their chief, Soulier Rouge. A few others have appeared recently from the City Pool Site adjoining the Coulee des Grues area.

As Underhill (1953, p. 137) has pointed out, this preoccupation with silverwork and jewelry correlates with the beginnings of the fur trade with organized factories and licensed traders. Since none has been reported from the Trudeau Site (Brain, 1970, 1974) or Anglo Farm (Ford, 1936, pp. 129-40), both documented eighteenth-century Tunica sites, it seems safe to say that this silverwork tradition was introduced some time after the Tunica left the Mississippi. Again one is tempted to attribute the beginnings of the industry to the Biloxi. Certainly such archeological and historigraphic evidence adds significance to the fact that the Biloxi had a native term for silver/money, while the Tunica used a possible French loan.

It seems likely that the crescentic breastplates of the Coulee des Grues burial were originally purchased from a trader, but the headbands and armbands were of native manufacture. Perhaps again these were the property of a chief. No other crescents have been found. Money, then, can be seen primarily as raw material for producing jewelry, but also as useful in purchasing European items. If one interprets the ochre at Coulee des Grues as a polishing agent (one still used widely by silver-smiths), the spring as a tweezers, and the battered tablespoon as a hammer (such spoons were still used by Tunica to hammer coins into rings as late as the 1950s), one can conceive of the possibility that this grave was also that of a local silversmith. The early date and gorgets suggest it may be the grave of Pariwah, a chief, but Tunica-Biloxi oral tradition holds he lies elsewhere, resplendent in gold and silver.

All in all, these data clearly point out several things: (1) Indian identity as such was cherished and preserved in spite of a great amount of technological change; (2) pan-tribal interaction seems to have been on the increase and of greater impact than European influence; and (3) certain elements of personal adornment and dress were becoming pan-tribal by as early as the very first years of the nineteenth century.

These factors remain in the culture of the Louisiana tribes even today. Indians tend to have more contact with Indians than with Europeans, and the tribes, especially the Tunica, Biloxi, and Choctaw, are closely intermarried. Although much non-Indian technology has been adopted, it often functions in a different context than in European culture. Native religions weakened, but traditionalists preserved whole blocks of myth-ology and tradition even after centuries of bombardment by Christian missions.

Lastly, this burial should not only serve as an indication of the kinds of forces that were in action in the eighteenth and early nineteenth cen-turies, but it should also remind the archeologist that technology (arti-facts) may not be the best data for understanding culture. Perhaps in the not too distant future archeologists will deal as much with the living as with the dead. It is hoped that this lesson has not been learned far too late.

ACKNOWLEDGMENTS

The author thanks Dr. William G. Haag for his default, whereby he sent the author and Roger Saucier to record the Coulee des Grues burial. The photographic talents and generosity of Roger Saucier have made this paper possible. It is hoped he approves of it.

R. K. Harris, for whom this *Festschrift* is intended, is responsible for my continued interest in historic Indian archeology, and for turning the Venetian bead into a useful archeologist's tool. He also impressed upon me the need to work on the later sites in the Red River region, and has aided in many other ways. It is hoped that this paper will acknowledge my many debts to him and Mrs. Inus Marie Harris.

Thanks go to Chief Joseph A. Pierite (deceased) and Mrs. Rosa Jackson Pierite of the Tunica-Biloxi tribe, and their tribal council: Joseph Pierite, Jr. (Chairman), Horace Pierite, Jr., Sam Mabry (deceased), and Mrs. Rose Marie White (Secretary), Mrs. Clementine Broussard, Mrs. Florence Pierite, and other Tunica. They have taught us a great deal about Louisiana Indian culture and in doing so have provided a key to the understanding of much that is to come.

Much of the substantive ethnohistory in this paper was a by-product of my close interaction with Ernest C. Downs and was gathered under the auspices of a grant from the Sachem Fund of the Mellon Foundation. The grant was administered by the Institute for the Development of Indian Law and directed by Vine Deloria, Jr. My thanks to all these people can hardly be sufficient to do them justice.

A special note of gratitude is extended to Dr. George A. Stokes, Dean of Liberal Arts at Northwestern State University, Natchitoches, Louisiana, for his editorial help.

BIBLIOGRAPHY

ANONYMOUS. 1944. "Survey of Federal Archives: Louisiana Indian Miscellany." Unpublished manuscript. Louisiana Collection, Louisiana State University, Baton Rouge.

BAUDIER, R. 1939. *The Catholic Church in Louisiana.* New Orleans: privately printed.

BRAIN, J. 1970. *The Tunica Treasure.* Peabody Museum Bulletin no. 2. Cambridge: Harvard University.

_____. 1973. "The Tunica." In *The Handbook of North American Indians.* Washington, forthcoming.

_____. 1974. *Trudeau, An Eighteenth-Century Village.* Peabody Museum Bulletin no. 3. Cambridge: Harvard University.

_____. 1976. "From the Words of the Living: The Indian Speaks." In

Clues to America's Past. Washington, D.C.: National Geographic Society.

———. 1977. *On the Tunica Trail.* Anthropological Study no. 1. Department of Culture, Recreation and Tourism. Baton Rouge.

BROWN, L. 1974. "Tunica Ethnography." Unpublished manuscript. Department of Anthropology, Brown University.

DARBY, W. 1818. *Emigrant's Guide to the Western and Southwestern States and Territories.* New York: Kirk and Mercein.

DOWNS, E. C. 1976. "Tunicas and Biloxis: Indian Policy versus Indian Survival." Manuscript in files of the Institute for the Development of Indian Law, Washington, D.C.

———. 1978. "Draft Petition for Recognition: The Tunica-Biloxi Indian Tribe." Native American Rights Fund, Washington, D.C.

FORD, J. A. 1936. *An Analysis of Indian Village Site Collections from Louisiana and Mississippi.* Anthropological Study no. 2, New Orleans Department of Conservation, the Geological Survey.

GREGORY, H. F., and WEBB, C. H. 1965. "Trade Beads from Six Sites in Natchitoches Parish, Louisiana." *Florida Anthropologist* 18 (3): 15-44.

HAAS, M. R. 1942. "The Solar Deity of the Tunica," *Papers of the Michigan Academy of Arts and Letters* 28: 531-35.

———. 1950. "Tunica Texts." *University of California Publications in Linguistics* 6 (2): 1-174.

———. 1953. "Tunica Dictionary." *University of California Publications in Linguistics* 6 (2): 175-332.

HSU, D. P. 1969. *The Arthur Patterson Site: A Mid-Nineteenth-Century Site, San Jacinto County, Texas.* Archeological Survey Report no. 5, Austin: State Building Commission.

HUTCHINS, T. 1784. *An Historical Narrative and Topographical Description of Louisiana and West Florida.* Facsimile ed. Gainesville: University of Florida Press, 1968.

MCCANTS, D. 1970. *They Came to Louisiana.* Baton Rouge: Louisiana State University Press.

SAUCIER, C. 1941. *The History of Avoyelles Parish, Louisiana.* Baton Rouge: Claitor's.

SWANTON, J. R. 1911. *Indian Tribes of the Lower Mississippi Valley and Adjacent Coast of the Gulf of Mexico.* Bureau of American Ethnology Bulletin no. 43, Washington, D.C.

———, and DORSEY, J. O. 1912. *A Dictionary of the Biloxi and Ofo Languages.* Bureau of American Ethnology Bulletin no. 47, Washington, D.C.

UNDERHILL, R. 1953. *Red Man's America.* Chicago: University of Chicago Press.

WEBB, C. H. 1962. "Early 19th-Century Trade Material from the Colfax Ferry

Site, Natchitoches Parish, Louisiana." *Southeastern Archeological Conference Newsletter no. 8*, pp. 30-33.

WILLIAMS, S. 1962. "Historical Archeology in the Lower Mississippi Valley." *Papers Presented at the 1st and 2nd Conferences on Historical Site Archeology, Cambridge*, pp. 55-63.

Recollections, Anecdotes, and Bibliography
Of R. K. Harris

WILSON W. CROOK, JR.

EDUCATED AT SOUTHERN METHODIST UNIVERSITY and later by profession to become a fireman and eventually railroad engineer for the Texas and Pacific Railroad, "King," as he is known to all his friends, has always been a ready learner and teacher. Continually sharing his knowledge and materials, King is a humble scientific pioneer with an open and inevitably searching mind. He participated in the first survey of Dallas County archeological sites, many of which were his own locations. He has worked in and is an authority on not only the Upper Trinity/Dallas area, but also the entire Caddoan region including the Red River area of Texas and Oklahoma, southward to the Waco region, especially the Abilene-Sweetwater-Merkel regions of western Texas, and eastward to Louisiana and Poverty Point in particular, Mississippi, and northern Alabama.

In 1969, after his retirement from the railroad, he was appointed curator of collections in the Department of Anthropology of Southern Methodist University. He was elected fellow, trustee, president, and regional vice-president of the Texas Archeological Society, and was founder, president, and publisher of the journal of the Dallas Archeological Society.

King has become in modern times the extant national authority on Historic period trade beads and the preservation and identification of gun parts, knives, glass and ceramic artifacts, copper and other metallic remnants, lead bullets, uniform buttons, and almost anything else archeological that is subject to decomposition. In addition, I have never seen a more experienced and careful excavator, with high quality notes, techniques, measurements, drawings, and photographs in scientific detail. His preservation treatment and reconstruction of bone, wood, metal, and ceramic artifacts are superb, thanks no doubt to his firsthand experience with many different types of artifacts; indeed, he is the type to be a fine museum curator. His records are kept with an eye toward use by future scientists: they are as scientifically detailed as conditions would permit. In many cases they are published, but always they are preserved for the future. With the sole exception of his own daughter, Linda, he is the finest pen or pencil field illustrator of chipped stone artifacts for mimeograph or printing that I have known in my years in the field of photoreproduction.

King Harris is Texas's own Cuvier, Boucher de Perthes, DuBois, Dart, Broom, Pilgrim, and Leakey, to say nothing of von Humboldt and Helmut de Terra, both of whom he resembles in approach. Having firsthand acquaintance with de Terra's visit to Texas sites and feeling that I know the others, I do not make the comparisons lightly; King is of similar stature and worthy of recognition as such.

King was an ecologist before the word was in popular usage, and his knowledge of flora and fauna often served him and others well in his archeological investigations. This is the man who taught me anthill archeology, gopher-hole archeology, underwater archeology with no highly sophisticated technological equipment, and quite a bit more, although I hope this was not always one-sided.

Regarding King's technique: he believed that one could no doubt do archeology by strip-mining an area by three-foot grid squares for life, but that there are more subtle routes to information which may save one some trouble. King showed me ways of avoiding this much work; the big red ants, for example, bring up small balls of soil from within a suspected site which may vary from gray sand to red clay—a most instructive lesson in subsurface geology with brainwork instead of backwork. We have found glass beads and flint flakes "rejected" by these helpful denizens. Gopher-hole mounds are sometimes even better, since they dig deeper and may twist across a site. The soil of these mounds, as King would show me, are indicators of what lies beneath, and we have thus discovered flakes and even projectile points.

King and I had our own variation on underwater archeology, which usually means scuba tanks and weighted belts. After heavy rains upstream from Lake Whitney, the water level would rise above the T-L beach and then subside (we would check with the Fort Worth Corps of Engineers); consequently, the artifact-bearing horizon would be eroded and exposed for our probing. Barefoot and with exploring toes in the murky shallow water we have recovered a surprising number of artifacts. If the artifact horizon was eroded out to the beach we would search it first, and only later go up to our knees in water.

Many of us have benefited from King's knowledge of local flora. He taught me the acrid taste of the bark of the pepperwood tree; the value of the foxglove plant used by the Indians to obtain a primitive digitalis for heart sufferers; how to procure the basic ingredients for the preparation of tasty sassafras tea; the composition of Indian pemmican or "iron rations" for war or fast travel (Texas-style from a combination of bone marrow, crushed pecans, and cornmeal); and how to make Indian-style pecan broth, which must have been most nourishing for the aged or ailing.

When he taught me other tricks of the woodsman, I began to suspect he should have been a professional naturalist or survival expert. One can, for instance, catch a plump field mouse by hand in a crack in the bank of a creek bed, and then reach in and pull out the dry grass lining of the nest as the finest one-match tinder available when everything else might be soaked by rain. I have seen King wading a shallow creek in rubber boots watching the cut-banks for archeological signs but, being an opportunist, unable to resist suddenly leaning down and splashing under water with bare hands to bring out a nice edible-size bream that had been hiding broadside in a two-inch rock crevice. During the grasshopper season, however, we made up for this exploitation by having great fun catching the insects (King bare-handed and I by sporadic luck with my cap), then dropping them into pools along the creeks. The hoppers floated and struggled, but the water would boil when the goggle-eyes hit the bait. He showed this tender-heartedness at other times too, and he does not lack the conservation philosophy.

Once in early fall King intrigued me by demonstrating the easy Indian way of survival fishing. When the sumac turned red-leafed and berried, he broke it and rolled it into balls, so that the juice oozed, and then put it in a sack weighted with stones and dropped it into a deep pool. Minutes later we could pick up the helpless drugged fish floating on top of the water. Crushed green hulls of nearly ready pecans, walnuts, and hickory nuts before the first hard frost turns them brown will work just as well, he assured me. Today this is illegal, but by learning how one can live in harmony with nature without modern technology I came to understand what could be done Indian-fashion to get food, and in this way began an independent route to understanding the life of the quarry we hunted archeologically. King knew the uses of ripe red hackberry seeds (Indian cherries) in the fall, the different treatment of fox grapes and mustang grapes, the utility of the root nuts of the abominable sting-nettle and the prickly pear apples. He showed me more palmettos in a secluded thicket in Dallas County in North Texas than I have ever seen on the nature trail in the famous Big Thicket or Palmetto State Park in southern Texas!

There were times also when I thought the calling he had missed was that of a champion hurdler or high jumper. These thoughts occurred upon seeing his easy clearance of barbed-wire fences when pursued by Brahma or Santa Gertrudis bulls while he was investigating potential sites. I may be younger, but one must give him full respect; his cigarette lighter and my cigarettes are still just across the fence in a southeastern Dallas County site where the bulls, having won their ground, never left their vigil and we finally left and never went back. Since that day long ago when science and fate thrust us together we have had unbelievable experiences, from learning unwillingly the tedious science of eye-straining magnifying-glass-and-tweezer archeology to what we called "snailology," which is now known in sophisticated circles as malacology. We would do anything for science.

King gave me my first set of shaped and sharpened excavation trowels and then worked me nearly to death using them in cursed three- and five-foot squares in dry and hard calichified clay. I got even, though, by coaxing him to do a similar thing with a geological pick. He also appreciated the similarly unrewarding labor and cost of breaking quartzite cobbles to determine the composition beneath deceiving surface cortex.

The man has an eye for artifacts that was best summed up by Ed Jelks, who once said, "King Harris can spot a flint flake in a ditch while riding forty miles an hour in a Travelall." Once in a great while, however, I was able to see that his archeological experience didn't make him *completely* infallible. The first occasion arose when the famous Wheeler early Archaic site was still existent and yielding: we always went out to look after rains to see what had freshly washed out. One such Saturday we went only to find that the pickings were very poor.

Returning to the fence gate, I noticed King's distinctive boot track in the wet sand just beside a complete four- or five-inch dart point plainly exposed. I mutely touched his arm, pointed at it *in situ*, picked it up, and pocketed it. A second occasion arose one day at the famous Wood Sand Pit multiple occupation site, which was being strip-mined by removing the sand and clay overburden to get the commercial gravel. We trudged along the edge of a twenty-five-foot pit, looking down at heaps of what we thought should have been artifact-bearing overburden which had been cast into the pit. Suddenly I stopped, pointed down to an almost perfect six-inch dart point on the dump below, and shouted, "There one is!" I clambered down and back up, at some risk, with the petrified palm-wood point. King fondled it, studied it, turned it over and over, and if he weren't as moral and religious as he really is, I would say he coveted it.

On another occasion I bought a perfect bronze cast of a Folsom point at the Denver Museum of Natural History while visiting Dr. H. M. Wormington with the intention upon returning home of letting King "find" it, then giving it to him as he realized it was metal and yet could not be. Eventually the time came and we went to the City of Kaufman Site after a rain (another over-the-fence-because-of-bulls day); and although it was poor hunting, I anticipated his exciting discovery of the point. By one pretext or another I would get ahead of him in the washes and partially conceal the bronze Folsom in his path. Three or four times he missed it, until finally one time even *I* couldn't find it again and had to tell him, and then only after the two of us spent considerable time on hands and knees did he receive his gift, but without my gaining the pleasure of his surprise.

Our joining forces was dictated by the fact that no one but he and I had done any research in the Upper Trinity preceramic Archaic, let alone published on it. Nobody could help or advise us; and our materials not only turned out to be unique but resulted in the publication and establishment of the Trinity Aspect of the Archaic and the Carrollton and Elam Foci. Even more heretical, we had both found Paleo-Indian points *in situ* (Plainview, Angostura, Scottsbluff, Meserve, etc.) in some earlier sites as minor but nevertheless consistent percentages. This was rather blasphemous then, until big people over the country began to come to us as the only published source of support. Soon evidence emerged to legitimatize our work: Graham Cave in Missouri carbon dated to 11,000, and Russel Cave in Georgia dated to 9,000. Thus even the University of Texas archeologists began to take second looks at the university's WPA collections from the excavated Archaic sites. Ultimately this revolution resulted in an issue of *American Antiquity*'s being devoted to the American Archaic with seven articles on the subject. Five quoted us and a sixth listed us in the bibliography. We became, of course, more controversial than that with the Lewisville discovery and its carbon-14 dates; but subsequent discoveries and dates in southern California, Mexico, and Peru have long since removed us from the center of the storm. In our humble amateur way we have simply broken ground enough times to be noticed. I might add, in an attempt to answer the question of how we did it, that a predilection for red soda pop, cans of sweetened condensed milk, and rat-cheese purchased at country grocery stores seems to sharpen the scientific senses.

Perhaps one of King's most admirable and successful qualities and the one which gains him entry past many a formidable door is his ability to talk straight and get down to earth in a way most landowners appreciate. I learned from this master that if you do it correctly they think either that you are crazy and simultaneously harmless or that you must be knowledgeable. Either way we gained a foothold in quite a few places where others failed—although I do remember one time when even the old pro was stumped. This exception was our expedition to investigate a reported Spanish gold mine on a Mr. Pancake's farm out of McGregor, Texas. On the way there we got our directions confused, so we stopped at a roadside farmhouse to ask. King, being the expert, walked up to the old house where an elderly lady was quietly rocking on the shaded front porch, doffed his hat, and asked in his best style. "Howdy ma'am, could you tell me where Mr. Pancake lives?"

Sitting in the car, I was just close enough to hear and to see that she just kept rocking with no answer. King presumed she was nearly deaf, so he began repeating the same question louder and louder and still received no answer. Finally (I am sure her perfect ears could no longer stand his shouting), she stopped rocking, looked him in the eye, and said briefly, "If you know him so well, then he lives where he's always lived!"

That was the end of the conversation, but not of the story. I have never seen King so defeated as when he humbly shouldered his crushed feelings and returned mutely to the car. Frustrated, we drove down the road until we encountered a farmer on a tractor plowing his field. I stopped, but King appeared immovable, so I got out, walked to the fence, and motioned to the tractor driver. He waved back, stopped his machine, and walked to the fence to talk.

"Can you tell me where Mr. Pancake's place is?" I asked, trying my best to imitate King's flawless style. He thought a moment, studying me, and replied, "What do you want of him?" Carefully I explained that we were legitimate archeologists from Dallas who had heard that Pancake had reported a Spanish mine on his place and had come to verify it. Again he thought a minute, squinted and looked at us, doubtless decided we were not revenue agents but in reality simply crazy and harmless, and then replied: "Well, I guess I can help you. . . . I'm Pancake."

I felt rather sheepish, but the mine did prove to be a Spanish trench dug in local limestone to get iron pyrites for sulfur in order to make black gunpowder. No gold was involved, but we were just as happy as if there had been, if not more so. I have since wondered about Mr. Pancake's other occupations, but satisfied myself with the knowledge that pure science is intangible and under it almost any activity can be defended and disguised.

It is of course a matter of record that King not only accomplished a phenomenal amount of field work but also is extensively published and even more often referred to in publications by others as personal communications. On some few of his publications I was fortunate enough to be coauthor with him, and thus I was asked to collate his bibliography and append it to this paper. One may judge from the bibliography that follows the professional profile of this man who has done so much for Texas archeology and yet calls himself an amateur.

PUBLICATIONS OF R. KING HARRIS

1936. "Indian Campsites of the Upper Trinity River Drainage." *Bulletin of the Texas Archeological and Paleontological Society* 8:113-33.

1939. "A Survey of Three Denton County Indian Village Sites." *The Record* (published by the Dallas Archeological Society), vol. 1, no. 2 (October 1939).

1940. "Dallas Area." *Texas Archaeological News* (published by the Council of Texas Archaeologists, Austin) 2:8-9.

"Two Indian Village Sites near the City of Denton." *The Record*, vol. 2, no. 1 (September 1940).

1941. (*with* K. L. Cowin) "A Report on an Indian Burial Blanket from Val Verde County, Texas." *The Record*, vol. 2, no. 6 (February 1941).

(*with* Forrest Kirkland) "Two Burials below the White Rock Lake Spillway, Site 27A5-19." *The Record*, vol. 2, no. 10 (June 1941).

"Additional Information about Dallas County Hand Axes." *The Record*, vol. 3, no. 1 (September 1941).

1942. "The Gilkey Hill Pottery Site." *The Record*, vol. 3, no. 9 (May 1942).

1945. "Bone Implement Burial, Collin County, Texas." *Bulletin of the Texas Archeological and Paleontological Society* 16:84-89.

1946. "An Interesting Copper Artifact from Garrett's Bluff." *The Record*, vol. 5, no. 1 (January 1946).

1947. (*with* Rex Housewright, Lester Wilson, Robert Hatzenbuehler, and Henry Hanna) "The Butler Hole House Site." *The Record*, vol. 6, no. 3 (November 1947).

"An Infant Burial." *The Record*, vol. 6, no. 4 (December 1947).

1948. "Trait Lists of Our Area—Lower Rockwall Site." *The Record*, vol. 6, no. 5 (January 1948).

"Trait Lists of Our Area—Butler Hole Site." *The Record*, vol. 6, no. 6 (February 1948).

"Trait Lists—Upper Rockwall Site." *The Record*, vol. 6, no. 9 (May 1948).

"A Pottery Site near Farmersville, Texas." *The Record*, vol. 6, no. 10 (June 1948).

"Two Cremated Burials, Site 27B1-1." *The Record*, vol. 7, no. 2 (October 1948).

(*with* Henry Hanna) "Burial 5, Site 27B1-1." *The Record*, vol. 7, no. 3 (November 1948).

"Preliminary Report on an Alto Focus Site in Kaufman County." *The Record*, vol. 7, no. 4 (December 1948).

1949. (*with* Forrest Kirkland and Robert Hatzenbuehler) "Refuse Pits Excavated in Site 27A1-2." *The Record*, vol. 7, no. 5 (January 1949).

(*with* Robert Hatzenbuehler) "Burial 5, Site 27A5-19." *The Record*, vol. 7, no. 6 (February 1949).

"Burial 7, Site 27A5-19" *The Record*, vol. 7, no. 7 (March 1949).

(*with* J. B. Sollberger) "Burial 6 and 7, Site 27B1-1." *The Record*, vol. 7, no 8 (April 1949).

"Preliminary Report Site 27B6-1." *The Record*, vol. 7, no 9 (May 1949).

"The Jordan Farm Site." *The Record*, vol. 8, no. 1 (September-October 1949).

"Excavation of Fire Pit Site 27B1-1." *The Record*, vol. 8, no. 2 (November 1949).

1950. "Preliminary Report on Site 18C7-10." *The Record*, vol. 8, no. 5 (March-April 1950).

"Preliminary Report Site 3 Walker County, Alabama." *The Record*, vol 9, no. 2 (November-December 1950).

1951. "A Preliminary Report on Site 18C4-6 in Denton County, Texas." *The Record*, vol. 9, no. 4 (March-June 1951).

"Two Mussel Shell Hoes from Site 19A1-2." *The Record*, vol. 9, no. 4 (March-June 1951).

"French or Spanish, or What Is It?" *The Record*, vol. 10, no. 1 (September-October 1951).

"Plainview Point from Site 18C7-3." *The Record*, vol. 10, no. 1 (September-October 1951).

(*with* Jack T. Hughes) "Refuse or Fire Pit Excavated in Site 27A1-2." *The Record*, vol. 10, no. 2 (November-December 1951).

1952. (*with* Wilson W. Crook, Jr.) "Trinity Aspect of the Archaic Horizon: The Carrollton and Elam Foci." *Bulletin of the Texas Archeological and Paleontological Society* 23:7-38.

"A Mussel Shell Paint Container from Palo Pinto County, Texas." *The Record*, vol. 10, no. 3 (January-March 1952).

1953. "Two Recent Trips to Sites in Fannin and Lamar Counties (Tex.)." *The Record*, vol. 11, no. 5 (May-June 1953).

"The Sam Kaufman Site, Red River County, Texas." *Bulletin of the Texas Archeological Society* 24:43-68.

1954. (*with* Wilson W. Crook, Jr.) "Traits of the Trinity Aspect Archaic: Carrollton and Elam Foci." *The Record*, vol. 12, no. 1 (February 1954).

(*with* Mr. and Mrs. John Perkins) "Burials 12, 13, 14, and 15, the Sam Kaufman Site 19B3-2." *The Record*, vol. 13, no. 1 (October 1954).

(*with* Wilson W. Crook, Jr.) "Another Distinctive Artifact: The Carrollton Axe." *The Record*, vol. 13, no. 2 November 1954).

1955. (*with* Wilson W. Crook, Jr.) "Scottsbluff Points in the Obshner Site near Dallas, Texas." *Bulletin of the Texas Archeological Society* 26: 75-100.

"A Flexed Burial, Site 19C5-15, Delta County, Texas." *The Record*, vol. 14, no. 2 (February 1955).

1956. (*with* John Perkins and J. B. Sollberger) "Burials 6, 7, 8, and 9, Site 27B1-1" (Upper Rockwall). *The Record*, vol. 14, no. 3 (April 1956).

(*with* Lester Wilson) "Burial 17, the Sam Kaufman Site, 19B3-2." *The Record*, vol. 14, no. 4 (June 1956).

1957. (*with* Wilson W. Crook, Jr.) "Hearths and Artifacts of Early Man near Lewisville, Texas, and Associated Faunal Material." *Bulletin of the Texas Archeological Society* 28:7-97.

1958. (*with* Wilson W. Crook, Jr.) "A Pleistocene Campsite near Lewisville, Texas." *American Antiquity* 23 (3): 233-46.

1959. (*with* Wilson W. Crook, Jr.) "C-14 Date on Henrietta Focus in Texas." *Oklahoma Anthropological Society Newsletter* 8 (3): 2.

1960. "Burial 1, Site 27B1-2 Rockwall County and Burial 5, Site 18D4-1 Collin County." *The Record*, vol. 15, no. 2 (May 1960).

1961. (*with* Wilson W. Crook, Jr.) "Significance of a New Radiocarbon Date from the Lewisville Site." *Bulletin of the Texas Archeological Society* 32:327-30.

(*with* Inus Marie Harris) "Spanish Fort, a Historic Trade Site." *The Record*, vol. 16, no. 1 (April 1961).

1962. (*with* Bob H. Slaughter, Wilson W. Crook, Jr., D. C. Allen, and Martin Seifert) *The Hill-Shuler Local Faunas of the Upper Trinity River, Dallas and Denton Counties, Texas.* Bureau of Economic Geology, Reports of Investigations, no. 48. University of Texas, Austin.

(*with* Inus Marie Harris) "Another Marker on the Trail of the Norteño: A Preliminary Report on the Gilbert Site." *The Record* 17 (1): 2-9.

1963. (*with* Dee Ann Suhm. Appendixes by Robert Hatzenbuehler, R. K. Harris, Mark E. Huff, Jr., and Norman Biggs) *An Appraisal of the Archeological Resources of Forney Reservoir, Collin, Dallas, Kaufman, and Rockwall Counties, Texas.* Report submitted to the National Park Service by the Texas Archeological Salvage Project, the University of Texas, Austin.

1964. "History of the Dallas Archaeological Society." *The Record* 20 (1): 1-10.

1965. (*with* Mr. and Mrs. Jay C. Blaine) "Activities of Members during 1964." *The Record,* 21 (1): 1-3.

"Club News" (41RW4, and 41RW2). (Editor's note on Society's excavation at Glen Hill Site in Rockwall County, Texas, and also at Upper Rockwall Site). *The Record* 21 (1): 3.

(*with* Inus Marie Harris, Jay C. Blaine, and Jerrylee Blaine) "A Preliminary Archeological and Documentary Study of the Womack Site, Lamar County, Texas." *Bulletin of the Texas Archeological Society* 36:287-363.

1966. (*with* Inus M. Harris, Jay C. Blaine, and Jerrylee Blaine) "French Clasp Knives: Types D and E." *The Record* 22 (1): 7-8.

(*with* E. Mott Davis, Kathleen Gilmore, Loyd Harper, Edward J. Jelks, and Bill Yancy) "The Site." In "The Gilbert Site: A Norteño Focus Site in Northeastern Texas," ed. Edward B. Jelks. *Bulletin of The Texas Archeological Society* 37:1-17.

(*with* Inus M. Harris and J. Ned Woodall) "European Trade Goods: Tools." In "The Gilbert Site: A Norteño Focus Site in Northeastern Texas," ed. Edward B. Jelks. *Bulletin of the Texas Archeological Society* 37:18-32.

(*with* Jay C. Blaine) "European Trade Goods: Guns." In "The Gilbert Site: A Norteño Focus Site in Northeastern Texas," ed. Edward B. Jelks. *Bulletin of the Texas Archeological Society* 37:33-86.

(*with* Loyd Harper, Ruby Harper, Inus M. Harris, Edward B. Jelks, and J. Ned Woodall) "European Trade Goods: Ornaments." In "The Gilbert Site: A Norteño Focus Site in Northeastern Texas," ed. Edward B. Jelks. *Bulletin of the Texas Archeological Society* 37:87-104.

(*with* Curtis D. Tunnell) "European Trade Goods: Miscellaneous European Goods: Kettle Bail Ears, Kettle Bails, Horse Trappings, Metal Scraps, Glass Fragments." In "The Gilbert Site: A Norteño Focus Site in Northeastern Texas," ed. Edward B. Jelks. *Bulletin of the Texas Archeological Society* 37:105-11.

(*with* Dee Ann Story, Byron Barber, Estalee Barber, Evelyn Cobb, Herschel Cobb, Robert Coleman, Kathleen Gilmore, and Norma Hoffrichter) "Indian Artifacts: Pottery Vessels." In "The Gilbert Site:

A Norteño Focus Site in Northeastern Texas," ed. Edward B. Jelks. *Bulletin of the Texas Archeological Society* 37:112-87.

(*with* Edward B. Jelks, Charles Nemec, Bobby Vance, and Lester Wilson) "Indian Artifacts: Tobacco Pipes." In "The Gilbert Site: A Norteño Focus Site in Northeastern Texas," ed. Edward B. Jelks. *Bulletin of the Texas Archeological Society* 37:188-90.

1967. (*with* Inus Marie Harris) "Trade Beads, Projectile Points, and Knives." In *A Pilot Study of Wichita Indian Archeology and Ethnohistory*, ed. Robert E. Bell, Edward B. Jelks, and W. W. Newcomb, pp. 129-62, figs. 52-54. Final Report for Grant GS-964, National Science Foundation.

(*with* Inus Marie Harris) "A Review and Notes on *The Rock Art of Texas Indians* by Forrest Kirkland and W. W. Newcomb, Jr." *The Record* 24 (2): 8-10.

(*with* Inus Marie Harris) "Cyrus N. Ray: Bibliography and Contributions to Texas Archeology." *Bulletin of the Texas Archeological Society* 38:130-34.

"Reconnaissance of Archaeological Sites along Red River in Fannin, Lamar and Red River County, Texas." In *The Archeological, Historical and Natural Resources of the Red River Basin*, ed. Hester Davis, pp. 32-34. Fayetteville: University of Arkansas Museum.

1968. (*with* Jay C. Blaine, Wilson W. Crook, Jr., and Joel L. Shiner) "The Acton Site: Hood County, Texas." *Bulletin of the Texas Archeological Society* 39:45-94.

"Benton Metal Points." In *Guide to the Identification of Certain American Indian Projectile Points*, ed. Gregory Perino, pp. 10-11. Oklahoma City: Leslie H. Butts.

Review of "Texas State Building Commission, Archaeological Program, Reports Numbers 1 through 9, Austin." *Historical Archaeology* 2:121-23 (Society for Historical Archaeology, the Museum, Michigan State University).

1969. (ed., *with* S. Alan Skinner and Keith M. Anderson) *Archaeological Investigations at the Sam Kaufman Site, Red River County, Texas.* Southern Methodist University Contributions in Anthropology, no. 5.

(*with* Inus Marie Harris) "A Study of Trade Beads and Native-Made Beads from the Vinson Site in Limestone County, Texas." Manuscript on file, Department of Anthropology, University of Texas, Austin.

(*with* Inus Marie Harris) "Fossil Shell Pendant from the Vinson Site in Limestone County, Texas." Manuscript on file, Department of Anthropology, University of Texas, Austin.

(*with* Inus Marie Harris) "Metal Buttons from the Vinson Site in Limestone County, Texas." Manuscript on file, Department of Anthropology, University of Texas, Austin.

(*with* Inus Marie Harris) "Metal Arrow Points from the Vinson Site in Limestone County, Texas." Manuscript on file, Department of Anthropology, University of Texas, Austin.

(*with* Inus Marie Harris) "French Blanket-Bale Seal from the Vinson Site in Limestone County, Texas." Manuscript on file, Department of Anthropology, University of Texas, Austin.

1970. (*with* Inus Marie Harris) "A Bison Kill on Dixon's Branch, Site 27A2-5, Dallas County, Texas." *The Record* 27 (1): 1, 2, 4.

1972. (*with* Inus Marie Harris) "A Glossary Guide for the Dallas Archeological Society." *The Record* 28 (1): 1-10.

1973. (*with* J. L. Shiner) "Historic End Scrapers in the Southern Plains." *The Record* 29 (2): 1-8.

(*with* Inus Marie Harris) "Analysis of Metal Artifacts from Garcitas Creek in Victoria County, Texas, Site 41VT-4. In *The Keeran Site: The Probable Site of La Salle's Fort St. Louis in Texas.* Texas State Historical Commission, Office of the State Archeologist Reports, no. 24, Austin.

(*with* M. P. Miroir, J. C. Blaine, J. L. McVay, and others) "Bernard de La Harpe and the Nassonite Post." *Bulletin of the Texas Archeological Society* 44:113-67.

1974. (*with* Claire Davidson) "Chemical Profile of Some Glass Trade Beads." *Bulletin of the Texas Archeological Society* 45:209-17.

(*with* Inus Marie Harris and Jay C. Blaine) "1860's Choctaw Village on the Brazos River in Hill County, Texas." Appendix 1 in *An Evaluation of the Archaeological Resources at Lake Whitney, Texas,* ed. S. Alan Skinner. Southern Methodist University Contributions in Anthropology, no. 14.

(*with* Inus Marie Harris) *Analysis of Metal Artifacts and Glass Beads from Mission Nuestra Señora del Santisimo Rosario in Goliad County, Texas,* ed. Kathleen Gilmore. Texas State Building Commission Report no. 14, pt. 1, Austin.

(*with* Herschel Cobb and Paul Lorrain) "Index of Publications of the Dallas Archeological Society." *The Record* 30 (3): 1-13.

1975. (*with* Inus Marie Harris) *Analysis of Glass and Jet Beads from Mission Nuestra Señora del Santisimo Rosario in Goliad County, Texas,* ed Kathleen Gilmore. Texas State Building Commission Report no. 14, pt. 2.

(*with* Inus Marie Harris) "A Preliminary Analysis of a Small Sample of Glass Trade Beads from the Floydada Country Club Site (41FL1) in Floyd County, Texas." Manuscript on file, Department of Anthropology, Southern Methodist University.

1977. (*with* Inus Marie Harris) *The Wylie Focus.* Wylie, Texas: Area Corps of Engineers, U.S. Army.

1978. (*with* Inus Marie Harris) "Clarence Hungerford Webb and Louisiana Archaeology." Annual Bulletin of the Louisiana Archaeological Society, vol. 4, in press.

(*with* Inus Marie Harris) "Distribution of Natchitoches Engraved Ceramics." Annual Bulletin of the Louisiana Archaeological Society, vol. 4, in press.

(*with* Inus Marie Harris) "The Atlanta State Park Site in Northeastern Texas." Annual Bulletin of the Louisiana Archaeological Society, vol. 4, in press.

(*with* Inus Marie Harris) *A Study of Glass Trade Beads from the Rosebrough Lake Site in Bowie County, Texas.* Denton, Texas: North Texas State University, forthcoming.

(*with* Inus Marie Harris) *Pottery from MaHaffey Site Ch.-1, Choctaw County, Oklahoma.* Report for Tulsa District, Corps of Engineers, U.S. Army, Contract No. D.A.C.W. 56-77-C-0129.

"Excavation of the Lewisville Site (18C7-13), Denton County, Texas." Narrative on tape with 18 color slides. Denton County Historical Commission.